THE MEN ON MAGIC CARPETS

THE MEN ON MAGIC CARPETS

SEARCHING FOR THE SUPERHUMAN SPORTS STAR

ED HAWKINS

BLOOMSBURY SPORT

LONDON · OXFORD · NEW YORK · NEW DELHI · SYDNEY

BLOOMSBURY SPORT
Bloomsbury Publishing Plc
50 Bedford Square, London, WC1B 3DP, UK

BLOOMSBURY, BLOOMSBURY SPORT and the Diana logo are trademarks
of Bloomsbury Publishing Plc

First published in Great Britain 2019

ISBN: HB: 978-1-4729-4259-3; TPB: 978-1-4729-4263-0; eBook: 978-1-4729-4262-3

2 4 6 8 10 9 7 5 3 1

Typeset in Adobe Garamond Pro by Deanta Global Publishing Services, Chennai, India
Printed and bound in Great Britain by CPI Group (UK) Ltd, Croydon CR0 4YY

To find out more about our authors and books visit www.bloomsbury.com
and sign up for our newsletters

To F & f & m

CONTENTS

1

VOODOO GAMES

Candlestick Park, San Francisco, 1964. The wind is whipping off the Bay on a typically cold night at the ballpark. Mike Murphy takes his seat in Section 17, just past the edge of the infield dirt beyond first base. The Del Courtney Jazz Band pipes up and the vendors shout their wares: Hamm's or Falstaff beers, Oscar Mayer hot-dogs with Gulden's mustard. Murphy is close enough to talk to the San Francisco Giants players in the bullpen. But he's not interested in hero worship. He wants to put a voodoo curse on the opposition, the LA Dodgers.

He tells two friends it's called a 'whammy' or 'occult backlash'. He's got this game. He's going to win it for the Giants. He's been practising for years, perfecting the very particular cries and exact hand gestures to transmit negative energy to players. He reckons he's a witch doctor. A baseball witch doctor, sending psychic waves to scramble minds and zap energy from muscles. A previous war cry had been so well-timed he'd knocked Bob Gibson, the famous St Louis Cardinals pitcher, clean on his backside while posturing on the mound. The story had become Murphy's 'party piece' and he claimed Gibson's tumble had been written about by baseball reporters. It was 'something extraordinary that had never happened before'. Murphy insisted that there was 'no doubt' his fall had been caused by the shenanigans, which had not been to everyone's taste. *Thwack*. A guy sitting behind him took exception and karate-chopped him on the head.

Clearly Murphy was no regular fan. He was the man the *New Yorker* would, in 1976, call 'the Mystic of Joy'. Also known as 'the Godfather of the Human Potential Movement', he co-founded the Esalen Institute, a famed New Age retreat and pillar of the counterculture movement in sixties' California. It was a centre for Eastern religions, philosophy, alternative medicines, mind–body interventions – and a fair amount of nude hot-tub bathing. You know, far out stuff.

While sitting in the bleachers at Candlestick Park, Murphy asked for assistance from the fellow Giants fans around him to explore his powers, straight-facedly explaining that the gestures had been developed by shamans in the Amazon basin to kill enemies. If they wanted the Giants to win, this would help. And so he exhorted the crowd to begin. He asked them to close their two middle fingers over the thumb, leaving the index finger and little finger pointing, like devil horns, towards their target. And he told them to shout and wail as they thrust their horns towards the Dodgers players.

That night would prove Murphy's most successful as a conjuring cheerleader. Murphy said he enlisted almost 200 fans. By the third inning they were rolling and rocking in Section 17, making an ear-splitting din. It felt like all their negative energy was flowing through him. Standing before his hordes, Murphy was the arrowhead. With several hundred horns pointing towards the tip, he began to feel dizzy. Whenever the wave of gestures and curses was at its strongest, the Dodgers began to make inept plays. Or so Murphy thought. It made little difference to the score. The Giants had not made a single run.

So Murphy decided to ramp up the psychic firestorm. His brethren were working themselves into a frenzy. In the eighth inning, the Giants tied. By the 13th, the Giants were up 2 to 1, following a crescendo of awful howls and thrusting. Murphy staggered out of the stadium, drained, exhausted and fearing a heart attack.

The next day the city's *Chronicle Sporting Green* ran a story with the headline: 'Michael Murphy dies at baseball game.'

*

Baguio City, the Philippines, 14 years later. Mental combat has begun for the world chess championship. Anatoly Karpov, the golden boy of the Soviet Union, is playing Viktor Korchnoi, a compatriot the regime loves to hate. Despite sitting opposite each other for hour after hour, day after day, they have not spoken. But somebody is talking to Korchnoi. There is a voice inside his head. It is incessant. Over and over and over it berates him.

'YOU. MUST. LOSE.'

Korchnoi recognises the voice. It's not his. It belongs to the man sitting in the front row of the audience since the match began. His heart starts to beat a little faster. He begins to sweat.

'YOU. SHOULD. STOP. FIGHT. AGAINST. KARPOV.'

The demands keep coming. Korchnoi is not afraid but he is angry. He understands perfectly what is happening. The man is trying to control his thoughts.

'YOU. ARE. TRAITOR. OF. SOVIET. PEOPLE.'

The man sits cross-legged, still, reclining with a hint of arrogance. He is dressed immaculately in a white shirt and dark brown suit. He looks like an accountant. Albeit a somewhat demented one. A slight smirk plays across his face. His eyes are terrifying. They bore into Korchnoi. He does not blink until Korchnoi snaps.

'If you do not remove that man,' Korchnoi shouts, 'I will with my fist.'

His mental assailant is winning. His name is Dr Zoukhar. And his reputation precedes him. Zoukhar is the KGB's mind-control expert. If Soviet state security wants to place a negative, damaging thought in someone's head, they call for Zoukhar.

It could have been worse for Korchnoi. They could have asked Zoukhar to stop his heart. The KGB could do that, too. Well, the hearts of frogs anyway. In the Kremlin's corridors of power, they believed that, before long, they would be able to do the same to humans.

The stakes were high. Zoukhar was there to help the Soviet Union convince the world that their way of life was superior. Put simply, communism surely trumped capitalism when the system was able to produce world chess champions.

That's why Zoukhar was staring at Korchnoi. He simply could not be allowed to win against the poster boy for true Soviet values. Korchnoi, hang-dogged and pot-bellied with a mistress in tow, was not the image they were going for.

'YOU. SHOULD. STOP. FIGHT. AGAINST. KARPOV.'

Zoukhar continued as the match progressed. Korchnoi, disturbed and losing, tried extreme measures to block the supposed brainwaves emitting from Zoukhar's bug eyes. On the advice of two members of an Indian religious sect, who he had consulted in preparation for the match fearing this tactic would be used against him, he did handstands away from the table in an attempt to make Zoukhar's orders fall from his head. His mistress sat next to Zoukhar. She kicked him. She tickled him. Until Karpov's fitness instructor sat on her.

Korchnoi lost. 'I expected to play one against one,' he said afterwards. 'Instead the whole Red Army, led by Zoukhar, was against me.' The press reported the match as 'parapsychological warfare in a sports setting'.

*

Both these stories are true. At first glance it would be easy to dismiss them as unconnected footnotes in a crazy chapter of human history.

There was Murphy, the zany hippy in bell-bottom jeans warbling occult orders, who would, in time, have the US government dancing to his tune. And then Zoukhar, the immaculately dressed communist spook, staring demonically for comrade and country.

The two men hailed from opposite cultures. Cultures so different that throughout this period America and the Soviet Union teetered on the brink of nuclear Armageddon, fingers twitching over red buttons in the East and West.

But for all their differences, America and the Soviet Union held a common belief. They believed in Superhumans. A race of cosmic beings who could, just like in the sci-fi movies, slow down time, speed it up, change their body shape, feel no pain, levitate, see into the future, and more. And, as we've seen, through boggle-eyed mind control and harnessing the occult, they truly thought they could put a thought in someone's head. Or stop the heart of a man at a hundred paces.

Both nations thought these powers would win them the Cold War. So battle commenced in an inner space race, in the course of which millions of dollars and roubles were splurged by both military powerhouses in an attempt to create a physical embodiment of Superman, Luke Skywalker or Wonder Woman.

From the West Coast of America to the far corners of the Soviet Union, yogis, shamans and psychics were sought out to aid these alternative war efforts. And sports, like that 1978 world chess match, were used as training grounds to test run their peculiar tricks. The men and women doing such oddball work were classed as Black Ops by the CIA or housed in basements patrolled by the KGB.

A Cold War thaw, however, had actually begun with more than a little help from the American gurus reaching out to their Soviet friends to try to change the world with a shared esoteric view. With the spooks and spies looking on nervously, the two secret psychic networks, who were supposed to be inspiring the military killers to win the war, got together to end it.

This meeting of minds was an attempt to decipher how brain and body could work in unison to achieve extraordinary things. And instead of using these mystical powers for the Dark Side of death and destruction, the American and Soviet misfits changed the 'rules', reckoning they could be taught and learned for good – to create a new breed of sports star. Someone *extraordinary*.

I found myself retracing the steps of the early believers, learning about runners who were put in trances to think they were dead saints; golfers who took to the course imagining they were Darth Vader; and basketball players who thought they could fly thanks to a teacher who called himself 'Yoda'. There were athletes who reported that they had seen competitors shape-shift – get smaller or taller, stockier or slimmer – in the blink of an eye. Others said they saw the play before it happened. Coaches and athletes began to trust in very weird things.

They were not alone. In 1978, 58 per cent of Americans said they had experienced some form of paranormal power. This was a year after Luke Skywalker, displaying the Jedi mind tricks the two nations were trying to harness, burst into the world consciousness with the release of the first *Star Wars* movie. In 1979 *Superman* hit the big screen. These movie series inspired a whole new generation of believers. One of them was me.

As a child, I wanted to be Superman. To possess super-strength, feel no pain, see through walls, fly – the lot. You probably did, too. Why not? It was fun to believe in something fantastic. And if it wasn't Superman it might have been Skywalker, Wonder Woman or some other comic-book hero. I had Superman pyjamas and a Superman bedsheet. Tucked under the pillow were my *Star Wars* figures. And I'd drift off at night imagining what it would be like to really do all those extraordinary things.

Then I grew up. We all did (well, most of us). That snapshot of juvenile innocence is probably the reason I would become infatuated with possibilities again. With every page of CIA documents, interviews with spooks and strange encounters with those who still trusted that the superhuman existed, I was transported further back to childhood, a place where reason, rationale and scientific rigour did not matter. It was good to go back. But how had I stumbled across this story?

I am a sports writer who has specialised in exposing corruption and greed, all-too-common traits that have sullied modern-day sport for many. But as well as investigating the grubby, depressing side of sport, I obsessed about how and why sports teams win and lose and attempted to predict the outcome of matches.

One day I was deep in thought about the lengths multimillion-dollar franchises might go to for victory. Cheating, sadly, was de rigueur. And at the very top echelon the fine margins between success and failure were pored over to mind-numbing levels. The British Olympic cycling team, as a tedious example, painted the floor of their mechanical area white to highlight dust. Any speck, they reckoned, could hinder their chances. If obsessive-compulsive disorders were rife, then, I wondered if there was anything really left-field a sports team had done to gain those extra percentage points of advantage? And that's when it hit me. What if a team, desperate to win, had attempted to harness something otherworldly, something really crazy to inspire their players or inhibit the opposition? Wouldn't that be, literally, mind-blowing?

As it turned out, it had been tried. An illusionist known as Romark (real name Ronald Markham) had been employed by Halifax Town, a nondescript soccer team in an economically broken part of northern England, to hypnotise their players to help them beat Manchester City in an FA Cup match in 1980. This was real David versus Goliath stuff.

John Smith, the Halifax striker, said at the time: 'I'm sat there with this guy called Romark, and he was saying, "You will go to sleep now, John Smith, and then you'll overcome the power of Manchester City. You will play the greatest game of your life." I'm thinking, "What's all this about? What a load of nonsense."' But John Smith, in mud up to his knees, helped set up Halifax's winning goal.

Surely a glittering career would follow for the mysterious Romark? Not quite. His next trick to prove his paranormal powers was to drive a car blindfolded through the streets of Ilford, in Essex. After a few yards he crashed into the back of a police van. 'That van was parked in a place that logic told me it wouldn't be,' he said.

Something else Romark didn't see coming was the fraud squad. He was imprisoned for embezzlement. He died in 1982.

I was undeterred. In fact, I was inspired. Here was somebody who had tried to use psychic powers to influence sports games. That was crazy enough for me. Had there been other teams or athletes who had benefited or been handicapped by esoteric methods?

I began to wonder what had become of the hippies in America and the Soviet Union who had wanted to change the world. Why had their cosmic skills become the stuff of myth and legend? Had their tactics influenced today's coaches? Did the superhuman who could do amazing feats really exist? Are they out there now, making miracles before our eyes? NBA players shooting impossible baskets, baseball sluggers launching it into orbit, footballers dancing through tackles as if they were ghosts?

This is the untold story about what happened to those dreamers, and a far out movement that fervently believed athletes could be faster, higher, stronger, and weirder. And why the spooks and spies continued to be so intrigued by their methods. This is the story about the search for the superhuman sports star. A quest that would become my quest.

2

BACK FROM THE DEAD

When I first met Mike Murphy I told him, 'I was really worried you were dead.' He laughed. His wife, Dulce, said, 'Some mornings, Ed, I think exactly the same!'

Mike is 86 years old. But he looked trim as he glided through the Italian restaurant he'd picked for our rendezvous in Mill Valley. He was wearing all black – a roll-neck and gilet to defend against the San Francisco summer wind. He had a smile for everyone. The waiters all seemed to know him. A few diners too, judging by a cheery wave here and there. I wondered whether they knew that, if he so wished, he could have them spinning on their backsides, dinner on their laps. All with a well-orchestrated howl or a black-magic hand sign.

There was nothing in the least hippy about him in appearance or manner. He was a suave octogenarian, hair swept back, with a deep tan. He could have been the owner of the place. And to look at old photos of him back in the days when he founded the Esalen Institute, there were no clues this was a man who believed in far out things then, either. No long-flowing locks or flowers in his hair. He was no cliché.

But it was the eyes that gave him away. They twinkled mischievously when he talked.

I was referring to his age with my opening gambit, not the newspaper article declaring his death after his voodoo games at Candlestick Park. It was another Michael Murphy who died that night: a 73-year-old whose heart gave out. But Mike being Mike, he believed he had something to do with it.

'Oh my god,' he squeaked (I noticed his voice jumped a few octaves when he got excited). 'I thought I'd killed the poor man! The energy that day was something else, let me tell you. It got weird.

'Sport is seriously occult. When I used to go to San Francisco 49ers football games, we'd pretend to sacrifice a goat. A shamanic ritual. This goes on when fans root for their team. They put a whammy on.' He paused. And for emphasis added, '*Whammies* are put on.' A smile played across his face. His 'whammy days' are over now, he said. The old ticker might not be able to take it.

'But you don't really think you killed that poor man?' I asked.

'I didn't intend to! I took comfort that his grandchildren later joined the Shivas Irons Society.'

Ah yes, the Shivas Irons Society. It was how I had found Mike. It hadn't been an easy task. I had started to think he really was a ghost. There were traces of him but I couldn't pin him down. A notion he would enjoy.

I had heard he had become somewhat reclusive, and the only connection I could find was the Shivas Irons Society. It was a 'fan club' set up in honour of the book that had catapulted Mike to global fame in the seventies. *Golf in the Kingdom* (1972) had sold more than a million copies and, at the risk of sounding like a billboard, was made into a major motion picture in 2010. It's the story of Mike when he was not long out of college, stopping off in Fife, Scotland, to play a round of golf before travelling to India to live in an ashram for a year. Or in his words, to go in search of 'the infinite mind'.

Mike was a trust-fund kid at Stanford University. The son of a lawyer, he wanted to be a priest, maybe a scientist. His parents thought a doctor would be best. But on the second day of spring classes in 1950 he went to the wrong classroom and ended up listening to a comparative religion lecture. It was providence. Mike was hooked. He quit his class, enrolled in Indian philosophy and devoured *The Life Divine* (1939) by Sri Aurobindo, an Indian mystic, yogi, guru and poet. It was a handbook for spiritual powers.

Aurobindo believed in superman: a race of 'gnostic beings' or 'cosmic individuals' capable of phenomena that came from an 'occult subtle energy'. It was accessing these superpowers that Mike dedicated his life to. They were also called 'siddhis'. One of which enabled him to put baseball pitchers on their ass. The more nefarious sorts in American and Soviet military regimes wanted to use them to win wars. In short, they were everything and anything that Superman, Wonder Woman and Luke Skywalker and his Jedi mates could do. They were changing shape, walking through walls, extraordinary strength, slowing down time, mind control, seeing into the future. You know, 'skills' that the layman would instantly dismiss as hokum.

After reading about the hypnotising of Halifax Town players, I had a thirst for more. And in the way in which so many quests begin these days, I logged on to Google. With excitable, racing thoughts about the possibility of more sports teams using hypnotists, psychics, curses and other voodoo to get ahead, I typed in 'psychic side of sports'. I had some vague hope that I would read about a football or soccer team that had asked its local clairvoyant to predict the outcomes of matches or warn of injuries to players. Maybe a baseball team had employed a witch doctor to make their players feel ten feet tall. What pinged back was a book.

A collection of siddhis in sport. Mike Murphy was the author. Further research on Mike started to reveal the Cold War inner space race and the Russians using Dr Zoukhar to use mind control to win a game of chess.

A lucky strike, eh? You bet. Particularly because, looking back, the search term I used was a little left-field. Later, as I was road-tripping around the West Coast of America, the folks I met would claim that it was not luck at all. No, I had somehow connected to an invisible force containing feelings and thoughts that were hurtling through, and round, time and space. Up there in the ether. Somewhere.

Anyway, you're going to hear a lot about siddhis in these pages. 'Siddhi' is a Sanskrit word, roughly translated as 'superpower'. The Hindus and Buddhists have believed since the very first millennium that spiritual practice – like yoga – was capable of giving rise to siddhis. They ranged from ability to master pain to being able to read minds at a distance. In various ancient Indian scriptures, examples of siddhis are listed in what Murphy has called 'the largest inventory of extraordinary human potentials the world has ever seen'. Sport, Murphy has always argued, has a 'genius' for encouraging them. Golf, in particular.

Unsurprisingly, *Golf in the Kingdom* is what might be termed 'bizarre'. In the story, while in Scotland, Mike meets a mysterious old golf pro called Shivas Irons. They play a late-night round together and strange things happen. Mike and Shivas talk levitation, clubs that swing by themselves and balls that change direction by the power of thought. Shivas is a sort of otherworldly guide to the mystical side of the sport. And there you were, thinking golf was about fat, rich white men in strange outfits ruining a good walk.

Shivas is an important figure in this story. After the publication of *Golf in the Kingdom*, Shivas became something of a legend in pro sports in America. For athletes and coaches who wanted to experience the extraordinary superhuman feats that he spoke of, there was a clamour to know whether he existed. Could his magic be bottled and sold? Could he be flown over to teach NFL or NBA players? Mike, with that twinkle in his eye, has never confirmed or denied Shivas's existence.

The Shivas Irons Society was set up to celebrate Murphy's mysterious character and to encourage other golfers to explore the game's 'transformational aspects'. Adam Brucker, who lives in Denver, Colorado, ran the group, which had 1,100 members in more than 20 countries. My first, rather tentative, question to him when we spoke on the phone was to ask whether Mike was still alive.

'He sure is,' Adam said. 'And he's in good shape, too.'

His response to my second query – 'Will he talk to me?' – was less enthused.

'Well, he gets pretty bombarded with requests and he keeps out of the public eye … but let me find out. The thing is, what do you want to talk about?'

I wanted to talk about possibility. Was *Golf in the Kingdom* based on reality? Could a basketball player really master levitation so he could hang that bit longer in the air to make the score? Could a golfer order the ball to fade, to dip, using just the power of thought, as if it were remote controlled? Could football players see the plays before they happened? Could athletes slow down time to achieve perfection? And was it really possible for Dr Zoukhar to use mind control to win chess matches? These were all siddhis. Maybe a non-athlete like me could do them. Wouldn't that be something? Couldn't we all use these powers to make the grocery shop a bit easier, or that weekly sales meeting with the boss go the way we wanted it to? Don't tell me you don't think levitation would be useful when reaching for the top shelf. Or, if you've not hit your sales targets, how about invisibility?

A long pause followed. I worried Adam thought I was crazy. Then he spoke.

'Sure. But tell me, are you more interested in the mystical or the mind?'

'Both,' I said, although I didn't really know the relevance of either.

'You've got to have body, mind and spirit coming together,' Adam said. 'You've got to put the time in. But you need a coach, a good practitioner to guide you along the way.'

'Like Shivas Irons, then?' I said.

'Right.'

Adam agreed he would put me in touch with Barry Robbins, a former nationally ranked softball player who was Mike's business partner. It sounded like I was being vetted.

'He lives down the street from Mike,' Adam told me. 'Oh, and probably best you don't ask Barry, or Mike, about the Russians.'

The Russians? Why would that be off limits all these years down the line? I wanted to know more about Dr Zoukhar and how deep the Soviets had gone in their search for superhuman powers. And by now I had a file of research that suggested Mike was a man who would know.

I spoke with Barry. He greeted me like a long-lost brother. Although he did keep calling me Edwin. Apart from that he was charming, and his effervescence crackled down the line. 'Won-der-ful!' was his response when I asked if I could talk with

Mike. He agreed to pass on his telephone number and told him I would call. I didn't mention the Russians.

*

By the start of the sixties Mike had returned to the States after 16 months in India, fully committed to Aurobindo's vision. And it just so happened that he had a big chunk of Murphy family land on the cliffs of Big Sur, overlooking the Pacific, which would do nicely as a base for his calling to teach superpowers. This would be the home of the Esalen Institute. For Esalen, read the Westchester Academy in the *X-Men* comic franchise, with Murphy as Professor X helping confused folks understand their strange powers. Murphy provided the land and his friend Dick Price, a co-founder, the cash.

Before its opening in 1962, the plot had needed a security guard. Hunter S. Thompson, the creator of gonzo journalism, got the job. 'He was 21,' Mike, who would have been around the same age at the time, told me on our first phone call. 'Unpublished. Fully armed. With a small arsenal. He seemed to love tracer bullets. He'd fire hundreds out into the night sky so every night was like the fourth of July.' Sometimes he'd fire his gun out of the unopened window of one of the houses that was on the grounds.'

Thompson was the first of many colourful and culturally significant characters in the Esalen story. Aldous Huxley, the English novelist, philosopher and psychedelic grand philosopher, followed. He was another inspiration for Mike, who in 1962 had attended a Huxley lecture at the University of California with Dick Price, entitled 'Human Potentialities'. Huxley, usually dosed up on mescaline, was a key figure in Esalen's establishment, before his death a year later from throat cancer.

Esalen, which took its name from a Native American tribe known as the Esselen, who buried and worshipped their dead in

Big Sur, was to become a base for the counterculture movement through the sixties and seventies – flower power, the psychedelic drug scene, civil rights movement, the sexual revolution. Controversial eroticist Henry Miller swam at the hot springs in the grounds. Beatle George Harrison once landed his helicopter there to jam with Ravi Shankar; and Timothy Leary, who Richard Nixon called 'the most dangerous man in America', taught regular workshops in how to get the most from LSD, claiming that women could orgasm hundreds of times during sex when under the influence. The Nixon administration, by the way, loathed Esalen and falsely claimed that Charles Manson had been a regular visitor.

Set in 165 acres and perched on beautiful rugged cliffs overlooking the ocean, Esalen was a place for people to find themselves. When they did, and it transpired they didn't like what they'd found, occasionally the cliffs came in useful. Other people found other people. The naked hot tubs, wiggling with flesh, gave it a somewhat racy reputation. It was not undeserved. The *New York Times* called it a 'cyclotron for gestalt and encounter therapy ... to get a generation of Americans into the all-consuming process of self-actualization'. Workshops pushed people to plough through sexual and emotional barricades. One was called 'The Value of Psychotic Experience', another 'Supernaturalism and Hallucinogenic Drugs'.

Murphy saw Esalen as a staging post for helping the human race in its evolution. It was committed to exploring ways and means so that Huxley's potentialities could become probabilities. That included people being able to achieve siddhi experiences.

This was a major thrust of what would be called the human potential movement. Its followers believed that any Tom, Dick or Harry had untapped potential, or hidden talents. They just needed to feel happier, more fulfilled and creative to realise it. Esalen staged the classes and seminars to help. And once people were happier, they would spread the word and help others to reach their potential. The goal was a groundswell of happy-clappy-chappies who could change society for the better.

Naturally, there were an awful lot of drugs taken at Esalen. Mike's words, not mine, although he did not partake. He limited himself to just eight 'trips' in his lifetime. He wasn't particularly indulgent in other activities either. He had taken a vow of celibacy in the 1950s, reckoning that he needed to conserve energies to enhance his mystical powers, only breaking it in 1962. And when he had a car accident soon after, cracking his ribs, he thought that the cosmic force was punishing him for his ill-discipline. So no free love cliché here.

But he was no killjoy. Mike was such a free thinker that the joke going around Esalen was that if Satan turned up, he'd welcome him with open arms and ask if he wanted to take a workshop. These were exciting and inspirational times. So were these days the birth of the human potential movement?

His tone in reply suggested it was a pretty dumb question: 'To say when this all started you have to go back 3,000 years to India, various forms of mysticism and the occult. I'm arguing that the universe is giving rise to complicit or latent divinity.'

I immediately enjoyed how Mike was so blasé. Here he was claiming that all of us had the ability to be gods or super-divine, with the tone of a man addressing a planning commission about erecting an outhouse.

If I want to find one of these superhumans, how many of these siddhis should I be looking for, you know, per person? More than two, surely? Three or four? Were some rated more 'super' than others? It was another line of questioning he swatted away.

'It's certainly too broad to require one, two, three, or indeed any specific number of siddhis. Better to stick with the definition I gave for "metanormal" on page 587 of *The Future of the Body*.'

The Future of the Body is a big read. So big that some might consider it useful to carry with them when walking downtown in case they get accosted. There are another 198 pages after page 587, where 'extraordinary metanormal functioning' is described as: '*Human functioning that in some respect radically surpasses the functioning typical of most people living today.*'

'Every aspect of human nature is primed to go beyond itself,' Mike explained. 'What's most interesting about sport is that's not why most people do it – it just happens. In real language, its grace is given. It happens.' Bruce Jenner, the decathlete Olympic champion, was, Murphy said, 'rising above [himself] doing things [he] had no right to be doing'. Jenner would later become best known as a reality TV star in *Keeping Up with the Kardashians* and for undergoing a sex change, calling herself Caitlyn.

'So what you're saying is that sports provide an arena for these strange and marvellous things to happen?'

'Yes!' he squeaked.

On the athletics track, golf course, the football field, the hockey rink or any other sporting arena you care to think of, there might be – *definitely* if we believed Mike – competitors who are comic-book heroes, displaying extraordinary powers every day of the week.

'One of the first things I can remember is that several [Esalen] founders came from other countries, like Huxley. And there was a guy from Czechoslovakia who said there were these experiments that were going on in Russia, or what was then the Soviet Union.'

So much for not mentioning the Russians. We had only been talking for five minutes, and here he was, spilling the beans with abandon.

Mike was getting more high-pitched as he spoke. He was clearly excited to be passing this stuff on: 'And they were working with alternative states of consciousness and various esoteric methods of consciousness expansion. It lit a spark in me.'

'Were the Soviets using this stuff in sports?'

'Yes!'

And then there was no stopping him.

'The Russian term is "hidden human reserves". That is very close to human potentiality. It was a giant, instant love affair between us and them. It was just like us on the West Coast. Russia has been full of this. But over there it went right up to the fucking Politburo. They were *into* this.'

'Wow.'

'We ended up working with the Russian Olympic Committee.'

'You were working with the Russian Olympic Committee about harnessing this stuff? During the Cold War?'

'Yes! And this is the great untold story. You'll find you're ahead of the curve on reporting this. I can regale an audience for hours on end with the stories people have told me.' His enthusiasm was infectious. A spark had been lit in me, too.

*

So I got on a plane to San Francisco to hear those stories, to understand why and how the Soviets had been first out of the blocks. And that's why we were sitting in the bustling, upmarket Italian restaurant in Mill Valley. Unfortunately, Mike wasn't as enthused as before. Well, not about the Russians anyway. That could have been the red wine or the late hour. Perhaps his previous lucidity had been down to the two root canal surgeries he'd had the day we spoke. 'You'd think I'd been in a prize fight. I look like a beat-up raccoon.' Maybe Adam's warning had been prescient, after all.

But Mike was in jovial spirits when we met for the first time. He was more interested in teasing me about English country life: 'Do you have a grocery store? A movie theatre? Wow, this is charming. England is charming. Are there landed estates around there? And people live there! I mean, families? Like Downton Abbey? With a lot of servants? Are there sheep? … A lot of sheep, hmm.'

Then Mike broke off. He had that twinkle in his eye again. 'You know you're on a very brave course. You've come to the centre of the story.'

Well, I thought I had. Mike then suddenly downgraded his assertion of 'working with the Russian Olympic team' to the more banal 'we introduced a horse whisperer' to their equestrian team.

I began to tease out information, despite Mike's apparently best intentions to divert. ('Do *you* have any land? An estate?')

After the rumours swirled around Esalen about the Soviets 'working with alternative states of consciousness', Mike wrote to various Czechoslovakian scientists to suggest an information exchange. It took months for the replies to come back. But slowly, bridges were built. 'We had found this evolutionary underground.'

Mike first visited the Soviet Union in 1971. It was the beginning of scores of expeditions (Adam suggested 40 or 50) over decades. Mike was unsure of the exact number. He was certain he was bugged and followed on every visit. He took what he called an 'occult tour' and stayed in the Grand National Hotel in Moscow. Through his correspondence, he was able to meet with Soviet researchers and scientists who were studying clairvoyance and past-life regression. But the trip ended early as he became spooked when his contacts, wary of who was watching, kept telling him, 'Next time we meet, pretend it is for the first time.' Mike was afraid of the KGB agents getting the impression that he was a spy.

Back in the US, his Russian sojourns had been noticed. CIA operatives scouted out his house. This was a time when those who were thought to be fraternising with Soviets would get a knock on the door to find some serious-looking suited gentlemen. You were then told: 'We know you're in contact with an enemy of the USA. In the future, they might try to turn you. Call us if they do.'

Mike made it sound like a badge of honour. 'I've been actively recruited by the FBI, CIA, KGB and IRA,' he dropped in casually.

'But what about sports, Mike?' I reminded him. 'Hidden Human Reserves?'

'Now what year did we get into that?' Mike said, looking at Dulce, his wife.

Mike and Dulce flew into Moscow in summer 1980, and then on to the region that would later become Georgia. Mike had been invited by the Soviets to give a speech at the International Conference on Sports and Modern Society in Tbilisi. It was held to coincide with the 1980 Moscow Games. Mike's speech at the conference in Georgia argued that the US and Soviet Union should work together to uncover human potential in sport. He urged them to 'explore hidden reserves' and 'vast untapped potentials'. It went down well. For years after, information and stories and ideologies were shared between the two groups. Mike's contacts grew, including some at the Kremlin, some in the underground movement, and some who moved between the two. One was Valentin Berezhkov, who used to be Joseph Stalin's interpreter.

In 1987 Mike would take a softball team to Moscow, which included Bill Walsh, the San Francisco 49ers coach, for the first official softball match between the two nations. The Americans were a bar team and had called themselves Les Lapins Sauvages (the Wild Rabbits), mistakenly thinking this translated to 'the Wild Hares'. The Russian team were called the Teapots and included Olympic gymnasts who did cartwheels in pursuit of the ball. That was about as 'super' as it got, although George Wendt, the actor who played Norm in *Cheers*, turned up (as he was in the city filming) on the promise of free beer.

Alas, Mike's contacts from his forays into Russia to meet occult practitioners, speak at conferences or play softball were now dead, literally or figuratively. Over the years he'd lost telephone numbers, addresses. And obviously there was no email back then. When I asked who could help tell me more about what the Russians had been up to, Mike suggested names and Dulce dismissed them until they agreed on one. Jim Hickman.

'He's here!' Mike yelped. 'In San Francisco! You've got to speak with Jim!'

I was getting somewhere. As we walked out of the restaurant and Mike had finished shaking hands with the waiters, he asked if I wanted him to hail me a cab. Knowing what can happen when Mike hollers and waves his arms, I thought best not.

Quickly Mike pulled me towards him before he left. 'This is the mysterious mistress,' he said. 'You're sleeping with her but you can't tell anybody. You call me any time. Be prepared, though, this is going to get weird.' And with that, he shook my hand, his eyes flashed and he disappeared into the night.

3

HIDDEN HUMAN RESERVES

It got pretty weird, pretty quickly with Jim Hickman, even if he wasn't in San Francisco, as Mike Murphy had said. He was in Bolivia. He lived there. Within five minutes of Jim answering my call, he told me: 'They created a replica of the Oval office and they would have people in there 24 hours a day concentrating on the US president in such a way to try to muddle his thinking.'

'They' were the Russians. Hickman spent many years in the seventies and eighties travelling in the USSR to research siddhis, the superpowers. Mike Murphy was often at his side. He told me they learned about strange, disturbing things. Even stranger and more disturbing than a whole bunch of Dr Zoukhars trying to influence the thought patterns of a head of state from great distances?

'There was much deeper work going on.'

'That's pretty deep, Jim!'

'We knew that we were only talking to the people they let us talk to.'

Those 'people' were probably among the 60 Soviet-based scientists who worked at what was called 'Special Department 8'. Their job was to investigate distant mind control. It was just one of 40 centres at Science City, Novosibirsk, in south-west Siberia, which housed thousands of scientists and their families from across the communist bloc in some sort of nerdy utopia. The road names included 'Calculators Street', 'Thermophysics Street' and 'Hydrodynamics Square'.

It was here that they also examined the existence of extra-sensory perception (ESP). The sixth sense. In one creepy experiment, told in the book *Psychic Discoveries Behind the Iron Curtain* (1970), Soviet scientists implanted electrodes in a mother rabbit's brain, took her young litter off to a submarine and, when it was deep below the surface, killed them one by one. At each synchronised time of death, the mother's brain reacted.

Hickman had initially travelled to Russia with a man called Stanley Krippner in 1968. Krippner called himself a parapsychologist and was well known at the time for trying to prove telepathy in dreams with help from the rock band Grateful Dead. Audiences at their Port Chester concerts in 1971 were asked to telepathically transmit pictures of artwork shown on a screen to some guy called Malcolm sleeping 45 miles away in Brooklyn. According to Krippner, Malcolm described the pictures accurately on four of the six nights.

It could be argued that this was one of the more extraordinary achievements of the human potential movement. The Grateful Dead and their fans, the Deadheads, were known for their penchant for drugs. Both were tripping the light fantastic to such a degree that they were unaware of critics chiding songs that went on too long and were out of tune. As the joke went: 'What does a Deadhead say when the drugs wear off? This music sucks.' So Krippner getting the band, and their doped-up groupie masses, to even agree to an experiment on snoozy Malcolm really was something, let alone to focus for several minutes at a time 'transmitting their images'. Lord knows what other pictures poor Malcolm was sent.

No matter, the Soviets heard about Krippner's experiments and invited him over. Hickman was 21 years old at the time and worked as Krippner's research assistant. Later he would meet Mike Murphy at Esalen, who taught him how to meditate and access the state where extraordinary powers resided. Hickman would go on to be a major player in Esalen's Russian research. Together, Hickman and Krippner were part of the vanguard of American believers trying to understand how the Soviets were attempting to develop a scientific form of voodoo.

This, then, was the Soviet Hidden Human Reserves project. And it didn't come cheap. In 1967 it was estimated that there were more than 20 centres across the Soviet Union, with a budget of around 20 million roubles ($21 million). And the order to invest on such a large scale had come straight from the Kremlin. The aim: to develop superpowers. Through conversations with Hickman and Krippner, I was able to begin to piece together just how they did it.

Krippner, now 84, shouted down the phone at me the first time I called: 'YOU'LL HAVE TO SPEAK UP! I'M HARD OF HEARING!' So we screamed at each other for ten minutes, which was not welcomed by my wife, considering I was eight hours ahead and she had just got the baby to sleep. He pointed me in the direction of the relevant papers and research documents.

The search for a superhuman might seem ironic in light of communism's ideals. Throughout the sixties there had been an almost *X-Factor*-style Soviet-wide hunt for psychic talents. Imagine lots of Simon Cowell-style scientists convening panels to examine people who said they could stop a frog's heart just by looking at it. That's not a joke, by the way. One of the 'winners' of just such a talent contest was Nina Kulagina, who said she could do just that, and she was the darling of the KGB.

Kulagina, who at age 14 had joined a tank regiment to fight in the battle for Leningrad against the Nazis in World War Two, was also said to be able to move objects through thought alone. She ended up having her own TV show. Matchsticks, salt shakers and cigar canisters were placed inside a fish tank and after she sat looking very stern for about 20 minutes or so, they would begin to move. It didn't sound like great TV. But in America, the CIA and Department of Defense were glued. What really gave them the willies was the frog heart experiment Kulagina conducted in Leningrad in March 1970. She was filmed staring, with the same intensity as Dr Zoukhar on Viktor Korchnoi, at the frog heart. It had been put in a jar full of Ringer's solution, which could keep it beating for an hour. The heart was attached to a machine to monitor the beats per minute. Kulagina, still silent and with hands placed on a table in front of her and the heart about five feet away, was also hooked up. Her heartbeat went up to 240 beats a minute. Her blood pressure rose and a US Defense report noted that 'heightened biological luminescence radiated from her eyes'. It took her seven minutes to stop the heart.

There was no shortage of so-called psi talent thanks to Russia's rich psychic heritage. One of Mike Murphy's favourite lines is: 'Scratch a Russian, find a mystic.' For centuries, shamans had been pillars of the community, claiming they were able to communicate telepathically, travel out of their bodies, see the future. 'They had much bigger cultural context than anyone in Europe or certainly the US,' Hickman told me. 'It was so much a part of their culture.'

It was the old world meeting the new. The scientific context was crucial in getting it past Communist Party brass who had upheld the tradition of 'sorcerers' or 'healers' being banned, forcing the movement underground. Scientists flocked to be part of the psychic boom. They saw it as an opportunity to prove what some of their ancestors might have believed. Paranoia and fear were also at play, of course. This research might give them a new weapon with which to win a war. Besides, they had to do something. They were worried that it was, in fact, the Americans who had started their own programme first.

A report in a French scientific journal in 1960 said that the US Navy had tested telepathy in 1959 from 'senders' on land to 'receivers' in a submerged submarine, the *Nautilus*. It was headlined 'The Secrets of the *Nautilus*'. A sailor with telepathic powers had been isolated in a cabin while the sub was under an Arctic ice pack and was apparently able to telepathically communicate with a technician on the East Coast of America at the Westinghouse Friendship Laboratory. They had communicated over a 16-day period, and a civilian scientist who worked on the project said they were successful for 'about 75 per cent of the telepathic tries'.

A declassified US Department of Defense document said these reports 'went off like a depth charge' in the corridors of power at the Kremlin. The Soviets were stunned. How had the Americans stolen a march on something that had been at the very heart of their lives? Dr Leonid Vasilev, Russia's leading ESP researcher, issued a rallying cry:

We carried out extensive and until now completely unreported investigations under the Stalin regime. Today the American Navy is testing telepathy on their atomic submarines. Soviet scientists conducted a great many successful telepathy tests over a quarter of a century ago. It's urgent that we throw off our prejudices. We must again plunge into the exploration of this vital field.

It started an era when America and Russia effectively egged each other on in their hunt for superpowers.

The Russians had dug up their 'underground' psychics again. And the KGB sent them to school. They wanted scientific evidence and set up the institutes to provide it. Yuri Andropov was the head of the security agency from 1967 to 1982 and left the Science City scientists in no doubt as to the importance of their work. If it meant research subjects died, so be it. Think *Rocky IV* when Dolph Lundgren, who could have been modelled on the vision of a Soviet superman, having pounded Apollo Creed to mush, says, 'If he dies, he dies.'

But it had all begun relatively tamely the same year the *Nautilus* story broke. With sticks and stones, in fact. In the early days, scientists first studied shamans, yogis, ascetics and witch doctors. They attempted to bless or curse objects likes jewels, pebbles or wood with negative energy and gave them to people. The experiments showed that their subjects started to feel depressed, weak or indecisive. Then it got a bit more hardcore.

At the Kharkov University Neurology Institute, the brains of rats were attached to electrodes and put in solution. The best Russian psychics, having been tried and tested in the research centres dotted around the state, were brought in to communicate with the brains. Emotions and thoughts were transmitted to them – the most popular was laughing but they also 'enjoyed' sums (it is not known whether the brains were better at fractions or algebra).

Unsurprisingly, some of the morally questionable experiments began to make the experts feel uncomfortable. One lab was even shut down in 1974 as the resident scientists en masse rejected what they called 'the negative work'. A mega-secret lab was set up in its place. This was widely believed to be at the Filatov Eye

Institute in Odessa, hidden underground in the sub-sub-basement. Only clandestine couriers knew how to access these secret paranormal institutes. KGB guards made sure there were no unwanted visitors.

There, death row prisoners were 'bombarded' with pulsing magnetic fields to see if they would become clairvoyant. Animals had been tested first and, according to Dr A.V. Kalinets-Bryukhanov, who ran the project, they believed the animals had developed the ability to see through walls. Surely this was a superpower in itself? Knowing whether an animal can see, oh, I don't know, a carrot the other side of some bricks? Alas, their small animal brains could not cope with the onslaught from the magnetic fields. Their brains simply disintegrated. The prisoners suffered the same, horrible fate.

Jim Hickman explained that institutes like that were not just carrying out experiments, but were training schools for extra-sensory perception. And the majority also had faculties for sports. 'What else was it for?' Hickman said. 'They used ESP extensively in sports. It was like a golfer before every shot imagining where it was going to go. But in the Soviet Union they were teaching that ability everywhere.'

The Soviets said it was a fundamental process. Given that the brain is primarily run by electrical impulse, they figured: 'Can we affect the neuro-signalling of a distant brain to affect their concentration and decision-making?' Mind control.

'So they'd send some of these people as part of their entourage with their chess champions,' Hickman said. 'To international chess matches.'

'Yes!' I blurted. 'Dr Zoukhar!'

'He was involved in that. And they'd sit in the audience and try to mess with the chess competitor's concentration.'

It was some tactic. One that Soviet sports teams were said to have deployed from as early as the late 1950s with a resident guru in tow. I chuckled at the thought of our modern-day athlete who surrounds himself with a coterie of specialists. Nutritionist? Check. Sleep coach? Check. Social media manager? Check. Voodoo mystic? Check.

Yet if the Russians thought one man's mind could control another's to impinge on sporting performance, what about the athlete controlling his own mind in order to improve?

'Now *that's* what they were into most of all,' agreed Hickman.

This was known as *psychic self-regulation*. With breathing exercises and a regime of visualisations, pain or tension could be almost completely eradicated. It was, for the layman, a form of hypnosis or meditation. In some cases, athletes would sit and do their breathing drills while listening to crowd noises from their event to make it as 'real life' as possible. Research had shown it was possible to control heart rate, blood flow and body temperature, just with the mind.

For competitive athletes, this was potent stuff. The catchily named Theory of Top Competition Sports in the All-Union Research Institute of Physical Culture in Moscow in the 1970s picked up this new ball and ran with it. In one of the research documents Stanley Krippner (he of the Grateful Dead dream theories) alerted me to, I read about Charles Garfield, a former American Olympic weightlifter turned psychologist, who experienced first-hand this Soviet psychic self-regulation at a health conference in Milan, Italy, in 1979. It was recorded in a 1990 research paper called 'Mental Imagery and Imagination' by Canadian hypnotist Lee Pulos. Before his trip, Garfield had already been helping cancer patients meditate to improve their prognosis. When meeting with Russian scientists and comparing notes, he found the ability of cancer survivors to focus and be positive about their condition was similar to the concentration required of athletes capable of high-level performances. If both groups sat down and had a really good, hard think about getting better and performing better, they did. The Russians were fascinated to hear of Garfield's work. So they shared their own.

Garfield agreed to be experimented on. First, he was asked by the Russian scientists in Milan how much he could lift. 'Three hundred and ten pounds,' he said. He barely managed 300. After a raft of examinations including brainwave measurements, he was told he would be given a 40-minute relaxation exercise. Then he would lift 365 pounds.

'I was told to stare at the weight and maintain a deeply relaxed state,' he said. 'Then they asked me to get a visual image of myself approaching the bench, lying down and lifting the weight. All in my mind's eye.' He was to rehearse that sequence over and over and over. No strain, no pain, easy-peasy. And then he lifted the 365 pounds.

In the build-up to the 1980 Olympic Games in Moscow, the general public found out about what America's Soviet rivals were up to. A report in Washington's *Ellensburg Daily Record* warned of 'Zen' and 'psyched-up' Russian athletes using superhuman powers that would leave the US team 'in the dust'. Dr William Kruger, a hypnotist clearly angling for a job, said, 'There are super-maximum potentials built into the human body and you get superhuman performance. America has not begun to benefit.' It didn't actually matter in the 1980 Games because America would boycott them in protest at the Soviet invasion of Afghanistan.

But the Olympic team weren't the only ones worried by who and what the KGB's institutes were churning out. The cat and mouse nature of the inner space race caused jitters. Eight years previously, the US Defense Intelligence Agency had produced a classified 174-page report called *Controlled Offensive Behavior – USSR*. Its author, Captain John Le Mothe, warned that the Soviets were training agents with 'psychoenergetic' abilities. Sidhhis. Le Mothe said they might be able to 'mold the thoughts of military and civilian leaders' and 'cause the instant death of any US official'.

The Soviets' goal, as you've no doubt worked out by now, was a race of superhumans to win the Cold War. Or at the very least they made the whole thing up as it was their turn to put the frighteners on the Yanks, perhaps 'proof' that they really had been able to place thoughts in their heads. Although their 1980 Moscow Games efforts suggested otherwise. They topped the medal table, winning 80 golds, 37 more than second-placed East Germany.

'They were using it to kill people,' Russell Targ told me bluntly down a crackling Skype connection late one night. He was the man tasked with trying to stop that happening. America was worried. But they had some pretty weird stuff going on, too. And Mike Murphy was helping.

*

WASHINGTON: The CIA financed a project in 1975 to develop a new kind of agent who could truly be called 'spook', CIA director Stansfield Turner has disclosed.

The CIA chief said that the agency found a man who could 'see' what was going on anywhere in the world through his psychic powers.

Turner said CIA scientists and officials would show the man a picture of a place and he would then describe any activity going on there at that time.

Chicago Tribune
Saturday 13 August 1977

Russell Targ was that 'spook'. There were others. One was called Uri Geller. You might have heard of him and his bendy spoons. There was a whole team of them based at the Stanford Research Institute (SRI) in Menlo Park, California as part of the CIA's Stargate programme to find psychic warriors, just like the Russians. But unlike the Soviet rabbits and death row prisoners who could see through walls, Targ and his buddies said they could see over oceans, underground, round corners and into the future. In Targ's case, this wasn't bad for someone registered blind.

Targ was a physicist. In the 1970s he looked remarkably like Egon Spengler from the original *Ghostbusters* movie franchise. He had the coke-bottle glasses and gravity-defying hair. He loved lasers. As a senior staff scientist at Lockheed Missiles and Space Company, Targ developed airborne laser systems for the detection of wind shear and air turbulence. So, you know, he was not dumb.

To you and I, the notion of someone sitting in their armchair at home being able to close their eyes, breathe deeply and then after a few minutes draw the location of Soviet missiles is crazy. But that was what Targ and his other 'remote viewers' said they did. That was the term they used. Another was 'ESPionage', and remote viewing was just one part of it. It is not second sight, travelling clairvoyance, the paranormal or fortune telling, he said. It is definitely *not* superhuman. My mistake. He cut me off rather abruptly when I said that during our call.

'Do *you* know what I'm about?'

'Well, yes, I…' I stumbled.

'Have you and I met before?'

'No.'

This seemed to please him.

'Anyone can do it,' he told me. 'I taught it.'

You can probably guess where Targ taught lessons in ESP. Esalen. This was 1972 and Targ and Mike Murphy had become friends. Murphy had hosted many five-day conferences on parapsychology at Esalen with Targ in tow. Scientists and parapsychologists would talk for hours about distant mental influence, precognition and other siddhis. When it was done, the scientists and parapsychologists would go back to work and try to prove it all.

In March of that year, Murphy was supposed to speak at an Esalen-sponsored conference at Grace Cathedral in San Francisco. He couldn't make it. Could Targ fill in for him instead? That phone call would lead to Targ becoming a government-funded secret. His lecture on Soviet and American parapsychology went down well with a watching NASA scientist, George Pezdirtz. Targ talked about how astronauts could learn ESP techniques as an extra safeguard against peril when being blasted into orbit. Pezdirtz agreed.

Targ was asked to pitch for a NASA grant. Yet there was nervousness among the space race bods. Wasn't this a bit, you know, 'oddball'? So they kept it hush-hush. Targ set up his programme at Stanford, the CIA heard about it – as they tend to do – and liked it. The Stanford Research Institute was just one of many remote-viewing centres dotted around the US during the Cold War.

The star of the show, though, was Uri Geller. The CIA had hoped that he would be America's answer to Nina Kulagina, the Russian psychic. In 1970 Geller, who had been a regular in the small theatres and nightspots of Tel Aviv with his displays of mind control, was catapulted to international stardom. During a show, Geller suddenly became ill. A doctor found his pulse was frenetic at 170 beats per minute. Geller told the audience that he had foreseen that Gamal Abdel Nasser, the president of Egypt, 'had just died or is about to die'. Twenty minutes later, Radio Cairo reported that President Nasser had died after a heart attack. Geller was an instant superstar. The CIA sent for him.

Over nine separate days between 1 December 1972 and 15 January 1973, Geller was tested at Stanford Research Laboratory by Targ. Geller wowed him and CIA suits. In another room, a die was placed inside a metal box and shaken. It was then put in front of Geller, who told them which number was facing up. He was right eight times out of eight. According to the CIA, the probability of guessing was one in a million. He then pulled off a one in a trillion chance. Twelve times in a row, Geller identified which of ten identical aluminium cans placed in front of him had an object inside. The others had been empty.

In August 1973 Geller was back at Stanford and, according to declassified documents, placed in an 'opaque, acoustically and electrically shielded room' with two locked doors. Half a mile away, a scientist drew a picture of the devil holding a trident. Geller was asked to guess what the picture was. He drew a trident, the Ten Commandments, an apple with a worm in it and a snake. Geller was inducted into the programme.

In 1987, with the Cold War coming to a close, Geller, under instruction from the Reagan administration, tried to influence the thoughts of Yuli Vorontsov, Russia's first deputy minister. The Americans wanted him to sign the Intermediate-Range Nuclear Forces Treaty after progress had begun to slow. Geller had been 'booked' as an entertainer. So he bent some spoons and read a few minds. But for Vorontsov he performed a special trick, which Claiborne Pell, chairman of the Senate Foreign Relations Committee, and his wife, Nuala, saw. Geller closed his hand on some grass seeds and, after a few minutes of concentration, he opened it. 'They grew,' said Nuala Pell. 'The Russians were stunned.' After that, Geller worked the room for a bit and then stood behind Vorontsov. He stared at the back of his head and repeated in his mind, 'Sign! Sign! Sign!' Vorontsov signed. Geller is modest about taking the credit, apparently.

Claiborne Pell was friends with Mike Murphy. They would go jogging together. Murphy, perhaps squeaking excitedly as he spoke, had told Pell all about what he had learned from his trips to Russia. Pell, who was a huge fan of Geller, was like-minded and the pair would discuss human potentialities. The Democrat, then, was a supporter of Targ's remote-viewing programme. In White House intelligence meetings he had spoken forcefully for the argument that 'if the Russians have it and we don't, we are in serious trouble'. It was an example of Murphy's influence on American policy and the military turning to the esoteric.

It didn't end there. The most famous case of the US military trying to cultivate superpowers was the Black Ops First Earth Battalion, popularised by the Jon Ronson book *The Men Who Stare at Goats* and the movie of the same name. It was a group of supposedly psychic soldiers who were capable of using non-lethal powers to end war. Basically, anything the Russians could do – mind control, slowing down time, seeing through walls and even walking through walls. In the film, George Clooney played one of them, a real-life terrifying man called Peter Brusso, who claimed he could throw grown men several feet in the air just by looking at them. Eat your heart out, Zoukhar.

The first commander was Jim Channon, who thought it a good idea that each of his 'warrior monks' should carry into battle pouches of herbs, flowers as a sign of peace, and indigenous music to calm and confuse the enemy. Where did Channon get his ideas from? You guessed it: Esalen. Channon had been given a small

Pentagon budget and two years to research ways for the US military to use New Age methods in warfare. He spent most of the time at Esalen. Channon claimed that Murphy became a teacher and advisor.

Murphy was also an advisor for the Jedi Warrior training programme at West Point Military Academy in the 1980s. It was code-named Project Jedi and had been inspired by the First Earth Battalion. The same super-soldier skills were taught: invisibility, seeing into the future and extraordinary intuition, like knowing how many chairs were in a room before walking in – but also stopping the hearts of animals.

Esalen's links to government and military spooks could be described as coincidence. Apart from the fact that Esalen and Murphy were actually extremely close to some very powerful people in Washington. A contradiction? If the counterculture was all about sticking it to the man, then Esalen was hopping into bed with him. Or rather, enjoying some naked hot-tub bathing in the famous Big Sur springs.

The definitive history of Esalen, called *Esalen: America and the Religion of No Religion*, describes succinctly the dual role the institute played: 'Through a catalysing passion for the occult, a long-term commitment to the administrative, fundraising and political work … and a kind of eccentric diplomatic genius, Esalen played its own part in the collapse of Soviet communism and the softening of American militarism and the ending of the Cold War.' They may have been hippy, but they were not dippy.

Ronald Reagan was said to be an Esalen fan. And why not? As Reagan portrayed the Russians as an 'Evil Empire' that needed a Star Wars missile system to keep them in check, Murphy and his cohorts were styling themselves as the Jedi rebels, capable of using their siddhis – the Force, if you will – for the good guys.

The trips to Russia undertaken by Murphy and Hickman were rich with information about Russia's desire for superpowers. That they could travel, and there were exchanges of information between the two states, was ascribed to periods of improved relations. The most well known was *détente* – French for cooling-off – in 1971. At other times, because the war was cold not hot, each side kind of let the other carry on with what they were up to, while being heavily monitored. Hickman had been forced to take lie-detector tests by the Russians (and the FBI, who would turn up unannounced anywhere in the world), the pair's hotel rooms were bugged, movements tracked and both the CIA and KGB were worried that Murphy and Hickman worked for the other side, or both. Murphy had a direct line to America's ambassador to Moscow under Reagan. His name was Arthur Hartman. He was another Esalen convert, having attended workshops, and would eventually train as a psychoanalyst.

Murphy, then, found himself in the middle of the Cold War race to create a psychic soldier. And it had all started with an interest in sport's capability to push the human possibilities; from swapping stories with his Russian counterparts at a softball game in Moscow to lecturing the Russian Olympic committee.

I thought about Adam Brucker's warning when I rang him for advice about speaking with Mike: 'Don't ask about the Russians.' Was this hinting at Murphy's Cold War activities when he was hopping between the two countries with the intelligence agencies watching his every move? Could it be that Murphy was, in fact, a spy? It was not a particularly complicated conclusion to jump to. After all, he told me he had been recruited by almost every secret agency going at one time or another. I called him to ask.

'It was *like* I was a CIA officer,' he said. 'I'd go jogging with Claiborne Pell and tell him all this stuff and it blew his mind. He was into this stuff. We did *not* go into it politically. It was for friendship. For culture. We didn't have government money at Esalen. My proposal was that the US and Russia explored hidden human reserves together.'

Bringing the two factions together was indeed what Murphy and Hickman said they were focused on. So they did. They thought they could change the world and end the Cold War. So they did. Well, they at least turned up the thermostat.

With their friends in Washington giving them a nod and a wink, a series of Soviet–American exchanges was organised from 1980. After the visits by Murphy and Hickman, the pair revealed they had discovered a 'Soviet Esalen', a group of believers and free thinkers who shared their ideas about siddhis and human potential. Contacts ranged from the obligatory psychic to Kremlin influencers.

As a result, astronauts and cosmonauts, writers, KGB agents, military veterans, politicians (like Claiborne Pell) and diplomats were frequently invited to Esalen. First they were told to sit cross-legged on the floor with pillows and just talk to each other. Then it was time to get naked and jump in the hot tub. The idea was to get Americans and Russians to recognise that, 'Hey, you're not so bad after all'. And that pushing the nuclear button would be a terrible mistake.

The brains at Esalen wanted to call this project The Institute for Theoretical Studies. Then someone pointed out that the acronym for that was TITS. It was changed to the Esalen Soviet–American Exchange Program. It still exists today, albeit under a different name – Track Two: An Institute for Citizen Diplomacy. It is run by Dulce Murphy, Mike's wife.

It was in the nick of time. The Doomsday Clock, the timepiece those cheery folk at the Bulletin of Atomic Scientists kept ticking to judge how close East and West were to obliterating us all, had nudged the little hand to four minutes to midnight and oblivion in 1981. Three years later it was pushed another minute forward.

'We had KGB guys and CIA guys at Esalen talking to each other,' Mike said. 'The KGB knew communism wasn't working. It was their job to know everything … they could fucking see it. When we hosted people, it was just confirming what they already knew.'

The exchange programme's biggest coup was to bring Boris Yeltsin to America in 1989. Yeltsin's aides had contacted Russian activists who were connected to Hickman and Murphy. At the time, Yeltsin was considered something of a political lightning rod in Russia. He was a critic of the communist regime and believed it had to change. It was a visit that played a part in ending the Cold War.

Some of Yeltsin's aides had benefited from the cultural exchange set up by Esalen and they approached the institute to ask if they would be interested in hosting him. 'I was against it,' Mike said. 'We were in with the [Mikhail] Gorbachev gang and they were making big changes.' Yeltsin wanted to overthrow Gorbachev, so Mike and Dulce both thought it wasn't a good idea to be sponsoring him. Mike didn't take part in the trip as a result: 'I didn't meet him [Yeltsin] but Dulce did. They were at the New York stock exchange and by chance I had the TV on and he was walking across the shot with Dulce.' This was what seemed to excite Mike more, before he added: 'It turned out to be a gigantic deal 'cos he flipped!'

Indeed he did. Yeltsin spent most of the trip drunk but when he visited a Houston grocery store called Randall's he sobered up pretty quickly. One of the Communist Party's big fibs was that America staged its wealthy image through fake stores. He was shocked by the bountiful aisles of meats, cheeses and vegetables. He asked why no one was queuing. He stopped shoppers to ask how much they earned per month and what they spent on food. Yeltsin became upset. 'They've been lying to us,' he said. 'This country is better.' Two years later he quit the Party, stood on a tank in Red Square and became a capitalist. The Iron Curtain came down. Now, it is true that there were many factors at play that ended the Cold War – Gorbachev's restructuring and *glasnost* were pretty significant – but Yeltsin's trip to Randall's helped to expose the failing Soviet economy and accelerated the fall in communist ideology.

In time, too, Russia's Hidden Human Reserves project dwindled. The advances in performance-enhancing drugs proved more powerful. Athletes didn't just feel superhuman, they *were* superhuman, dosed up to the eyeballs so they bulged manically like our friend Dr Zoukhar's.

'It was superseded by the drug culture,' Hickman said. 'With good reason. You get hurt, they shoot you up with drugs, and you can keep playing. You can't do that with mental stuff.'

Stanley Krippner agreed: 'THEY USED INJECTIONS. BUT DON'T CITE ME ON THAT. I HEARD IT SECOND HAND.' Most of us had. It has been well documented that athletes' drug use under state-sponsored programmes was rife in the East. In fact, it still is.

So did that mean the search stopped when the Cold War ended? Had the cosmic playbook been torn up in favour of under-the-counter prescriptions for uppers, downers and in-betweeners? I wondered what had happened to the psychic spies and the First Earth Battalion's warrior monks, who found themselves out of a job when the Cold War ended. What did they do? Where did they go?

4

DARTH VADER CAN'T HIT A SEVEN IRON

A hundred miles south of Los Angeles, just a hop from the Mexican border, round the corner from the International Banana Museum and down a dusty track, lives Peter Brusso. It's desert. He calls this barren, arid place 'bumfuck Egypt' because it's almost impossible to get a cell-phone signal. 'You found me,' he said cheerily as I got out of my car. It was approaching 120 degrees. 'Quick, come on in, the air con's on.' I was anxious to get inside. The first thing I noticed about Peter was that he was huge, maybe 230 pounds. He must have been very pleased when George Clooney was cast to play him in *The Men Who Stare at Goats*. The second thing I noticed as I walked through the door made me take a step back.

'Er, Peter, you've got a lot of, er, weapons on the wall?'

'Of course.' He said it as if I'd pointed out he also had windows and a front door.

'Do you mind if I count them?'

'You English are so prim and proper! I love that. Go ahead.'

There were 64 knives or axes, two semi-automatic weapons, one fly-swatter and a banner that said 'Kill 'em all and let God sort them out'.

'You forgot the two knives that I'm wearing now,' Peter said.

Peter was also wearing his First Earth Battalion t-shirt. The First Earth Battalion, or FEB as he called it, was all about non-lethal force, trying to make war less violent. Turn up with flowers and some happy-clappy music and resistance would be futile. Occasionally their band of super-soldiers would (try to) walk through the odd wall, make themselves appear invisible and place thoughts in the head of the enemy, but it was most definitely not about the sort of guns and knives – with serrated teeth thicker than my fingers – that Peter hung like pictures.

But then Peter was also a trained killer. He served in Vietnam and did ten months in Cambodia. He was a 'spook for the CIA' and more recently had trained US marines in martial arts at Camp Pendleton in San Diego. You can see countless videos of him on YouTube 'killing' his students in mock knife fights. And there is also a video of him beating up Jon Ronson, the author of *The Men Who Stare at Goats*. This 'fight' is replicated in the movie with Clooney going to work on Ewan McGregor.

'Oh, Jon squealed like a little girl,' he chuckled. And I chuckled too. Silly Jon, I thought. But Peter narrowed his eyes and I stopped laughing.

'Stand up,' he said.

'Why? What, er…'

'Come on, stand up, it's the price of the interview. Just let me beat you up for a bit … you need to see how *this thing* works.'

He brandished a piece of plastic. About as long as a pen, and half as thick, it looked like the neck and head of an overweight cockerel. With a hole through the middle. It was called 'the

Predator'. It was a weapon Peter had made based on commander of First Earth Battalion Jim Channon's research at Esalen on chakra points and Eastern mind and body philosophy.

'Attack me,' he said.

Apparently, Jon Ronson had tried to resist Peter's 'advances' for about 30 minutes. In the video it's edited down to seconds. I thought there was little point in wasting time. So I lunged, half-heartedly, with my hands outstretched. Quickly, he had somehow manoeuvred my thumb through the hole of the Predator. And he was twisting it around. And it hurt like hell.

'Great, isn't it?'

Before I could answer, he jabbed the base of the Predator's neck just below my heart and between my ribs. I doubled up.

'So it can also be great on any bony areas ... and soft tissue, too.' And with that he placed the serrated edge of its head on to my ear lobe. But then he stopped.

'If I twisted it now or applied any force, it could rip off your ear.'

'OK,' I gasped. 'Good. You've made your point.'

I should say that Peter is not a thug. He is smart. Really smart. He was an engineer and has separate PhDs in physics, nanotechnology and metaphysics. He has a congressional medal for recycling a nuclear warhead (who doesn't, though, right?). And you know those rolling advertising boards you used to see in sports games? Peter invented those.

But I didn't come to talk about his inventions. Or to be beaten up. There's another video on YouTube. It's of Peter using the power of his mind to throw Ronson to the ground by barely touching him. In it, he tells him, 'I'm literally going to move through your body and you're not going to be able to stand there.' And that's what happened. Ronson flew backwards and reported a pain in his armpits, neck and chest. 'I was flying across the room,' he wrote.

Peter said he was projecting his thoughts into Ronson's head. I wanted to know whether a sportsman could do this.

'It can be done with a sports person very easily,' Peter said. 'When I fought in martial arts every day I literally knew what my opponent was going to do. The fundamentals were described in the FEB. I believe sports people access the same kind of skills that we do in combat – clairvoyance. You know what's going to happen, we're transmitting and receiving mentally. We do that all the time – if you're driving down the road and you've got a guy ready to turn? You just know he's gonna pull out in front of you. And then he does. It happens all the time.

'I'm not a "sports" guy. Martial arts is a way of life. We teach people to kill people, not to score a point. Big, big difference in your approach.'

Peter believes that anyone is capable of doing what he did to Ronson. You just need to have a calm, clear and quiet mind. But if anyone can do it, why wouldn't, say, a boxer learn this skill? He would be unbeatable.

'I said to Jon, "I'm an old fat guy. What are you scared of me for?" He was paralysed with fear and that's 'cos I was projecting this fear into his mind. And he grabbed hold of that fear and ran away with that thought. It became more powerful.

'The answer is yes. I've walked out on to a mat and thought-projected on to my opponent: "There's absolutely nothing you can do to stop me from killing you. Absolutely nothing." And as I walked towards them with my hands down they're paralysed. You walk right in and grab them by the throat and take them out. I've experienced it. I've done it in combat even.'

Peter didn't really answer the question. I had rather hoped he would name this mythical boxer. But instead he talked about himself. So I just let his mouth run.

'You paint the picture you want your opponent to see. There's been times when I've been beaten on the mat, and I know I'm out of gas, that I have to paint a picture of such strength and to do something so different that they get scared. It's all a bluff. There's other times when I knew I had to bluff so I pretended I was hurt and they get all boisterous and over-cocky. *Then* they die.'

Let's just leave that last sentence hanging for a bit…

Then Peter said, 'You can practise [mind control]. Do you have a dog?'

'No.'

But my neighbours have two. Pete said I could mind project on them 'pretty nicely'. When they start getting agitated, barking and snarling, I should 'send' them a mental picture of a steak. 'It works like a champ,' he said. 'They'll think, "Yeah, we wanna eat. This guy wants to give us a steak. Where is it? Where's the food?"' Peter didn't tell me what would happen when the dogs realised they weren't going to get a steak. He kept talking.

'Animals project all the time. From rabbits to rabbits. We can read rabbits' minds. We can talk to them. We can read animals' minds easy. Plants are even better. You know flora and fauna can actually be your greatest friends?'

Reading the minds of rabbits, talking to plants. All well and good, but I didn't understand why, if Peter said anyone could do it, more people weren't using this in sport. If I was a curious, open-minded athlete I would want to learn how to do this stuff.

'You've answered your own question,' Peter said. 'They are just not that open-minded in sports. There's a very particular type of person that you are looking for.' Peter waggled his head and looked very pleased with himself. He was challenging me to ask the next question.

'OK, so who am I looking for?'

47

'The person you want to find in sports or who has an aptitude for what you're talking about is something called a "switchable". That's a person that changes their neurology depending on the environment they're in.'

What Peter was talking about was how human beings learn a skill. We do it one of four main ways. Visual: using images. Aural: by listening. Verbal: in speech and writing. Kinaesthetic: using your body or sense of touch. Peter was arguing that a superhuman sports star would be able to 'switch' effortlessly between the styles.

'I'm a switchable. We pick up learning styles of others, we're more likely to receive other people's internal information. It's like a goalkeeper in soccer saving a penalty shot. He's reading stuff from the shooter – maybe he's received energy or a thought projection. So he knows which way the ball is going to go.'

That ability to receive internal information and to influence it was very First Earth Battalion. Without it, you were no use to them. But when the Cold War was coming to an end, there just didn't seem the need for a battalion of psychic super-soldiers any more. The US military had been scaled back overall because, simply, the chances of war with another country had reduced drastically. And domestically there was no appetite for interfering overseas after Vietnam. Peter's warrior monk days were over. Back then he was as curious as I was now about whether it could work in sport. So he thought hard about choosing a sport that was predominantly mental, with participants that had an unhealthy dose of neuroticism and, importantly, were rich (a man's got to make a living). Golf it was, then. The sport where amateur players to professionals had the disposable income to try anything once in the hope it would improve their game.

He started coaching in 1990. Peter's methods were, naturally, a little different. He wasn't interested in how a player swung the club or putted, he wanted to get inside their heads. And for Peter that was pretty easy. He called it 'being Brusso-ised'.

'I told these guys, "I will get ten strokes off your game in four hours or less or you don't pay me,"' he said. 'I guaranteed it. I'd never played golf in my life.'

Peter started off teaching the local golf pro. 'He said to me, "This is incredible, it's East meets West, the Holy Grail!"' Then he put another local pro on the senior Tour who had been trying and failing to make the cut for two years. 'We took seven strokes off him! Fucking *sev-en*.' He taught a long ball champion to hit the ball further than he'd ever hit before. Peter was making almost $4,000 a week and was coaching players all over the West Coast. So, how did he do it?

Darth Vader. Probably best let Peter explain.

'I asked them to close their eyes and imagine they have a big, juicy lemon. Freshly picked. There's a knife next to it. "I want you to cut that lemon, pick it up and look at it, the juiciness. Now take a big bite." And they had the actual reaction.' He mimicked the face of someone eating a lemon. 'If that can't tell you there's no difference to what's real and what's imaginary, nothing ever will,' Peter said. 'So if you can see it in here [pointing to his head] you can experience it out there. So I told them, "Stand up and, in your mind, put on Darth Vader's cape. How would he stand? How would he walk? Feel the power he has. Now when you've got that club in your hand I want you to close your eyes, put on the cape, stand like Darth Vader, and I want you to choose a target, see the flight of the ball and see it hit the target. Keep playing it over and over in your mind until it's perfectly clear, and then hit the damn thing. Do that bullshit wiggle or whatever that thing is before you hit the ball if you have to." That's all I wanted them to do. Oh my god, they were hitting the target eight times out of ten.'

There was only one rule: you couldn't keep the Darth Vader cape on all of the time. It had to be off between shots. Why? Because if you walked round in daily life thinking you were Darth Vader you might not prove to be so popular.

None of this was luck, Peter said. Darth Vader stomping around West Coast golf courses in the early nineties was down to Peter 'knowing how people's brains work' – basic neurology he learned in the First Earth Battalion. 'The point of the lemon story was to prove that your mind doesn't know what's real or imaginary. Think about that lemon. Go on … your mouth will start to water.' He was right. If you do the same now, yours will too.

If golfers thought they were Darth Vader, they felt invincible? 'Not just that,' Peter said. 'Darth Vader is not the type of guy to miss the target, right? It also gave them a focus for that visualisation. They were imagining what the shot was going to look like. The brain was prepared. So it replicated the shot in real time.'

Word started to spread about this mystical East-meets-West golf teacher. Peter was in demand – a reincarnation of Mike Murphy's legendary Shivas Irons. And soon the pros started calling him up. His first was Tommy Moore, who was on the Tour for three years. He tragically passed away from a rare blood disease in 1998, aged 35.

'Most athletes are telling themselves what not to do. Tommy was no different. He was annoyed 'cos he hit the shot off centre of the green. I said, "What's wrong with that?" "It's not in the centre." "Well, did you visualise hitting in the centre?" "No." Your brain only knows what you're focusing on emotionally. It doesn't know right or wrong, good or bad. So I taught Tommy and he did really good.'

After Tommy, there was Tom Watson. You may or may not have heard of Tom Watson, depending on how much you are into golf. But let me tell you, Watson was kind of a big deal. In the 1970s and 80s he was ranked as the number one player in the world, replacing the legendary Jack Nicklaus. He won eight major golf championships and was top of the earnings list five times.

But in the late eighties and early nineties he was not winning so much. He was looking for a boost to help him return to the glory days, to keep up with the new breed of player coming through. So he turned to Peter Brusso and Darth Vader.

'He was real superstitious,' Peter said, with a sneer, as if this was a bad thing. Surely it would help him get into character when he put the cape on?

'Maybe. We used Darth Vader because he was recognisable. Everyone knew who he was.'

'But was it always Darth Vader?'

'No. It can be any powerful caped person you want.'

'But always a caped person?'

'Well, they have to be powerful,' he said, slightly irked.

Their first tournament together was the Pacific at Torrey Pines near San Diego. I imagined Peter in his FEB t-shirt – maybe with two knives hidden somewhere – rolling around the course willing his Dark Emperor to do great things.

'I think he came close to winning. And people were asking me who I was. But Tom's number one thing was: I wasn't allowed to say who I was or what I did. He didn't want people to know he had a coach out there. It would be perceived as a weakness.'

I thought it more likely that Tom didn't want his peers to know he was imagining he was Darth Vader. It would have been perceived as something else entirely. Unfortunately, Peter and Tom didn't quite get along. Peter felt Tom was not committing to 'the tech' – slang for Peter's methods.

'I threw him on the ground once,' Peter said. 'I took his ass down. Big time. Boooom! He acted stupid and negative so I had to reset his mind. So I did a classic combat hip throw and he was laying on the ground and I was standing over him: "Now we're not gonna talk like that again. We need a real reset here and you need to be afraid I'll do this again." And his eyes got all big: "You assaulted me." "Yeah, and I could kill you in a heartbeat too. But let's not go there. I'm here to help you."'

Then there was the time when Peter threw Watson's seven iron into a lake. 'He called this club "Damian", like it was the devil, because he couldn't hit [with] it,' Peter snorted. 'So why put it in the bag? I threw that in the fucking water. He didn't like that, either.'

'But otherwise you got on OK?' I asked.

'Well, yeah. But he kept going back to the superstition. He'd wear the same clothes. He had to eat the same breakfast…'

'What, like porridge?'

'Dunno. Whatever. Golfers never change. So being into a new tech for a short time freaks them out: they worry it might fuck their whole game up – they're too superstitious.'

Peter became disillusioned with golf and golfers. He taught a football college place-kicker. And a ten-pin bowler, Darth Vader in tow once again. But eventually he decided sports were not for him. 'It's hard not to think hitting a little ball around with a stick is bullshit,' he said.

Peter had, seemingly with little effort, improved the performances of golfers. It had worked with Tommy Moore, and his long-ball champion in less celebrated environments. But not Tom Watson. There's a line between the successes and failures. On one side you have a lower level of performance than the other. Watson was a superstar, the others were not.

This thought bugged me. Surely the best sportsmen and women would be more likely to be capable of the siddhis than the average Joe, especially if Peter was right. 'Anyone can do it,' he said. The more focused you are? The more committed? Traits that the best of the best absolutely must have in abundance.

There were a group of people who agreed with that, of course. Mike Murphy and his Esalen cohorts. Sure, they had been busy saving the world from Soviet tyranny, but Murphy was adamant that it was on the athletic field where these skills would be more beneficial, rather than the battlefield.

5

BIG RED

It was another cold, rainy mid-1960s day in St Louis. The St Louis Cardinals were playing the Pittsburgh Steelers. David Meggyesy (pronounced 'Mega-see') was the Cardinals linebacker. He had his 'psyche on'. He always had his psyche on. He had to. He was a hitter, a demolition man whose job was to jeopardise his safety for the good of the team.

From a kick-off, his role was to run halfway across the field and smash into the third man from the kicker on the Pittsburgh team. He watched the flight of the ball in the leaden sky, took a couple of steps back, rocking on to his heels as if he were a human catapult, and then he began to sprint.

Meggyesy's target did not see him coming. Maybe because he was a rookie. Maybe because he thought the linebacker had failed to do his job. He was running at full speed, too, but was not looking to his left or right. Mistake. He had his head down and was focused only straight ahead. So Meggyesy decided to go low.

It was the sound of the Pittsburgh player's knee exploding in his ear that Meggyesy remembers most vividly. It was a 'jagged, tearing sound of muscles and ligaments separating'. I tried to imagine that sound when Meggyesy's huge hand swallowed mine when we met. But I couldn't. I was still trying to comprehend what it would feel like being hit by the proverbial train in front of me. The sort of collision that had happened every minute of every game in the football pros since time immemorial. Meggyesy is 74 now, but he still has the lean, mean frame. Yet he's not mean at all. So I decided best to call him Dave, such was his friendly nature.

'Football's violent, eh?' he chuckled. It was a nervous laugh betraying the conflict he had felt throughout his seven-year career, one you can see in his face, which is kind and measured. It was his job on the football field to be violent. But he hated the violence. When he put that Pittsburgh player on a stretcher, he felt sympathy. He wasn't supposed to feel sympathy. That player was collateral damage in the football war. And the war had to be won at any cost. Owners and coaches, the bullet-headed lords that ran the sport, absolutely demanded that of their players.

The Pittsburgh incident was the final hit in a way. Sick of football, in 1969 Dave retired – aged just 29, when supposedly at the peak of his powers – to write a scathing exposé of the football culture called *Out of Their League*. It was published in 1970. He was an instant pariah and disowned by the sport. Coach of the New York Jets Weeb Ewbank said that he had fallen for 'communist hogwash. These are the things that poison our young youth.'

Dave loves that quote. 'It's great, isn't it?' he said. 'The "young youth". As opposed to the old youth.'

The young Dave was also an instant celebrity. He had not only chewed up and spat out the hand that fed him but he had, in the eyes of the nation, committed a sacrilege on America's sweetheart sport. No one had dared do that before. He appeared on the Dick Cavett TV show with Janis Joplin and Margot Kidder, wearing a purple tie-dye t-shirt, jeans and cowboy boots. He had an unruly mop and he stroked a bushy beard. There was sniggering in the audience at first, then they realised that Dave was no dumb jock. He spoke eloquently and thoughtfully. He explained how all of the ills of American society were right there in the locker room: college players were being paid under the table in brown envelopes; team doctors were shooting them with uppers and downers to beat the pain; coaches bullied players to play with severe injury by calling them 'fakers'; there were orgies organised by married players; teams were split along racial lines.

By the time Dave left his college team – Syracuse – his career had almost been ended by the horrific injuries he was supposed to forget about. He had often been misdiagnosed. He broke a wrist, separated both shoulders, tore an ankle so badly it broke the arch of his foot, suffered three major concussions and almost lost an arm to amputation because of the wrong treatment.

The bottom line, he felt, was that the system did not care about the individual. After he quit, Meggyesy set about trying to beat the system.

'Coaches develop a talent,' Dave wrote in his book, 'for emasculating a player over and over again without quite killing him. Most coaches – Vince Lombardi was the classic example – give their players a tantalising hint of what it might be like to be a man, but always keep it out of reach.' Criticism of Lombardi, a deity of coaches and whose name adorns the Super Bowl trophy, was tantamount to blasphemy.

Dave shrugged it off, just as he did when I met him, with a weary puff of the cheeks: 'Lombardi was against everything I was saying. A lot of it's still relevant. There will always be coaches who coach that way. The bawlers, the bullies. This is really important to understand.'

Dave laboured this point. He said that I had to appreciate that, although his book was now considered a story about how things used to be, not a lot had changed. Players were still commodities who, if they didn't play on through physical or mental pain, were letting everybody down. Few franchises were making the link between a happy and safe playing staff and winning. Even fewer recognised that a coach screaming and shouting at players would not result in trophies.

He was right. The NFL had not moved on. Read this quote from the NFL rookie symposium in 2012: 'Nobody cares about your problems. The fans don't care. The media doesn't care. And the ownership doesn't care. They care about results.' Those words belonged to Chris Ballard, who was the player performance director of the Kansas City franchise. Seven months before he told his players this, one of them, Jovan Belcher, had shot his girlfriend nine times and then driven to the team parking lot and shot himself.

In one way, Dave was a coach's dream. He always put the team first. But in another he was 'a little bit too different'. He was too hippy. Coaches liked football players who had haircuts they could use a spirit level on. Dave's was flyaway free, as was the company he kept away from the field. The team hierarchy were twitching uncomfortably.

He was an anti-Vietnam campaigner. He hosted anti-war meetings at his house and paid for buses to take protestors from St Louis to Washington. And this piqued the interest of the FBI. His phone was tapped, he was followed and an 'extensive dossier' was compiled. The FBI then tried to force him out of the Cardinals. It worked.

'The owners of the Cardinals told me that I'd be released if I didn't stop,' Dave told me. 'I was told that the government was using the intelligence services of the military to investigate citizens. The government of course denied it. People don't realise that the government was really freaked out by the anti-war movement.'

'So they had you down as a communist, then?' I asked.

Dave laughed. 'A little bit, yeah. Some guy hung a bedsheet over the stand at one of our games and it said "The Big Red Thinks Pink". That was the Cardinals' nickname, so they were saying the players were commies. It was pretty funny.'

But not that funny. Instead of starting games, Dave was deliberately benched. His position at the Cardinals had become impossible. 'It was devastating for me,' he said. 'I felt betrayed.' So he quit.

His subsequent attempted destruction of the sport that had made him, but almost broke him, was shocking and fascinating. But what I was most interested in was what he didn't write about. Use any term you like – 'lifted the lid', 'warts and all' – every misdemeanour and stomach churner was in there. But what was left out? What was it that even this most zealous of whistle-blowers didn't have the guts to say? It was why I had come to meet him in San Francisco – having tracked him down via Barry Robbins, Mike Murphy's friend. I had been told that Dave had experienced the superpowers.

Dave never tried for them. They just occurred. And they occurred more times than he could actually remember. 'Minnesota, I guess,' Dave nodded to himself, slightly bashful. 'And who else? Cleveland, Baltimore. They happened all the time. They weren't rare occurrences.'

Meggyesy was convinced that when he slipped into a 'kind of trance' he was able to see the plays before they happened, the speed of the game slowed down and players were shrouded in an 'aura'. These siddhi states happened with such regularity that he didn't sound sure exactly which game they occurred in. But I believed him all right. He spoke of them without fanfare.

'I could sense the movements of the running backs a split second before they happened. I played a brilliant game. I had a sure knowing where the next play was going – patterns of player movement, including energy halos.'

I was excited by Dave's reveal. Here was a guy who had not displayed just one siddhi, but three at once, although I was not too sure of the benefits of seeing players surrounded by light. For that I had to check good old Sri Aurobindo, Mike Murphy's inspiration and the 'discoverer' of the siddhis. It was, according to the great mystic, an indication of the 'opening of an inner vision'.

But Dave remained matter of fact. I wondered *why* he thought these things happened to him. 'Funny, I think about that question occasionally,' he said. I asked whether his LSD trips with the anti-war protestors had played a part. That line of enquiry was not dismissed. 'It expands the mind,' he said. 'Marijuana, too.'

It came back to childhood, he said. A symmetry that had a sadness to it. His upbringing on a farm in Ohio, where there were eight of them living in one room, was brutal. His father, a Hungarian emigrant, beat him black and blue for the 'crime' of being left-handed. Sometimes he used an axe handle, sometimes a razor strop. It depended how drunk he was. This violence, ironically, prepared Dave for his life in the NFL. And the long hours spent cow-watching in the field behind the family home aged six prepared him for what he calls 'the inner life'. For a kid, he was a pretty deep thinker.

'My job as a kid during the summers was to "watch the cows", meaning I would take the bovines, steers and cows out to the back fields to make sure they did not get into and feast in the grain fields, corn, wheat and rye. I was alone for six hours or so each day. I think in retrospect I would meditate in a way, think about "stuff" – God, plants, fields, the sun, the cows; all that was surrounding me – and a self-conscious witness perspective of "Me" emerged, as I would call it now.

'When I was eight or nine the Shredded Wheat cereal boxes would have information cards in them. One card had a drawing of an Indian holy man, a yogi, who sat on a platform 20 feet in the air 24 hours a day. The commentary was about this person being a yogi, a spiritual holy man as we would say today. I vividly remember that drawing and description, it had a big impact on me. A sense of huge wonderment came in, and questions: what was this all about? What was he doing sitting there? What was a yogi? I was fascinated.'

Dave had never talked of this before with his locker-room buddies, nor with many 'outsiders', which I clearly was, having not experienced anything he had described. This was his way of life. And the siddhis had just been a manifestation of that. It seemed strange that he wilfully left them out of his book, and the belief structure that gave rise to them. Why? Was it for fear of being labelled crazy?

'Yeah, exactly,' he said. 'No one talks about them. How do you ask *that* question? Did time slow down? Imagine the athletes' responses? Come on!'

The trance-like state, then. How did that come about? Was he meditating? This is what he called 'getting his psyche on'.

'A lot of it was preparation, you know? We watched a lot of film, really analysing what a team would do – the formation, field position – these were the factors to internalise to figure out what they would do. So that gave me a real focus. For an individual, it was like, "If they do this, how do I respond? How do I react?" So that was the level of detail you got into. From a psychological standpoint, by the end of the week you're really thinking about every possible situation as a team and individual. That's honed down. By the Saturday I was doing mental rehearsal: "If they do this, what do I do?" So you play that out and visualise that in your mind.'

So Dave had already played in the match in his head 24 hours beforehand. Think about that the next time you watch a sports event. Someone, somewhere out there might, just might, have seen it all play out in his or her downtime before it's happened. To them, it's now just a real-time action replay.

'But prior to the game you're still really nervous,' Dave said. Players had different ways to cope. One guy would bang his head against the wall. Dave had a ritual of tying his shoelaces 20 times. 'It was a way of focusing,' he said. The way Dave prepared didn't always fit with the mood of the locker room. Before one game, he was focusing on his breathing, 'getting centred', and had his eyes shut. The coach thought he was asleep and tore a strip off him.

That disconnect bugged him. But there was a place for people like him, those who were different. In 1968 he visited Esalen to take a class called 'More Joy'. It taught techniques to help people return to a baby state, where they might gurgle and giggle at someone blowing a raspberry. Dave kept schtum about this when he returned to the locker room.

Inevitably, his path crossed with Mike Murphy. They first met properly ('probably 1970') when watching the Chicago College All-Star football game on TV with Hunter S. Thompson, who didn't fire off a few rounds into the set when the result did not go his way. For the first time, Dave had found a kindred spirit in a sporting context. Mike understood the way Dave ticked, and what he wanted to achieve. Encouraged by Mike and feeling emboldened by the knowledge that there were people who shared his view, Dave decided to do something about the disconnect that had made him feel like an intruder during his football career and after it, too.

Help, or rather inspiration, came in the form of a psychologist called Abraham Maslow, who was all the rage at Esalen. Maslow pondered why people in his field spent all of their time studying humans who were 'deficient' – those with depression, addiction or whatever. Why not study those who were at the bottom of the bell curve? The most creative, those capable of high performance. What was it that made them exceptional? His famous 'Hierarchy of Needs' theory – a sort of checklist for being brilliant – attempted to answer those questions.

Maslow wanted to know how and why people achieved siddhi states, and for that he is remembered as crucial to shaping the early Esalen vision. If Murphy had the ideology, Maslow provided the clout. His books in the 1960s routinely sold more than 100,000 copies. Here was an esteemed psychologist saying, 'Yes, I agree with you.' He therefore gave the Esalen advocates confidence by rejecting the widely held belief that altered states of consciousness were symptoms of a mental disorder or that they didn't exist. Maslow categorised them as a 'force' or called them 'peak experiences'. He described peak experiences as 'rare, exciting, oceanic, deeply moving, exhilarating, elevating experiences that generate an advanced form of perceiving reality, and are even mystic and magical in their effect'. In early research, Maslow set about interviewing and questioning 'healthy' people – instead of those considered to have psychological disorders – who had had peak experiences. He found that common triggers were art, nature, sex, creative work, music, scientific knowledge, and introspection. And, of course, sport.

'Mike was very close friends with Maslow,' Meggyesy said. 'He was in on the human potential movement at the start at Esalen. Maslow's view was that people had the experiences I had all the time. *All the time.* But he said they were accidental. Mike's question was this: "Does it have to be accidental?"'

Murphy and Meggyesy wanted to train athletes and coaches to actually access siddhi experiences. To reach those states 'more often than not'. In 1973 the Esalen Sports Center was born. And they got up to some crazy stuff.

6

THE GREAT WILD MAN

There was a time when if Mike Spino walked through a hotel lobby, people would tremble in their shoes. Spino was old New Jersey Italian Mafia stock. His uncle was known as 'the Finishing Clerk'. You didn't mess with a guy called the Finishing Clerk. So you didn't mess with Mike Spino.

'You ever seen the movie *Goodfellas*?' he asked me over the phone. 'Remember the guy who gets the wire and tries to strangle someone? My uncle – he didn't do that … much.'

Walking towards me through the lobby of the Holiday Inn at Fisherman's Wharf, San Francisco's tourist hot spot, Spino, 85, was not the least bit intimidating. He was the loveable uncle you most looked forward to welcoming at Christmas lunch. He waved enthusiastically all the way from the check-in desk to where I was seated, trundling along in huge white sneakers, a blue blazer and cream chinos.

'I'm not going to mess with you, Mike,' I said.

And in a wonderful New Jersey drawl he said, 'I wouldn't if I were you,' laughed, then shook me by the shoulder and said, 'It's great to see you.'

He asked whether I'd met with Mike Murphy. The pair went way back. Spino was the Esalen running coach. He taught

Murphy and Jim Hickman. They would run in the hills around Big Sur, meditate, then run some more.

I told him we'd met: 'It was strange because he didn't really want to talk about the Russians.'

'I wouldn't ask him about that.'

'Why does everyone keep saying that?'

'It's all part of his mystery. You never know with Mike. He believes … this is the sort of stuff he believes,' he paused, incredulous and holding back a laugh, 'there's some big game last year, the pro game, and the guy missed the extra point. He thinks that all the people watching it were willing him to miss it. That's what he believes. At least, that's what he'll say he believes just to get a rise out of you. Ha.'

'But do you believe it, Mike?'

'Well, I'll tell you what the Russians did. In tennis matches they'd put people in the stands and think evil thoughts about the other guy – that they had ants in their muscles.'

But Spino, despite his Mafia upbringing, was not one for the darker elements of this force. He was a lover not a fighter. He had a serene manner about him. 'I'm a poet, you know,' he told me, nodding like a sage. Sometimes he wrote about the 'otherness' of pounding the road alone. He said that running, as an activity, was capable of launching people into alternative states of consciousness, where it felt like their feet weren't touching the ground or that they were flying.

It had happened to him. In 1967 he had gone for a six-mile run at top speed. 'My body felt like a skeleton … I felt like the wind. When the run was over I didn't know who I was. Was I the one who had been running? Or the ordinary Mike Spino? I sat down and wept.' He cried because he was happy at experiencing a 'magic'. There were also tears of frustration at the 'impossibility of giving this experience to anyone'. But he would sure as hell try.

Spino, who had been on the track team at college, and Murphy came together during the jogging boom in the 1970s, when you couldn't set foot in the park of an American city without risk of being mown down by a stampede of amateur runners.

Athletics coaching was Spino's forte. He directed the pre-Olympic training camp for the Atlanta Games and coached hundreds of All-American runners at Georgia Tech and Life University, regularly filling trophy cabinets. He was the Peter Brusso (minus the knives) of athletics. Instead of using Darth Vader, he tailored visualisations to the runner to make them feel as if they were untouchable. If one was a patriot, he would get them to imagine being draped in the US flag on the podium, hearing 'The Star-Spangled Banner'. Or he might have them believe they were a famous distance runner, like Sebastian Coe. If someone was a massive *Star Wars* fan, Vader might, in theory, have been useful, but when I asked him Spino laughed and said, 'No, never tried that one.'

Other techniques included asking runners to imagine that in their right hand they had a special button, which when pressed would give them a boost of energy. They would have to shout out 'ping!' when they pressed it to get maximum benefit. Or they could imagine they had a rope around their waist and they were being pulled along.

People bought it. In the seventies Spino ran workshops for businessmen who, in line with their competitive nature, wanted to excel at the new running craze. Once, the Finishing Clerk had to get involved. 'Some rich guy from Atlanta hadn't paid, so I had to send him down there,' he said. 'He just said, "Look, what ya doin' to the kid's not right."' Spino winked at me. The guy (unharmed) paid up.

It would be Spino's job to make the vision of Mike Murphy and David Meggyesy become a reality – Esalen as a school for the sporting siddhis. He was the director of the Esalen Sports Center (ESC) for four years. The ESC wanted to cultivate, teach and encourage the superpowers. It was their version of the Russian programme, minus the rabbits.

Instead, they co-opted folks like Will Schutz, a former Harvard psychology professor who used to sing 'You Are My Sunshine' to conjure up spirits to diagnose why or how an athlete was not performing at his best. Schutz ran the 'More Joy' workshop that Meggyesy attended. Dr Lee Pulos was the hypnotist who had studied the Russian methods and worked with the Canada Olympic team and National Hockey League teams. And they also had Tim Gallwey, who would be, to the testosterone-fuelled sports nut layman, the most 'woo-woo' of them all. He believed athletes shouldn't try. Imagine a football coach, soccer coach, whoever, passing that on to players: 'Today, guys, I don't want you to try too much.' More on him a bit later.

'I saw some amazing, extraordinary things,' Spino said, shaking his head as if he could barely trust his own recall.

Some of it was not subtle. Spino's training regime for Mike Murphy – who had no previous aptitude for athletics – had been so effective that he had started running in national competitions. At one meet, Murphy was in the lead and being tracked. So Spino employed a rather liberal idea of 'mind control'. He started screaming at Murphy's rival.

'HEY! YOU!' Spino cleared his throat. 'MOTHERFUCKER! YOU *CAN'T* RUN, MOTHERFUCKER! YOU *CAN'T* RUN.'

It backfired. Murphy heard Spino's outlandish tirade at his rival and started laughing uncontrollably. He lost the race.

Murphy called Spino 'the Great Wild Man'. I thought this could have been because he had sported a large mop of unruly curls, handlebar moustache and love of poetry. Byron, but in track shoes. The young Spino, always in jogging suit, looked exactly like the seventies' runner cliché from TV commercials. But Spino, the curls gone and his hair now lightning white, told me, 'It was because I tried to motivate him to kill himself running up the sand dunes in Santa Cruz one day.'

The true Wild Man, however, was an Australian called Percy Cerutty. Spino was Cerutty's protégé. 'He was my hero,' Spino said. 'I based a lot of my techniques on what he taught me.' Cerutty was a brilliant coach who guided the Australian Herb Elliott to legend status in distance running. Some of his methods sounded nuts. So the ESC absolutely had to have him on board. But even at free-thinking Esalen they didn't know what they'd let themselves in for. 'He was almost too much. Everyone at Esalen was very much in their own head. But Percy was prone to sudden explosions of temper, yelling and screaming at people. You might be out for a run around Esalen and he'd suddenly jump out of a tree and start screaming at you.' This was not some weird motivational technique, by the way. 'It was my job to keep him calm,' remembers Spino.

Cerutty had wanted to be a runner but in school he would become ill after races, suffering severe migraines. He was considered too weak to serve in World War One and ended up working for the postal force. At the age of 43 he suffered a mental breakdown and was told by a doctor he had only two years to live. With what would be typical bluster, he thought the doctor was wrong and set about saving himself. He read books about mysticism and psychology. He ate only raw vegetables. Then he set about a second athletic career, setting Australian records for 30, 50 and 60 miles. In 1959 he began one of the most bizarre and controversial coaching careers the sport had seen. From a wooden shack on the sandhills of Portsea, near Melbourne, he ran the International Athletic Centre. Athletes who agreed to be coached by him endured an extraordinary regime, which was neatly recorded by the *Australian Dictionary of Biography*: 'He made them read Plato, poetry and the Bible, fed them raw oats and wheat germ, sent them on punishing runs through tea-tree scrub and rugged, sandy terrain, and insisted that they set goals which could be achieved only by pain and sacrifice. He made them swim year-round in the ocean and shed all their clothes in the open at least once a day.' But that was only the half of it.

Before a big race, Cerutty would 'tribute' or pay homage to his athlete by running himself to exhaustion. He would also experiment with different running techniques. There is footage of him trying to mimic the gallop and canter of a horse, hopping and skipping as if he were running on hot coals. (Spino showed them to me later. He watched them with reverence. 'You probably think he's crazy 'cos it looks so weird.' It was hard to dispute.)

'He used to hate athletes warming up,' Spino laughed. 'He'd mock them: "You ever see the lion warm up? Does the lion warm up? Yeah, they warm up good, don't they?"' Spino slapped his thigh and wiped his eye.

To inspire his athletes, Cerutty used what Spino called 'great thinkers'. All around his training base there were statues of philosophers, martyrs, writers and poets. 'He had this thing about putting a great person in your head, being that person and learning to be like that great person.'

The story went that when Herb Elliott raced in Dublin in 1958, Cerutty had convinced him that he was St Francis of Assisi.

How did he do it? By locking him in a hut for two and a half days before the race and putting him in a trance.

'First of all Percy did his tribute,' Spino whispered, as if he were passing on a mythical tale. 'He said, "I'm gonna *really* try to kill myself. That's a tribute to you." But then he also just kept him in this shack or hut. He was obsessed with great men and great thoughts and great people. "You'll be like that." He channelled St Francis of Assisi to Herb because Herb was a Catholic.

'This was a meet just for him to run against a guy called Ron Delany. And Delany would warm up for an hour, so Percy was already muttering about lions. When the reporters saw Herb was about to come on to the track, they were all hustling him and asking Percy, "Is he gonna break the world record today?" And Percy would jump on these guys, screaming, "Don't anybody talk to him!" Because he had him in a trance. *He was trying to get him to the track in a trance.*'

That day, Elliott broke Derek Ibbotson's 1957 record for the mile by 2.7 seconds, running 3:54:5. It was the biggest improvement on a time in history.

Cerutty's reputation went before him, and soon other coaches would travel from the other side of the world to seek his advice. Bob Timmons was the American coach of Jim Ryun. Ryun had been the first high-school athlete to run a mile in under four minutes. He would win a silver medal in the 1968 Olympics. But Timmons was not getting the best out of his man so, according to Spino, he wrote to Cerutty, asking him if he could travel to Portsea to visit him.

When Timmons arrived, he was slightly unnerved by the sign at the entrance: 'You don't have to be crazy to enter but it helps.' Cerutty was nowhere to be seen. Timmons looked all over, but Cerutty was watching him. He was hiding in a bush and when the moment arose, he jumped out and started strangling the American: 'You hopeless bastard! You've killed that young boy, you're not inspiring him!' Shocked and confused, Timmons left.

When the ESC flew Cerutty over from Australia in 1974, he was approaching the end of his life. He lived on a diet of chicken livers and sherry and was prone to passing out unexpectedly. Spino lived with the original Wild Man and drove him to the conferences that the ESC had organised for people to hear about his theories and methods to achieve athletic perfection. There was that problem, though, with Cerutty's temperament.

'I used to introduce him at these events,' Spino said. 'I'd say, "Look, at least half of you are going to want to leave after the first five minutes, but you're never going to have this experience again. Pleeeeeease hang in there. Please. Still about 20 per cent of the people walked out. He would get up there and start talking, slowly at first and then he would start ranting: "YOU HOPELESS BASTARDS! YOU AMERCIANS ARE BETTER DEAD!"

'That was his catchphrase – "better dead". People would want to call the cops. And I'd be shouting at him, "CALM DOWN! CALM DOWN!"'

Cerutty died in 1975 from motor neurone disease. 'He had such style, such class,' Spino said. 'Sometimes I'd find him passed out before he was due to go on stage, and when he came round he'd say, "Leave me, I'm fine." He was a great guy.'

When not calling people hopeless bastards, Cerutty was supposed to be educating athletes and coaches, amateur and professional, about sport being used as an alternative to yoga. The ESC believed that sport had to change radically. Training was too focused on strength, aggressiveness and winning. It was too macho. They called it 'America's disease'. Instead the ESC wanted to 'project a higher vision of man'. This was a coming together of the core principles of Esalen, Murphy and Meggyesy. Sport should be about emotional and spiritual development. Not too manly and not mean at all.

America's disease was testosterone-fuelled football players in the locker room screaming at each other, headbutting walls and, like Meggyesy, willing to succumb to life-threatening injury to win the game. The ESC way would be for those players to be sitting cross-legged and chanting 'ommm' so that they could take to the field in a more tranquil and focused frame of mind. It was the taking part, not the winning, that counted.

Given Cerutty's temper tantrums and belief that athletes could run thinking they were a Catholic friar who gave up wealth to live a life of poverty, it would be fair to say that he effortlessly bridged the divide between these two beliefs.

It was this emphasis on spiritual development that seemed to me to be the beginning of the quest for the superhuman sports star in the US. The ESC's proposal, written by Meggyesy, to the Esalen board of directors in May 1973 outlined its desire to 'explore the athletic experience as a means of achieving higher levels of awareness'. It was at these higher levels of awareness where the siddhis could be found. 'Many athletes have reported paranormal experiences and other altered states of consciousness while engaged in sports,' the document claimed.

Murphy had been 'taking confession' from athletes ever since the publication of *Golf in the Kingdom* in 1972. He had a whole library of them, some from the biggest names in sport. What Russia's scientists were trying to prove had been happening at an elite level for years. And they had formed the basis for what ESC were trying to achieve. Sport, and other cultural pursuits as Abraham Maslow had found, could lead to higher states of consciousness. And if an athlete is in a higher state of consciousness, they are more likely to win. Murphy had collated numerous examples and clippings from athletes of almost 30 siddhis.

Sugar Ray Robinson, frequently classed as the greatest boxer of all time, claimed he was able to see into the future. In a dream the night before he fought Jimmy Doyle in 1947, he foresaw his opponent's death. He was so disturbed he wanted to call off the fight. 'It's just a dream,' his camp said. Catholic and Protestant priests talked him into going ahead. 'He died right there in the ring,' Robinson said. 'It was premeditated. That ain't the only time. I've had many experiences like that.'

Morihei Ueshiba, the founder of the martial art aikido, was said to be able to make himself invisible. Murphy cites film footage of Ueshiba trapped by two attackers. In the next frame he is facing the opposite direction. Murphy found that there were 'scores' of reliable witnesses who had seen Ueshiba elude attack in that way. One wrote: 'Completely surrounded by men with knives, Ueshiba disappeared and reappeared at the same instant, looking down at his attackers from the top of a flight of stairs.'

What about a human passing through solid matter? Or walking through a wall, like the military psychic soldiers of the First Earth Battalion? Yup, Murphy had that covered, although somewhat obliquely. He quoted Pelé, the greatest soccer player ever: 'I felt that I could dribble through any of their team … that I could pass through them physically.'

In 1970 Bobby Orr was said to have called on abilities of thought projection to hypnotise Chicago Black Hawk players during a four-game winning sequence on the way to the Stanley Cup finals for his Bruins team. Then there was John Brodie, the San Francisco 49ers quarterback.

Murphy had met with Brodie in 1972 at a training camp in Santa Barbara. Brodie spoke to him in hushed, conspiratorial tones. 'Some days there are miracles out there,' he said. 'Yeah, miracles.' These miracles were shape-shifting. Brodie had seen players change their shape and size for a split second. 'Five or six times,' he whispered again. 'I know so. A running back got bigger once, then smaller.'

He also told Murphy that he had been able to move the ball to where he wanted it to go using psychic power. This was extrasensory perception. 'It has happened to me dozens of times,' Brodie said. 'An intention carries a force. A thought is connected with an energy that can stretch itself out in a pass play or a golf shot or a 30-foot jump shot in basketball.'

Murphy recorded that Jack Nicklaus was convinced that Arnold Palmer, the golf legend that Nicklaus usurped, could also 'will' the ball into a hole using the power of his mind, some sort of ESP that moved the ball where he wanted it to go.

Murphy was encouraged by Brodie. These extraordinary occurrences were what Aurobindo believed in – the race of 'gnostic beings' or 'cosmic individuals'. They were to be found on the sports field.

So the ESC set about trying to harness and teach these abilities. They held their first convention in San Bruno, California, in 1973. It was a huge hit. An overexcited journalist at the *New York Times* wrote that it was a turning point in sports history, comparing it to the French Revolution. The *Chicago Tribune* was more restrained, declaring that the vision should 'become a national ideal'.

'We'd need 300 people to break even at these conventions,' Spino told me. 'But we'd get 500. They were great days. It was a real movement.'

At Oregon University in 1974, 1,000 athletes and coaches turned up to hear the ESC's therapists, healers, yogis and gurus talk and teach. A track event followed the seminars with the Kenyan runner Ben Jipcho, who won silver in the 1972 Olympics steeplechase, taking part. At this meet, Jipcho did something that Spino and Murphy have never forgotten.

Murphy had talked about him when we met in Mill Valley. He said that after the race, Jipcho had glowed, as if there were some sort of paranormal force enveloping him. 'He had this aura,' Murphy said, blinking at the memory. 'It was as if he was from another planet. And his smell! Oh my! He smelt wonderful! You know how sick people smell really bad? This guy was physical perfection and he smelt *incredible*!'

I told Spino what Murphy had said. He was more interested in what he did on the track. 'It was extraordinary, one of the most amazing things I've seen. He ran a mile in 3 minutes and 54 seconds. That was quick in those days, believe me. He ran five races in an hour and a half with a 54-second last lap on the last race. And the thing was, he looked like he was *walking*. Time slowed down. Amazing.'

Despite the popularity of that event and Jipcho's feat, the ESC faltered. Based in Esalen's San Francisco centre, it ceased to be in 1976 with finances getting tight. There had been warnings from the start, though, that it might struggle for longevity. When Murphy wanted to talk to John Brodie again, the 49er dismissed it as 'drunk talk'. Brodie had been spooked by the 'spooky things' Murphy had talked about. They were to be spoken of in private only. Not to be shouted about at conferences or seminars. It was America's obsession with the macho holding him back, Murphy thought. It just wasn't the done thing to talk about shape-shifting or paranormal experiences on the field or in the locker room. Just as Meggyesy had proved when he had left out his other-world experiences from his book.

Coaches who attended events would balk at some of the advice. 'What's this crap?' they'd say. 'Don't mess with my guys. They just need to get out there and play hard.' It was the 'win at all costs' attitude that the ESC's new-fangled thinking just couldn't fathom.

In that regard, the *Chicago Tribune* had been clairvoyant in its review. Although upbeat, it questioned how the ESC would 'crack the notably thick skulls and authoritarian structures of coaching fraternities'. The very disease the ESC wanted to cure played a role in killing them off. They couldn't combat conservative and entrenched mindsets.

'The problem,' Spino said, sighing, 'is that there isn't the language for athletes to *talk* about stuff. It freaks them out. It freaks others out to hear them talk about it. So it stays secret, underground. We'll always be in the margins.'

Where did this leave the quest? In the late sixties and seventies, the environment to create such a 'gnostic being' was rich. The problem was it was outside the professional, elite arena. Or soon pushed out of it. Dave Meggyesy was isolated and branded a 'commie', Mike Murphy was the ringleader at the hippy Esalen, Percy Cerutty was too sweary. 'Otherness' was not welcomed. At the top level you did things by the book, turned up on time and kept your nose clean. Athletes should not have opinions. Their focus should be solely on the good of the team. They were not individuals. And why would any of them rock the boat?

For as much as there had been a sea change in American society with the counterculture, sport was also changing, but in a different way. Money was flowing in as at no other time in history.

It was becoming big business. The television deals and sponsorship packages that would make administrators, coaches and athletes rich beyond their wildest dreams also made sport a more closeted, fearful world than ever before. Why would anyone admit to shape-shifting or being able to see into the future when their Nike deal might be in jeopardy? OK, maybe the odd athlete here or there might do so, but a coach? The man who said 'follow me' and 'do as you're told'? No chance.

And that was key. The Esalen Sports Center wanted to teach the siddhis. But they could only really do that if they could get through to the coaches. I thought of one of Mike Murphy's favourite quotes. 'Evolution meanders,' he says. It could have been that the ESC had been ahead of the curve.

In the years after the ESC's closure, what had happened to the movement? I picked up the phone to an excitable Mike.

'HEY, YOU, ER … YOU *FUCKING* YOGI, GET OFF YOUR FUCK-IN' … ER, UM, GET IN YOUR LOTUS POSITION AND LOOK AT THE BASKET.' What Mike was trying to confirm for me, with an entertaining impersonation of the average fan, was the difficulty I would face when trying to get an answer to that question. For a coach or athlete to talk about such alternative methods in the modern day would be career suicide. 'It's like the gay movement back in the sixties,' he argued. 'These secret mystics will not ever come out of the closet if it will hurt their team or franchise or, in the case of the players, make them look like idiots or loony tunes. You don't want to give anybody an excuse. There's billions of dollars in this. These players are going to get rich. They don't want a reputation as a dingbat.' Granted. But surely someone, somewhere had been inspired by Murphy and the ESC? And had, either at the time or several years later, tried to apply the principles to a sports team? I hesitated to ask, considering Murphy had sounded adamant that no one would want to talk. I also didn't want him to tell me that there was some high-school track coach who was trying it out in the Midwest somewhere. It needed to be someone working in the pros. Mike didn't even pause.

'Well, there's Pete.'

7

SPORTS AND COSMIC FORCES

Let's go back in time again. 1975. A small group of students lounged around the Gold Room at the University of the Pacific, Stockton, California. Some of them sat on rugs on the floor, others reclined in armchairs. Pictures of past university presidents adorned the walls. But this wasn't downtime. This was a class. It was called Sports and Cosmic Forces: The Inner Game. The teacher was Glen Albaugh. Pete was one of the students. Pete had dark, floppy hair, a *Brady Bunch* smile and an infectious exuberance. That day, as most days, they were meditating. Breathing deeply. Getting present and centred. They focused. And they drifted off into a trance. The goal? To summon the spirit of a character from Mike Murphy's *Golf in the Kingdom* – Seamus MacDuff, the spiritual guru of Shivas Irons.

When we meet at a Mexican restaurant in San Rafael some 40 or so years later, Glen Albaugh tells me they didn't manage it. Seamus didn't show, except for the time when Glen asked an actor friend to dress up. 'Some of them believed it,' he laughed. Glen, now 85, has a dodgy shoulder, a dodgy knee and walks with the help of a stick. He speaks with the soft, wise tones of a master on all things alternative in sport. He had a reputation as a teacher for encouraging 'self-discovery' and for a 'free-flowing' style.

'Famous class,' Glen said. 'It only had about 25 people but hundreds said they attended. We were trying to understand why some people performed at higher levels than others. People called it "hokey" but it was serious stuff.' I wanted him to talk about the one special student who did go on to perform at higher levels.

'Pete was curious, really curious,' he said. 'And so darn atypical.' Atypical didn't seem to cut it, considering what he told me next.

'He was looking for people who could levitate,' Glen said, matter-of-factly. 'He *really* was. There are people who have that connection and I believe it. I think Pete probably does but we haven't talked about that in a *loooong* time. You know, he's open to all kinds of possibility. He really thought he was a channel. And he investigated the Philadelphia Experiment, which was pretty secret. I think Murphy wondered whether he had both feet on the ground. He was developing his coaching philosophy at the time.'

'What do you mean by "a channel", Glen?'

'Communication on a cosmic level. At a higher level, like … I don't know, you'll have to get him to tell you the story about the Long Body. He believed those things. I think Murphy, who has a great sense for these kind of things – more so than anyone else in the world – he feels that within Pete there's a special communication that only the occult can recognise.'

A special communication that only the occult can recognise. It's worth repeating. That phrase made the hairs on the back of my neck stand to attention, as if a ghoul had just tapped me on the shoulder. It's also worth defining occult.

Occult – Noun
　　Mystical, supernatural or magical powers, practices or phenomena

Immediately, I was captivated by Pete. I had visions of this character holding a séance to contact the other side. Or trying to summon superpowers with weird rituals to guarantee sporting domination. At the very start of this story when I wondered if anyone, anywhere, had tried something really off the wall, it was this kind of stuff that I had in mind. To what lengths would people go to win? If I had been standing on the edge of the rabbit hole before this point, I was now in freefall.

There were more questions, of course. What was the Philadelphia Experiment? What was the Long Body? But I guess the most important at this stage was: who the hell was Pete?

Pete was Pete Carroll. I had heard of him. But being an English investigative journalist ordinarily preoccupied with the nefarious goings on in sports like cricket or soccer, not American football, I had to look him up to learn more about his career. Of course, when I did I realised he was a huge personality. Far bigger than I could have possibly imagined. He was no high-school track coach, that's for sure.

Peter Clay Carroll was born on 15 September 1951. After abandoning hopes of an NFL career as a player, he sold roofing materials in the Bay area in San Francisco. But it wasn't for him. So he decided to become a coach – and that's why he ended up in Glen Albaugh's class. It was a good decision. He is now one of the most successful football coaches of all time. This is how his own website describes him.

> One of only three coaches to win a Super Bowl and college football national championship, Pete Carroll is head coach and executive vice president of the NFL's Seattle Seahawks following one of the most successful runs in the college football history while at University of Southern California. With his unique 'Always Compete' philosophy and approach, Carroll has a combined 42 years of highly decorated NFL and collegiate coaching experience.

Normally, people like me might take the profile of somebody on their own website with a pinch of salt. But Pete is the real deal. Arguably it is actually a pretty modest bio of his career. ESPN in 2017 ranked him at number 18 on their list of top NFL coaches of *all time*. Vince Lombardi, the doyen who fired a broadside at Dave Meggyesy's criticism of the sport, was number 1. Bill Walsh, the San Francisco 49ers coach who was part of Mike Murphy's softball team that took on the Russians in Moscow, was at number 5. At the University of California (USC) and the Seattle Seahawks Pete had been a phenomenon, transforming middling teams into record-breakers who crushed every team in their path. USC won 34 games straight from 2003 to 2005. Seattle appeared in back-to-back Super Bowls from 2014, winning one. At that time, only three coaches since 1995 had led a team to consecutive Super Bowls.

Carroll's profile on his website – and the ESPN ranking rationale, come to think of it – doesn't, unsurprisingly, mention his research into the Philadelphia Experiment or offer an explanation of the 'Long Body'.

For the record, then, the Philadelphia Experiment occurred when the US Navy, in 1943, tried to make a warship disappear. They did it – or they didn't, depending on who you believe – by uniting the fields of electromagnetism and gravity into a single field. No, I'm not sure I know what that means, either. Paranoia of what the Soviets were up to – sound familiar? – had apparently inspired the test. It was, supposedly, part of Project Rainbow, a CIA plan to make US military hardware trickier to spot on radar.

Today, it could be considered one of the more outlandish conspiracy theories. The story goes that the experiment worked so well that the USS *Eldridge* vanished. It wasn't just 'invisible' to the naked eye but was 'teleported' to another harbour, in Norfolk, Virginia, about 270 miles away. The process was then reversed and, hey presto, the *Eldridge* was back in Philadelphia intact – aside from some minor problems like crew members disappearing into the ether, others going mad, catching fire and being fused into the structure of the ship.

The US Navy, which has consistently denied the experiment took place, received so many requests for information that it drew up a standard 'response letter'. Politely, the Office of Naval research pointed out that the legend took hold because of a simple misunderstanding of the word 'invisible'. Ships are routinely 'demagnetised' to combat magnetised mines and torpedoes. The letter didn't mention that the story was dreamed up by a disgruntled UFO researcher keen on five minutes of fame. Just as well Pete concentrated on the football, then.

As for the 'Long Body', the archives of the *LA Times* from 2007 have the answer, revealing Pete's interest in the Iroquois, Native Americans who have inhabited the north-east for up to 4,000 years. When at war they were renowned for defeating opposition twice their number because of their extraordinary ability to be, well, a team. No doubt you're relieved to hear that this is not as bonkers as warships disappearing into thin air. Carroll was head coach at USC when the *LA Times* story ran and the city was firmly in the grip of the Carroll miracle.

> Carroll stumbled on a concept called 'Long Body', a way the Iroquois thought of the tribe. One feels pain, all feel pain. One triumphs, all triumph. Long Body. He began applying this idea to football. 'Things were occurring,' he says. 'I didn't know – I had a meeting with players and coaches, and I was telling them about this Iroquois concept. Connection of the tribe. They live together, they hunt together. They become one. So I'm telling them about this concept – this is really far out – and I say, 'As we go through this camp, go through this season, we're going to get so close, we're going to connect in this true fashion. Long Body. It's going to take us to places we've never been before.' And at the end of my talk I say, 'As we get through it, I'll explain it more to you, and I know this to be true so much right now that thunder will strike—'
>
> At that moment, Carroll says, he struck a table with his fist and a clap of thunder shook the building.

It was a rare slip from Carroll. Hardly surprising. The journalist had followed him round for weeks, yapping at his heels like a terrier. Another hint one finds when trawling the archives of Pete being 'alternative' was that he was considered a 9-11 'truther'. According to *USA Today*, in a 2013 meet with the US Army's chief of staff, Peter Chiarelli, Carroll wanted to know of the 'veracity' of the various conspiracy theories surrounding the attacks on the Twin Towers. This was unusual behaviour for a serving NFL coach, to say the least. By and large I found that he almost never talked about the superpowers that can be found in athletes, not to mention being a channel for the occult or other 'different' methods or opinions. Just like Dave Meggyesy. I guessed that he feared he would be dismissed as crazy, that he might lose his job and owners or colleges would never take a risk on a coach who believed in such concepts.

It is fair to say that most NFL coaches, albeit the successful ones – like those on the ESPN ratings list – would have done the same had they harboured such interesting thoughts and beliefs. That is, of course, if what Glen and Mike were saying about Pete was correct. I mean, let's just backtrack here for a second. Mike Murphy, the guy who said he had knocked over a baseball pitcher through the power of thought, reckoned that it was Pete who didn't 'have two feet on the ground'. Pete Carroll. One of the most revered football coaches ever.

Naturally, this was great news for me. It was great for my story that, seemingly, there was a coach right at the very top echelon of professional sport who was practising what Murphy et al. had preached. And I had found him just as I was fearing being taken down a track of amateurs and small-timers. I thought that Pete might be able to answer the question: does the superhuman sports star actually exist?

I was, however, a little torn. Pete Carroll was one of the most sought-after interviewees in the sports world. America was obsessed with him and the Seattle franchise. 'Everything they do is explored in minute detail,' Glen said, which made the chances of him talking to an investigative reporter from the UK almost non-existent. So it was one thing actually getting face time with Pete. And it was something completely different getting him to actually talk about a subject that he didn't talk about. As I said, what went on in those classes at Pacific and his esoteric interests had, from what I could see, gone unreported. Football coaches, or anyone calling the shots in pro sports, have little time for the sports writer who asks the dumb question. The coach can raze an inquisitor with a waspish tongue or hate-filled glare so he or she feels only capable of communicating with the Lilliputians. I would have to ask, as Meggyesy had said, *that* question.

This was not my only worry. Would the mysterious Pete Carroll be flying so high, communicating with the cosmos and channelling God knows what, or who, that he wouldn't come down to my level to talk to me? Let alone getting off the pedestal that America had put him on as one of their sporting heroes. It threatened to be a 'so near yet so far' moment. Indeed, it felt like my story had taken on new form. I had to get to Pete Carroll. And I had to get him to admit to precisely the beliefs that Glen and Mike said he had. So, did Glen have anything with more substance for me to work with?

Glen and Pete had bonded through a love of competition and their interest in the inner game of sport, the battle between mind and body. 'I *lurrrve* competition,' Glen said. 'Can't do it at the moment, but I love it.' Glen winced, growled and repositioned his knee. 'Did you know Pete and I used to play tennis?' he continued. 'We were pretty even. You rent the court for an hour and when the hour is up the lights go out. And we're in the middle of a point, you know, and it was in the second set, set point, and I'd won the first set. The ball's on my side, I hit it and the lights go out.

'So I say to Pete, "I know the ball's on your side."

'He says, "Probably hit the net."

'"No, I think I got it back."

'So we're crawling around on the floor looking for the ball. He found it on his side. He said, "It was out."'

At Pacific, Glen and Pete explored possibilities. Glen was the teacher and advisor; Pete was a graduate assistant just starting out on what Glen called his 'coaching odyssey'. And Glen was well qualified. He had known Michael Murphy since he was five years old. They went to high school together. Then they lost touch. They only came together again when Glen read *Golf in the Kingdom*, which was one of the texts he set for the Sports and Cosmic Forces class. Another was *The Inner Game of Tennis* by Tim Gallwey, who had led workshops for the Esalen Sports Center. Pete loved this book so much he wrote a foreword for a later edition. Glen, who probably wouldn't have described himself as a hippy back in the day, had been in the ESC orbit, too.

'*Golf in the Kingdom* changed my life,' Glen said. 'I had to find Murphy again. And since then we have done many things together. He's an extraordinary human being.'

'Were you ever involved with Russians?' I asked.

'Yes. Difficult time politically because of the Cold War. Mike was going regularly. I didn't get there till '89 – when the break-up was coming. I went with Bill Walsh, the legendary 49ers coach. We had a few discussions about the work they'd done with the esoteric stuff into alternative consciousness.'

'What about "Hidden Human Reserves?"' I asked.

'We'd heard they knew things we didn't. I didn't find that. I think we were at least equal and our field was just starting out.'

One of the 'many things' that Glen and Murphy did together was to invite a Russian contingent to a conference called The Further Reaches of Sports Psychology. It was held in 1993 and was based on typical Esalen principles of spreading the word about human potentialities. Pete Carroll was there.

'The Russians were bringing a guy who might have been a sports psychologist or wrestler, I can't remember his name … long time ago,' Glen said. 'Their lead guy said, "You know, he's out there?" And I thought he might fit in with Pete.

'So we met in San Francisco, and this is a true story, at the St Francis hotel. Two delegations. The Americans, our people, had all flown in or drove in. Immediately, this Russian and Pete saw each other and sat down. They had never, ever before seen each other and they had six mutual friends and half of them, I think, were in the cosmos. I mean, they were both on magic carpets. I think at the time Pete might have thought he was a channel, as I said.'

There can't have been much room on that magic carpet with Murphy, Glen, the rest of the ESC crew, Pete and the Russian guy all jostling for space. The Russian guy was believed to be Leonid Gissen. Gissen was not a wrestler. He was a sports psychologist who had won an Olympic silver medal for the Soviet Union in the men's rowing eight at the Helsinki Games in 1952. And he was very strange.

Gissen had an ability to see inside people's bodies and tell them about their injuries, past or present. He could tell people what teeth had cavities in without them even opening their mouths. The story goes that Pete had placed his hands under a napkin and Gissen was able to tell him which fingers he had broken. A lucky guess? Maybe. But Pete's father was with him at the conference and Gissen, when Pete asked what was wrong with him, replied he had cancer *in the place he had cancer*.

Comparing Pete with one of the more alternative Soviet contingent, who had come from a rich cultural and, thanks to the Cold War, scientific heritage of believing in and trying to capture the occult, sure did add to the mystery of Pete. Glen said such experiences were all about exploring possibilities and had no qualms about calling them 'left-field', which may or may not be an understatement when considering levitation and disappearing warships. But they didn't tell anyone what they were up to. They couldn't. 'If we did that the first thing that would happen was all the players would walk off the football field,' Glen laughed.

Pete's appetite for exploration was 'voracious', according to Glen. The catalyst had been a siddhi experience he had in high school when playing baseball. Pete called it the 'homerun story', the outline of which he had emailed to Glen.

While preparing to go to the plate a simple harmless thought came to mind. 'We're down 3–1. No matter what I do with this bat I can't affect the outcome of the game!' Just a simple realisation that, as I recall, gave some temporary relief from the pressure of the moment. What followed was one of the most vivid occurrences I ever experienced as an athlete. As I settled into the batter's box, and prepared for the first pitch, everything seemed normal. But, as big Mike started his wind-up, everything seemed to change. His wind-up was unusually slow, his arm speed seemed like it took for ever, and as the ball left his hand it slowly started spinning as the most perfect looking 'slider' I had ever seen. The rotations were so obvious you could almost count them. As I started my swing there was never doubt about making contact, everything was perfect. The contact was sweet and the sight of that ball jumping off the bat so perfectly was like you dream about. The ball shot directly over the pitcher's head, dead centrefield. This ball was going places well beyond any fielder's glove. It was too perfect to be caught! There were no fences on the field in those days, just a track and the old football field. The trip around the bases was a joyous glide that all ball players dream about, a homerun! As was always the case at my house, we shared every detail of the game and any fleeting moment of heroism was dissected completely. These were always my favourite times with my mom and dad, as they loved the stories and the recounting as much as I did. I did my best to describe all that took place in the moments surrounding the homerun but found myself struggling to impart the uniqueness of the experience to my parents.

This story is important not only because it showed Pete had an ability to achieve siddhi states but that, until he met Glen, he didn't understand what had happened that day. And, as he learned more, his thirst for knowledge about those types of experiences was almost unquenchable.

'He had a relentless pursuit of knowledge. And he was all over the place trying to figure out how he could use it all in his coaching,' Glen said. 'Always sending me stuff to read.' Often there just wasn't the time. To cram in *Cutting Through Spiritual Materialism* by Chögyam Trungpa, a Buddhist meditation master, Pete read it while driving back and forth down the freeway, book nestled in the steering wheel.

'He's a random thinker,' Glen said. 'I remember being in his office and the door's open and he had the singer … oh, what's his name? … James Taylor on, the television is on, the radio is on and he's talking to me. And people are coming by to say "hello", looking confused. I said to him, "I know you're a random thinker and you're paying attention to me, but you can't do this with other people."'

Glen advised Pete on his thesis, which collated unusual experiences in sport. They felt there was a correlation for the best athletes having more than the average guy or girl. It was another nod to the ESC and Murphy. The crucial intervention came in 1976 when Glen took Pete to San Francisco one night to meet Murphy and Tim Gallwey for the first time. Murphy spoke about Shivas Irons, siddhi superpowers and the occult, Gallwey about reaching the high levels of awareness that hosted such experiences. They had dinner together. Pete was entranced. Immediately afterwards he said, 'This is the beginning. This is it. This is what I'm going to do.' He was going to dedicate his career to inspiring athletes to join him on his magic carpet.

So just as Glen had taught and advised his student at Pacific, where he studied for three years as a graduate assistant from 1973, he continued to do the same as Pete's coaching career began criss-crossing the States. In 20 years he took in Arkansas, Iowa State, Ohio State, North Carolina State, back to Pacific, on to the Buffalo Bills, the Minnesota Vikings and the New York Jets. At these franchises he held assistant roles or second-assistant jobs and was revered as a defense specialist. He was made head coach at the Jets in 1994, being promoted from defensive coordinator. He was 43.

He lasted one season, sacked after the Jets lost their last five games. But he was doomed from day one. At his first team meeting in front of players, coaching staff and management, he failed to make an impression on the owner, an 80-year-old oil billionaire called Leon Hess. Hess was a hard-nosed businessman who gave no quarter. He was startled by the new man's approach. A 'pumped' Pete bounded in with unbridled enthusiasm and, in Hess's eyes, talked in New Age riddles. This was a team that would 'search within itself' to be positive, something that was to be prized ahead of the ubiquitous 'win at all costs' attitude. Pete sounded as if he wanted to be everybody's friend. Hess was dumbfounded. This was American Football, not a happy-clappy West Coast retreat. He should have known he was getting something different. When he was defensive coordinator, Pete would award a stuffed beaver to the player who caused the most fumbles in a game. The beaver, of course, represented 'hard work'. It became a point of pride for a player to have the beaver in his locker for a week. The beaver would be taken to games and thrown around in celebration when the Jets caused a fumble. Hess did not say anything to Pete during the meeting. Or after it. In fact, Hess didn't speak to him for the remainder of the season. He quietly fumed about reports that Pete would be walking down the halls of the coaching facility, bouncing a basketball, conducting interviews with the press on-court between games of three-on-three and organising family picnics and 'beer and bowling' nights. Pete has since admitted that his approach on day one was 'unorthodox', a label he would struggle to shake.

After the Jets he went to the San Francisco 49ers, as defensive coordinator, where he worked with Bill Walsh, Glen's Russian road-trip buddy. 'They met every morning before the other coaches got in,' Glen said. You don't need to guess what they talked about most.

The head coach job at the New England Patriots followed. But it was a disaster and Pete's coaching career began to unravel. Glen said the Boston media were out to get him from the start and that he was undermined by the general manager, who didn't allow him the final call on signing players. 'He didn't stand a chance. They were vicious.'

That was true. The *Boston Globe* archives from the time appear to reveal an orchestrated campaign against Pete. He was labelled 'the Poodle'. In October 1997 one correspondent, discussing the Denver Broncos coach and Pete, wrote, 'The big difference – and this is a BIG difference where I come from – is that I very much like [Mike] Shanahan and very much dislike Carroll.' Another in the same month penned: 'Bill Parcells is a better coach than Pete Carroll and will always be a better coach than Pete Carroll. Bill Parcells is the best coach the Patriots ever had or ever will have'.

So Pete's biggest problem, in the eyes of the media, was that he wasn't Bill Parcells, who he had replaced. Parcells was the archetypal bully coach who had learned all about discipline when coaching with the Army football team for four years from 1965. At New England, players were fined if they were not five minutes early for meetings. According to the *New York Times* Parcells was 'manipulative and nasty', someone who didn't give a second thought to berating a player or coach or secretary. No one was safe. He once threw iced tea over a reporter who asked one of those dumb questions I was talking about. But Parcells took the Patriots to the Super Bowl in 1996 so all was forgiven.

Parcells was a man who had ruled by fear in every job he'd had. He was exactly the type Dave Meggyesy and the ESC had railed against. Pete was the tousled-haired Californian surf dude who wanted to give his players a hug and play three-on-three with his coaching staff whenever they got downtime. The Boston media could not accept the culture shock. And their jibes were getting to Pete, too. 'I don't even own a surf board,' he said.

Pete would play music during training drills. Players were asked their opinions. If the Patriots lost, Pete would not watch the video of the defeat with his players to analyse what went wrong. That was too focused on the negative. He even spoke to them about trying to create an environment where individuals could reach for the superpowers, like seeing the game in their mind before it happened. It was all anathema for the Patriots, one of the original ultra-masculine, victory-obsessed teams. None of this would have happened before, let alone under Parcells.

During his three years at the Patriots, Pete received regular pep talks via fax from Glen, reminding him to stay true to the philosophies he had been so inspired by. He showed some of them to me. They revealed a close, respectful bond. But ultimately they were about one man trying to protect his friend when a jointly held belief system was under attack.

Shivas Irons says that an integral part of practice must be focused on staying in the present. It comes down to being present for every interaction we have with everyone, for every day, for every moment. How does this sound?

My guess is this week and 'for ever more' you must be decisive, confident, high energy, motivated, direct and in Zen ordinary consciousness (present centered). As you say, 'shoot the bullets at me'.

Murphy says that the highest order of consciousness is staying in the present and that means the coach must be focused at all times. The leader must remain detached from judgment, but passionately stay connected to the players.

Glen suggested inviting the media to practice, meetings and off-season workouts to observe 'first hand the pace, intensity, structure and learning curves' of the players. He also tried to enlist the help of sports psychologists in an effort to stem the negative energy aimed at Pete's regime. It didn't work.

It wasn't just the media who didn't buy his approach. The playing group was split down the middle: half for Parcells, a winning coach who had left too soon because of a disagreement over signing players; the other half wanting to give Pete's methods a try.

Unlike Parcells, Pete wanted to treat his players like adults. But they weren't so keen to behave like them. Three players were carpeted for visiting a nightclub before a crucial game. One got a speeding ticket on the way to a practice that he was three hours late for. Another story that did the rounds was that Terry Glenn, the Patriots wide receiver, had been ordered by Pete to run laps for breaking the rules. Only Pete caught up with him, told Glenn that he didn't have to do the punishment but to tell everyone he had. Pete even poured water on Glenn's shirt to make it look as if he'd perspired. The inference was that Pete and his ways were too soft for the NFL. The 'win at all costs' disease that the Esalen Sports Center had been so concerned about was to claim another victim.

Drew Bledsoe, the Patriots quarterback from 1993 to 2001, summed up the reason: 'When Parcells stepped into a meeting room, he had this intimidating presence. Pete is enthusiastic and fun but did not have the same intimidation factor Parcells had.'

Pete was sacked after the Patriots failed to qualify for the play-offs in 1999, winning just two of the last eight matches. He had guided them to the play-offs in his previous two campaigns but the buddy-coach tag that had bugged Pete since he was an assistant at Pacific wouldn't go away. He had once knocked on Glen's door in tears after the football coach there, Chester Caddas, said he was 'too soft' to make it. 'Wrong,' Glen said. 'It wasn't softness. It was compassion – because he felt it very important to develop his relationship with his players.'

The more Glen told me, the more excited I became about Pete's methods. The leap to the Seattle Seahawks, where he was close to building a dynasty, was big from those early failures. I wanted to understand exactly how Pete had made the philosophies of the Esalen hippies and thinkers thrive in an environment where they had no right to be.

'Do you think Pete will talk to me?' I asked Glen.

'That would be challenging. He's selective. Mike has told him you're authentic, and I can tell him that you're authentic but...'

'Would it appeal that I'm an outsider?'

'You are. I think that's to your advantage. He's so damn atypical. Been like that for ever. When a coach, Edward, has developed a trust as Pete has done with his players, and the players know he's not going to cut their nuts off – as some coaches like to do – then you can really coach hard. You can really get stuff done.'

I emailed Pete. I used the outsider angle. I said I was desperate to hear about his philosophies and how he implemented them. I told him I wanted to tell the story of the history of the 'movement' to the present day, and the search for the superhuman. I told him I had no agenda.

He didn't reply.

That search had stalled after the closure of the Esalen Sports Center because nobody wanted to talk about the siddhis or the states of transcendence required to access them. And when I looked through my notes from the interviews with Mike Murphy, Mike Spino and Dave Meggyesy, they all said the same thing. There wasn't 'the language' to adequately describe what happened to these athletes. So no one tried to explain it. It was simultaneously too hard for the believers to talk about and too easy for the sceptics to make them sound like fools. Murphy had told me that Pete was nervous about talking about it. Fair enough. He didn't want to come across, to borrow Mike's words, as a 'loony tune'.

There was an impasse. The movement had become stuck between a rock and a hard place. Or, to put it another way, between the ears of those who had lived it. An outsider like me couldn't hear about it because so few would talk. And I sure couldn't see it.

Glen had an idea. He invited me to watch him teach a young golfer the mental skills that would help him to access the siddhis. He made it sound incredibly simple, despite the apparent language barrier. 'All you have to do is see the shot,' he said. 'I mean, er, that's not all, but it's really helpful. To engage your senses, to feel, to get into your imagination. This kid? He's got it, he can do it. He sees the shot before he hits it.'

8

I AM THE MATADOR

'What do you have there?' asked Glen.

'Pitching wedge,' said the kid.

'Let's get an eight iron and first of all let's remember the inner game warm-up. So take some swings, feel your weight shift, close your *eyes*, let your club bounce off the ground … now feel the club head, let your club find the path of least resistance, let it go where it goes, where it's trained to go, *feeeeeeeeel* the rhythm and tempo. See the target, keep the image … all right? Ready? Just hit some shots with your feet together. Hit the target. Full swing.'

The kid did as he was told.

'Now stand on your right foot. Right foot only. One leg.'

'Like that?'

'Ya. There you go, ya, ya. It might be hard in this wind.'

The kid, who was a little shy and had a tendency to mumble, nailed the ball down the fairway; it left his club with the satisfying ping of a tuning fork. He was still standing on one leg. He barely wobbled. It was mighty impressive considering the thuggish San Rafael wind that battered the course, the Peacock Gap on Biscayne Drive. Glen turned to me and smiled, as if to say, 'Told you this kid was good.'

'What he's doing here is discovering how to do that,' he said. 'He's figuring it out.'

The shots actually got better.

'Wow! He's a good player, Edward. You see it takes only two swings. Now left foot.'

Miguel Delgado was the kid, although he didn't look much like one. He was 6 foot 3 inches with dark, brooding matinée-idol looks. He was a sophomore from Notre Dame. His ambition was to be a pro. Glen was his inner game coach. It was his job to get him, as Glen said, 'present and centred'. (Glen rolled his Rs occasionally, which made him sound a bit like Elmer Fudd. It was particularly charming when he used that phrase.)

That was the point of the drill. To enable Miguel to achieve a level of consciousness that made it more likely that he would achieve the extraordinary. Like see the shot before he hit it. Or feel it in his body. Or slow down time. But Glen said that this first state, which he called 'the athletic mind', was 'just the price of admission'. After that, nothing was guaranteed.

'It's internal feedback,' Glen said. 'We have six or seven other inner game drills to help them get in touch with the athletic mind. There's a chance of high-level play when you get there. And you're playing without thinking, when you're mindful and absolutely centred, and you have to practise being there.

'You have opened up skills for, say, the basketball player coming down the middle of the court. And they've got five or six things they can do but they're not thinking about any of them 'cos they're practised to respond and they're playing with a sense of flow. Sport is much like a compelling novel. You're captured by the writer, you think you know how it's going to end, but then you get to the next chapter and they've fooled you. Sport is the same. We are prepping for the novel situation. You never know what's going to happen so we coach them to stay in the present and to have a chance to respond to the "novel" situation. It's a metaphor I use because almost everybody has read a good book.'

Such a drill might look odd to the casual observer. That's what Glen wants. 'The ultimate seriousness is non-seriousness.' He once told Pete Carroll that, when he was going through his personal coaching hell at the New England Patriots.

The 'athletic mind' is also known as the 'quiet mind'. To you and I that is most recognisable when we get in a car to drive home or to the shops. Have you ever taken that trip and realised you don't remember half of it? That's because you had achieved a quiet mind. We are more alert and more perceptive. We just don't realise it. As Peter Brusso said: sometimes you just *know* the other car is going to pull out in front of you. Brusso, by the way, was in my thoughts quite a bit during Glen's lesson. You'll see why later.

A quiet mind was, apparently, essential in sport at the top level. Glen believed it, Pete Carroll believed it. But what did it actually mean? It's about an individual protecting himself from damaging or negative thoughts. Which is why it is called the inner game. Mind versus body. The golfer who is still fretting over the mishit iron on the previous hole is less likely to make a good shot from the tee on the next. The golfer who is worrying what will happen if he lands the ball in the sand trap will – guess what? – more than likely land it in the sand trap.

So instead, golfers, tennis players and football players are told to occupy their mind with quiet thoughts and feelings. They might focus on the feel of the club or the racket. Or they might just focus on their breathing, the sound of their breath or heartbeat.

Sounds simple, eh? Well, back in the seventies it was revolutionary stuff. It was the brainchild of Tim Gallwey and, of course, Shivas Irons. Gallwey's book *The Inner Game of Tennis* was published two years after Shivas became a legendary figure in sporting circles, but the similarities between the ethos of the two was striking.

'You've got a free throw with the clock ticking down. What do you say to the shooter?' Glen shouted at me.

'Er, um…' I stuttered.

'Nothing. Shoot it. You certainly better not say anything about technique. It's up to the player. You see, Pete Carroll understands that. A lot of coaches don't.'

Another favourite saying of Glen's was: 'When there's a hurricane, stand in the eye. It's calmest there.' That's another he gave to Carroll when at New England. The athlete or the coach has to remove himself from the pre-game, in-game and post-game hyperbole to stand a chance of performing at optimum level.

Glen should know. He had been teaching this stuff for years. And not just to college dreamers, either. He taught the guys at the very top. Before he felt the urge to return home to Stockdale, a district of Bakersfield, California, he was on golf's pro tour.

'I was trying to figure out how to do this full time,' Glen said. 'I started quite late with it and had a good player on the second tour down – I was still teaching. But what happens is, he wins lots of tournaments and then I get all the phone calls coming in because they think I have a magic formula. So I kinda knew what I was doing. I picked up a couple of people. Started a business. I thought then as I do now, that golf has squeezed the joy out of the game with technique, people are spending too much time on their swing rather than just playing. I hooked up with Scott McCarron, Kirk Triplett, Charlie Wi. Did a lot of travel up until 2008 before getting tired.'

McCarron, Triplett and Wi were more than good. Between them they had more than 30 professional wins.

Some golfers have visited Glen and not returned. 'Happened the other day,' he said to me. 'I just don't think he "got it", you know. It's more nuanced, of course, than telling a golfer to block out negative thoughts. Of course it is.

'One guy came to me who was highly skilled, hits it very far, and was overwhelmed by emotion. So over a series of meetings the first thing we do is try to explain to him what happens when he is overwhelmed by emotion. Emotion doesn't tell us it's coming – it comes fast, positive or negative. Typically, frustration comes, then anger, then depression, and then he plays like shit 'cos he can't get past it. So the next thing we have to develop is awareness of when it comes – it ain't going to stop coming, it will keep coming and coming for the rest of your life. But to manage emotions is really important.'

Tim Gallwey referred to this as the two selves: Self One and Self Two. It is a Zen Buddhist concept, as outlined rather amusingly by *Sports Illustrated* in 2016. It went a little like this: One is your mind. Two is your body. And Self One is constantly on Self Two's case. If the golfer or tennis player stuffs up a shot, he will scream at himself, 'Oh man! What are you doing?' A good example of this is the British player Andy Murray, whose two selves had been on such bad terms that tennis writers desperately opined that he make a peace pact. In the end, he visited a sports psychiatrist. It helped Murray make it to world number one.

Hang on, what's wrong with Self One telling Self Two to get its act together, you might say? It needs a darn good talking to. Wait. Have you thought how bizarre it is for a human being to be vocally admonishing himself for something he did? You do realise you're talking to yourself? And when this happens the precious, tranquil quiet mind has been blasted away by anger, shouting and chaos. Or, in other words, our mind is perfectly, horribly capable of sabotaging what our bodies are perfectly, beautifully capable of doing on their own. That's another reason I was thinking of Peter Brusso. He said the same thing but in perhaps less flowery terms. This was page one of the First Earth Battalion manual.

It was time for more drills. Glen told Miguel to swing the club at 60 per cent of his power. 'Like slow motion.' Again, it looks strange. This is about internal feedback. It's building an awareness for himself about the speed of the swing. Self-coaching. Then it's on to 'Think Box' and 'Play Box'. The Think Box is five or six yards behind where the ball is. This is where Glen had told Miguel to do all his thinking. What club is he going to hit? Where is he going to hit it? What will the shot look like? Where is his target? He can only leave the Think Box when he can see the shot.

'You don't have to stay there very long,' Glen lectured Miguel. 'But then I want you to take a really good breath, the kind of breath you take when you get on the green, so you are centred. Feel it in the diaphragm and it'll get you present and centred and then it's over … and you're … *into Play Box*. When you step over that line you're in the Play Box.'

Think Box, then, was where Miguel could see the shot he was about to hit. After a few moments of heavy breathing, looking down solemnly and fiddling with the club, Miguel gazed out towards the course and puffed out his chest, breathing out loudly. He looked as if he might be about to start weeping. Anywhere but a golf course, folks would have come up to ask, 'You OK?'

'What do you see?' enquired Glen.

'The ball flight,' said Miguel.

'Ball flight?'

'Yeah. It's a par five and I'm going to see everything: the ball flight, the wind will take it a little right.'

Miguel hit the ball. It seemed to me the wind took it a little right. And he seemed to like it anyway.

'That was good,' he said.

'No,' Glen replied. 'It's never good or bad. It's, "I retained the image." There's no bad shots – it's just the shots you get. "I retained the image", or "I lost the image."'

'It's just the shots you get.' That could be Shivas Irons talking. Visualisation was central to the spiritual and cosmic elements of sport. When Mike Murphy met Shivas, the teacher eventually revealed to him extensive journals that discussed his desire to turn visualisation into a 'consummate art'. Shivas believed that the path of a ball would lead to streams, or 'streamers', of energy stemming from the player to the target. It is along these streams that the ball travels.

Murphy wrote of Shivas's notes: 'One reason for the quiet surrounding [golf] is that players and onlookers alike sense that something occult is under way and that they should not interfere.' Shivas's notes said that the energy streamers 'can be affected by the players or gallery'. Shivas also wrote about enjoying 'new powers', which made him feel as if he had invisible arms like the Indian god Shiva enabling him to swing with 'extra arms and legs'.

So it wasn't just about 'seeing the shot'. It was about believing you were somebody or something else. Like Percy Cerutty channelling St Francis of Assisi, or Peter Brusso telling his golfers to imagine they were Darth Vader. You thought Brusso was a real nut, didn't you? But here it was, being taught by a guy who had worked with the best.

'You remember a long time ago we talked about the walk of the matador?' Glen asked Miguel.

'The what?'

'The walk of the matador,' Glen repeated in reverential tone.

'The walk of the matador? I don't remember that.'

Glen tried it in Spanish. Or what he thought was Spanish. Or maybe what I thought was Spanish. '*El paseo del matador?*'

Nothing from Miguel.

'Well,' Glen tried again, 'the way you were walking into the last three or four shots was like the matador.'

'Like the bull,' Miguel offered, finally getting it – sort of.

'Ya ... the matador walks in, and he struts, and he's dressed like the matador.' Glen really warmed to his theme. He's puffed out his chest, his chin is high. 'Is he afraid of the bull? Yes, because the bull could kill him. He is dressed like the matador, he struts like the matador. But what if he doesn't strut? So when you walk in *you are the matador*. You say, "Watch me. Here I come: 300,000 people watch the matador!" You could be the matador, Miguel *Delgado* [he said his name with a Spanish flourish]. *You could be.* Walk into the shot with that presence. You've got to capture that. Be the matador. Let's add one thing to your routine. Go back there, the line's here: Think Box and Play Box. Think about the bull.'

'I like the matador,' Miguel said. 'I walk in with confidence, strength. I think, "I'm the man."'

It's the most he's said all morning. I felt like I should offer encouragement at this point, noting that I had probably spoken even less than Miguel.

'I love it,' I said. 'It's great. It's powerful. I think you should do it. Use it. Definitely.'

So Miguel walked back into the Think Box. He mumbled something. He could have been reminding himself that he was a bull-slaying maniac. Or he could have been uttering something unmentionable about the English writer who had suddenly started advising him about his golf game.

'I am the matador,' he said. He pinged a shot off the club. It didn't look like it was a good one.

Glen laughed. 'The bull got him!'

'I felt good, though.'

'I know.'

Then he hit three more shots.

'I am the matador [ping]! I am the matador [ping]! I am the matador [ping]!'

Glen turned to me. 'Do you believe him?'

'Er, not sure. I think so.'

'Maybe I should say it in Spanish?' Miguel suggested, perhaps self-conscious about what other golfers might think of hearing him.

'Yeah, yeah, say it in Spanish, say it in Spanish,' I squealed. I surprised myself at this level of excitement. Glen raised a lone eyebrow in my direction.

'*Soy el matador* [ping]*! Soy el matador* [ping]*! Soy el matador* [ping]*!*'

As Miguel walked to the clubhouse, Glen and I held back. He wanted to talk to me about the work he had done.

'What we were doing today, but we don't use the word, was being *mindful*. Being present and centred. We don't use the word "mindful" or "mindfulness" because players – athletes – don't want to hear it. When Pete is teaching hard-nosed football players, you can't talk about that. He got burned for that in New England. But Miguel, he loved the matador, didn't he?'

'Sure did,' I said.

'Yeah, he bought into that. So I'll encourage him to practise that. Even something like that, if it's not automatic then don't use it. Be careful. Has to be automatic. This is the thing with coaches in sport. They give so much information and something as innocuous as that, you notice where the shot went the first time he tried it? He topped it. It interfered. It was fun but it interfered.

'This is what Pete gets. You've got to get through the stages of learning, you can't miss anything. The first stage is slow, and you think about it. The thinking mind doesn't hit any shots, but when you think about it you are training your brain to do it. The second stage is when you can feel it and you can see it. You might have to come back every now and then to stage one, but you can do it automatically.'

Glen asked whether I'd had any luck in talking with Pete. 'Not yet,' I said. He looked pensive. I hoped he was going to come up with an idea. Maybe that he would put in a call directly and urge him to talk to me. No. But he had another solution. He said that I needed to get to someone who was close to Pete, who he would listen to. 'That's not me so much any more,' he said, sadly. But there was someone.

'Pete works with this guy,' Glen said. 'He's probably the best in the world. The stuff he does really is cutting edge and he's taken Pete to another dimension.'

9

THE SECRET TAPES

When Michael Gervais, emboldened by the PhD in performance psychology in his back pocket, first walked into a pro locker room, he got a shock. It was a National Hockey franchise. The coach, the sort who might 'cut your nuts off', was not so happy with a fresh-faced Gervais entering his domain. 'And if you're fucked up in the head,' he bawled, 'go see this guy,' thumbing in Gervais's direction.

Things have got easier since. Today, Gervais is probably the most in-demand sports psychologist in the world. More colloquially, he's known as 'the sports shrink'. His clients include top athletes from almost every sport America has ever heard of, artists, musicians and Fortune 100 CEOs. The *Huffington Post* said – and at this point it might be best to try to replicate that gruff, macho voice of the guy who narrates action-movie trailers – he works 'in the trenches of high-stakes environments, where there is no luxury for mistakes, hesitation, or failure to respond'.

A bit over the top? Not really. Gervais is attracted to danger. If a protagonist is risking life or limb, Gervais is the guy in his ear telling him everything is going to be OK. That's why he is the Seattle Seahawks sports psychologist. The violence, the brutality and the potential for harm motivates him. But even the NFL is tame compared to other work.

He is part of Red Bull's high-performance team, advising athletes who do dangerous things at great speed or great height or both. You know the sort: climbing up a glacier without a safety rope, cliff diving, base jumping. Or wingsuit flying.

Ever heard of Felix Baumgartner? He was the base jumper who in 2010 thought it would be a good idea to attempt the highest-ever freefall from 24 miles above the earth. He managed it. But he almost didn't go through with it at all. Baumgartner, in a somewhat skewed list of things to be worried about, became frightened of his space suit. And his space helmet. He would only have to look at them to break out in the sort of cold sweat that pervades when you or I look down from, say, the fifth or sixth storey of a building. It became so bad that Project Stratos, as his insane jump was called, was about to be cancelled. So they called Gervais.

He solved it. He got Baumgartner, panicking and breathing heavily, all dressed up in the suit, and asked him to spell words backwards and do simple maths calculations. Then he told him, 'You'll have to fall asleep in this thing.'

It took some guts – understatement alert – for Baumgartner to jump out of a balloon with the Earth arcing ominously below. No one actually knew what would happen to him when he broke the sound barrier. But it also took some guts for the sports psychologist to encourage him to go ahead. Imagine that on your conscience if, when he got up there, he had a panic attack. Baumgartner didn't. He was A-OK. Helping football players must be a breeze by comparison.

Gervais and Pete Carroll started working together in 2011 after mutual friends had told them they were of one mind. They talked for hours and really hit it off, so Carroll invited Gervais to join the Seahawks. 'Let's build a masterpiece together,' was his grandiose offer.

And that's what they have been trying to do since. There have been no half measures, it seems, particularly talking about what they have done. Gervais is a one-man inspirational bumper-sticker generator. Really long bumper stickers.

'We don't talk about winning – we talk about being engaged at a really rich level to get the most out of life. We're not defined by a win or loss but defined about how it feels to be us. That's how we measure success. We know we have to win, to sell, to be sustainable. But the primary focus is resonating.'

It sounds like good stuff, doesn't it? Not that I had the faintest idea about what he actually meant. When you read more about him and listen to his podcasts, you just hope that he is copywriting some of it. Not that he probably needs the money, judging by the expensive-looking kitchen that flickered on my laptop screen when we connected on Skype. He looked impossibly healthy and buoyant. 'I'm doing great,' he told me. I was huddled over my wife's make-up table in the late-night gloom, praying my baby wouldn't wake to disrupt our talk.

Gervais was modest about Baumgartner, the Seahawks, being the main man in his field: 'Yeah, some of the projects I've been on have had great success. The truth is that it's a little bit of everything, it's not just one person.'

I'm not going to lie here. I was a bit nervous talking to Gervais. Maybe even a little paranoid. He tilted his screen – showing me a bit more of that desirable kitchen – so it appeared that he was looking down on me. Was this a psychologist's trick? Was he trying to intimidate me? Later, of course, I realised these were the irrational foibles of a mind that was not in the least quiet. It was shouty. Very shouty.

'*WE HAVE TO BE GREAT MATES! MAKE HIM LIKE YOU!*'

I was pinning my hopes on Gervais getting me to Carroll, you see, so we absolutely had to get on.

Ironically, as this inner game-style Self Two berating took place, Gervais was talking about two people 'connecting'.

'If we are really trying to get to the source of success,' he said, 'it's all about the relationship. And enduring relationships are founded on a deep regard for the other person, and when two people have a high regard for each other you become compelled to help them be the best. In football it's 53 players doing that and 22 coaches.'

'*MAKE HIM LIKE YOU!*'

Then I thought, that's Pete Carroll's Long Body he's talking about. Had I said that to Gervais he would have probably thought, 'This guy might know what he's on about.' But I 'missed the mark', as he would say, because I was too 'self-focused'. Dammit.

Instead I made a mistake. In my panic (desperation?) I forgot all about the warnings of the need to find the right language. It was, as Dave Meggyesy said, 'How do you ask *that* question?' Well, here's how not to do it. I went too big, too early.

'I want to know how Pete Carroll has taken Mike Murphy's ideas and run with them?'

There was a pause. Gervais, calmly and with impeccable politeness (which actually made me feel worse), said, 'I don't think he's taken those ideas and run with them.' And silence.

I floundered. I searched in my head for the response to get me back on track. But there was nothing.

'*OH! NOW YOU'VE GONE QUIET, HUH? YOU USELESS…*'

Gervais came back: 'No, *not* at all.'

111

A few seconds of awkward white noise later, the baby woke screaming. I had been released from the purgatory. Having decided that I had absolutely nothing to lose, I quickly asked Gervais to put me in touch with Pete. 'I've emailed him a few times but no response, Mike. Could you put in a word?' Gervais was probably thinking that Pete had done the right thing. 'I'll take his temperature tomorrow,' he said. 'Let's see what comes back.'

So we logged off. Gervais went off to enjoy his massive kitchen. I scuttled away to becalm a fractious infant. I thought I had blown my chances with Pete. Gervais, if he even bothered to mention me, would warn him, 'Don't waste your time with that English guy, he doesn't have the language.' The shame.

I emailed Gervais two days later. 'Hi, Mike. Did you take his temperature? What came back?' Mike? … Mike?! … MIIIIIIIKE?! He didn't reply.

What I should have been concentrating on, however, was Gervais's claim that Pete was not a Murphy follower. Had Murphy the mystic man got it wrong? Had he overblown their relationship? Glen told me they had known each other for four decades. And what of Glen? He was his guru. His teacher. Hold on, surely Gervais had got this wrong? At the very least he was on his guard against a shrill sports writer he had never met, wittering back at him on a computer screen from a darkened room.

I called Glen in a panic. I didn't tell him about my conversation faux pas with Gervais because I was too embarrassed. But I wanted to be sure about this.

'How much did Pete buy into Mike's ideological view, Glen?' I asked. 'Because he really *believes* in superman.' Glen talked over me before I could finish the question: 'Completely, completely.' He told me he was going to send me correspondence between him and Pete from way back. 'It's from when he was at the Jets right through to when he went to USC. There's not been so much since those days, but there's a lot of information for you to look through.'

Glen sent a clutch of papers. Some of them were press cuttings from Pete's revolution at the Seahawks; there were more of Glen's notes cajoling his protégé to stay true to his beliefs in New England; and early emails between the two. They revealed Glen's pride, like a parent collecting clippings or treasuring letters home from college, at Pete's achievement.

The most revelatory, however, was a 31-page transcript of a taped meeting between Glen, Pete and two men called Sean Brawley and Ken Ravizza in Pete's office at USC when college football was beguiled by the Carroll phenomenon. Before he arrived in 2000, USC had not won a national championship since 1978. Over the next nine years they won two. In the 2004 season they went undefeated. Pete's win–loss record finished 97–19. Under Pete, USC would win a staggering 84 per cent of games. That number meant it wasn't just Los Angeles that was infatuated with Pete, the whole country had its head turned.

It hadn't always been that way. When Pete was hired by USC following his failure at the New England Patriots, there was uproar among the college's football fans. The USC Athletics Department reportedly received 2,500 emails, faxes and phone calls from alumni. They weren't getting in touch to say 'good decision'. Pete had been, according to his critics, a consistent failure at the NFL and had been out of the college game for nearly 20 years. College donors even demanded he be sacked – before he had coached one game – or they would withdraw funding.

It was some turnaround, then. One that, as Mike Murphy might argue, only someone with occult powers could manage. The USC meeting, which gives a fascinating insight as to how Carroll actually achieved success, happened 'in probably 2005', according to Glen. Brawley was Tim Gallwey's 'only certified' inner game instructor. Ravizza was one of the first sports psychologists who, in the 1970s, had said a big fat yes to the siddhis after a soccer goalkeeper told him he'd looked down on himself, from about ten feet, playing the entire game.

They were the only four men in the room. The tapes had never been heard before by anyone (bar the transcriber) who wasn't there that day. They presented Pete at his most candid, before the vice of a ridiculing media and skittish owners perhaps squeezed him from speaking his mind about what he really believed in. He spoke about his own idiosyncrasies that had driven him to succeed, how to love players and to get them to love each other (back to the Long Body again). But, crucially, they showed his willingness to embrace the 'weird'. The pages did not just confirm his rejection of authoritarian coaching regimes. It wasn't just about treating players like men or being someone who could put an arm around an athlete. He talked about 'brainwashing' and what I thought sounded like the ultimate siddhi – mass thought projection.

What really jumped from the transcript was Pete's confidence (maybe even relief, after his failures at the New York Jets and New England Patriots) that his way had been proven to be the right way. After his sacking from the Patriots, Pete took time out. He did some consultancy work for NFL franchises, some writing in the media, and a lot of reading. But he didn't enjoy it. After six months he went to the New York stock exchange and got a buzz. 'The fighting, the phones were ringing, people were calling across the floor.' He loved it. He realised he was a 'total energy junkie'. He had to coach again.

He was also reminded of his passion for competition. And this underpinned everything. Every piece of research he ever did – from levitation to trying to summon the spirits of characters from Mike Murphy's book – was about being competitive. 'You know,' he told his intimate audience, 'I never shoot baskets to see if I can make a shot. I shoot baskets to see if I can make five in a row, or ten in a row. I can't go in until I hit five straight, and then I'm like, "OK, I have to do it again. I have to do that three times in a row."' Pete was an obsessive.

And he was obsessive when it came to putting this philosophy on paper. It flowed out of him. He wrote stories, chapters, one-liners, illustrations of philosophy, love and competition. Some of them he drew from his dreams. 'What came out of that is, "I'm going to do things better than it's [sic] ever been done before."'

Pete's inspiration for that line came from an unlikely source: Jerry Garcia, the front man of the rock band Grateful Dead. I wasn't expecting them to crop up again. Pete was a Deadhead. Perhaps he was there that night in Port Chester in 1971 when Stanley Krippner was conducting his telepathy experiment. Garcia had said that the band didn't want to be the best ones doing something, they wanted to be the *only* ones doing it.

In the transcripts, it didn't take Pete long to get on to the subject of being perceived as soft. Something, he admitted, he perhaps was when at the New York Jets in his first NFL head coach role. A player called him out for not yelling at him after a defeat. 'He was going, "What's this shit? What do you mean we did all right today?"' Pete learned to tailor his approach to the individual. That was a key difference between Pete and other coaches. This sounds elementary, but it's worth remembering the culture of football that had made it almost impossible for the Pete Carroll way to survive. You had to be a Vince Lombardi. A Bill Parcells. Pete believed in picking his spots, knowing when to go hard, knowing when to go easy, and because he had created an environment of trust with players, they knew that when he did shout and bawl he wasn't just doing it for the sake of it. If they were not working hard enough, Pete said he would 'jump their shit', which I took to mean a stern talking-to.

'You always come back the other way,' he said. 'You always show them that this isn't how I am always. So you come back and you love them. You get after them and you love them. And you show them that you'll go from A to Z for them. And the reason that you're after them is because you want them to be so good and you know they can be. And you convince them they can be whatever you expect them to be. You convince them that they are capable of being great, or good, or a role player, or whatever you are trying to convince them of. You don't relent. You keep on rolling, and eventually they know.'

It almost brings a tear to the eye. Sniff. Particularly when you recall Dave Meggyesy's quote about how football coaches give players a 'tantalising hint of what it might be like to be a man'.

This 'love them' approach makes much more sense than the 'out there' stuff that Pete had been reluctant to talk about. Yet here's the thing. Without the 'weird stuff', would he have ever struck upon his philosophy? It seemed to me that without a curious mind being prepared to consider all possibilities – and let's face it, smothering football players with love was most definitely *not* mainstream in football – his education as a coach would have been half-baked. Pete admitted that, to reach the top, you did have to be a bit, well, weird.

'I've been fortunate. I've done a lot of weird stuff. I've had a lot of weird-encounter things. I've listened to some wild stuff that has really opened me up to figure out what's really important to me. Yeah, there's a lot of stuff.' Then he paused. 'Remember the Russian guy? I'm always trying to find the truth of real shit.'

The 'Russian guy' was Leonid Gissen, the former rower who was able to see inside people's bodies at the Further Reaches of Sports Psychology conference in San Francisco in 1993. It was simultaneously frustrating and gratifying to have it confirmed that Glen's and Mike Murphy's characterisation of Pete held water. Even if the actual nitty-gritty detail was missing. This would be a theme as the transcripts continued. To the outsider, though, Pete sounded more and more like Murphy's captivating description.

The only way I can think of describing it was that when Pete was coach at USC, he was the leader of a sect. A nice sect, let's make that clear, one that just wanted its team to compete. He was the guy at the front telling everyone what to do, and they just went off and did it without thinking. Like in a trance. It sounded, well, cult-like. Mainly because Pete used the word 'brainwashing'. There was a definite tone of hubris as well, something that made sense for someone so successful at the time at leading a team, getting people to do what he wanted and being revered.

'What's really clear is that these guys are brainwashed,' he said. 'I've said that a couple of times, and I have to be careful with the phrase, but that is what is going on. These guys are absolutely brainwashed. They don't know any better. They don't know how to even speak any more. If I say something, it just comes out of the next ten guys. We have the same conscience.'

Then he spoke about mass mind control. It was in response to a question about a media interview he had given when USC had been denied progression to the 2003 national championship game because of a quirk in the ranking systems. Despite being rated the number one team in the country by the Associated Press and college coaches, USC were demoted to the third-best team by the computer algorithm that decided the two best teams. At the time it was hugely controversial. Pete said of the system, 'I don't know how it works.' And he didn't care. What he did care about was how the snub gave him an opportunity to ram home his message about the USC programme. That at its core was a bunch of players not getting stressed.

'They're brainwashed,' he said. 'They don't get concerned about stuff that they can't control. We don't worry about [the championship game].' Not worrying about the game that, surely, was every coach's ultimate goal? This was not elementary stuff. Nor was it elementary that he was trying to get USC's followers to believe that the championship game didn't matter.

'I knew I had a chance to make a statement and that a lot of people would hear it – [a chance to] control the mindset of a whole lot of people. So I did it to the max. I went back a month later and watched the interview that everybody responded to. I thought, I didn't say hardly anything [sic] of substance. It was really cool. It was like political leaders do it – they control the mindset of their constituents. That's what that was.

'What you want to do is create an environment where people do things because they want to do them, because if they have to do it they will creatively avoid [doing it]. I say brainwashed because it's the shortcut way of saying that. But they do stuff because they want to. When you're in a program where you've got the whip you can only go so far – that's the US government and Armed Services. They just said, "Fuck it, this is the way we're going to do it. We won't get them to the highest level but we'll get them all in line." Now, the Special Forces groups, they go to that point but then they go to a whole different level because they need people to go to their optimum, and you cannot go to your optimum when you're under the oppressive whip thing.'

Pete was talking about brainwashing and mind control. It almost sounded like he believed in the Soviet idea of thought projection when, perhaps, it could be more easily explained as 'good, sensible management'. No doubt that was how he would have explained it had there been a journalist in the room, a doubter. But among friends and fellow believers, he could talk freely. Carroll sounded like a student of the Esalen–Soviet pact. And the evolutionary line was clear, too. Murphy and Esalen had researched what the Soviets had been up to; they tried their own programme with the Esalen Sports Center in the hope of inspiring or creating athletes and coaches who had sensitivity to the siddhis. And Pete Carroll had been a student of that world.

The words that struck a chord with me were 'go to their optimum'. The optimum was the realm of the siddhis, the alternative states of consciousness that had tantalised Murphy, the Esalen Sports Center and before them the US military themselves with their remote viewers like Uri Geller and the First Earth Battalion, who were peace, love and carrying flowers as a symbol of goodwill. Pete Carroll's football project was based on the same principles. And you could not get to that state without peace, love and goodwill for the individuals under your care.

Pete's philosophy chimed with the original mission statement from the Esalen Sports Center: 'Traditional athletic and physical education programs often articulate and reinforce values such as authoritarianism and winning at all costs.' The language was the same. But how did he actually put it into practice? I emailed him again. No reply. But it was OK, because hiding away in the chunk of Glen's papers was the answer.

10

ZEN PLAYBOOK

The Seattle Seahawks used to be a joke. 'What do the Seahawks and the Post Office have in common? Neither deliver on Sundays.' And another: 'The Seahawks don't have a website because they can't string three Ws together.' The Seahawks weren't a terrible team. They were just, well, average. Mediocrity personified, muddling along from one week to the next raising their fans' hopes in one game only to dash them again. For 39 long, barren years they didn't win a Super Bowl. They got mighty close once, in 2005, but otherwise they didn't get the proverbial sniff. Then Pete Carroll showed up.

Pete left USC and was officially hired as the Seahawks head coach on 11 January 2010. He signed a five-year contract. Unlike his tenure at New England, Carroll insisted that he was the main man. He made all the decisions. He was even made executive vice-president of football operations. This meant that Pete hired the general manager. Normally it is the other way around. In just four seasons under Pete, the unheralded and unfashionable Seahawks became world champions. Few had predicted it apart from, apparently, Pete himself. After leaving USC for the NFL outpost, he had told people that something extraordinary was going to happen.

Pete had wasted little time in stamping his authority on the Seahawks. He completely renovated the team roster, making 200 player transactions. Despite a 7–9 record in his first season, Seattle still won the divisional title. That was historic. No team had done that with such a win–loss rate before. As if that wasn't proof enough that Pete was doing something right, the Seahawks then stunned the sport by taking down the New Orleans Saints in the wild card play-offs. The Saints were the reigning Super Bowl champions and it was considered an extraordinary upset. The Chicago Bears would end their season in the next game.

By contrast, 2011 was a disappointment. Seattle failed to make the play-offs. Perhaps this was down to Pete needing the time to train the brains of his players to accept the 'athletic mind'? It couldn't happen overnight, as Glen Albaugh had said at the Peacock Gap with Miguel. A year later, Pete was in profit in the 'wins' column for the first time at Seattle. Their 11–5 record suggested they were a coming force but a heartbreaking loss to Atlanta Falcons in the divisional game – they had led by two points with 30 seconds left on the clock – had analysts wondering whether they had blown a Super Bowl chance.

Pete remained upbeat. 'We've got a chance to be really solid,' he said at the time. 'Maybe it winds up we're not good enough, I can't believe that. I think we're going to win a lot of games.'

Pete had built slowly at Seattle, signing players who he knew would be open-minded to his ultra-positive approach. And then he set about his brainwashing. In personality, he was just the same as he was in his first head coach job at the Jets. He bounded about the place, back-slapping, making jokes and being the players' buddy. Historically this was an NFL no-no. But players spoke about how they had bought into Pete's competitive and fun environment.

Indeed, fun was central to the Seattle programme. Training sessions had themes. The week began with 'Tell the Truth Monday'. Pete had wanted his players to talk openly, without fear of rebuke, about how things were going on and off the field. The idea was to create a 'we're all in this together' atmosphere. Wednesday was 'Competition Wednesday'. Pete's prime parking slot would be up for grabs for, in one example, the player who caused the most fumbles of the ball in one session. Next was 'Turnover Thursday' where the focus was on winning back the ball. A video of the session was then replayed, edited with funny, irreverent or topical clips; Bruce Lee sending an opponent flying through the air, a kangaroo punching a man in the face, piranhas swarming over prey. 'No Repeat Friday' was about players being so precise in the execution of the plays that they were not made to do them again.

Seattle had good players, too, though. Russell Wilson was lauded as a quarterback and the defensive backfield of Richard Sherman, Earl Thomas and Kam Chancellor were so good they had their own nickname: the Legion of Boom. And you know you've made it in sport when you've got a macho-sounding nickname. Sherman was one of the most vocal players in favour of Pete's ways: 'We're his guys – guys he picked who have really embraced his way.'

The combination proved irresistible in 2013–14. Seattle won their first four matches. They would extend their home wins record to 15 straight, and ended the regular season 13–3. The New Orleans Saints and then the San Francisco 49ers were defeated. Denver Broncos were waiting in the Super Bowl. How did he start the week of preparation for the Seattle team's biggest game of their lives? A basketball shoot-off. The winner got a trophy. The game against the Broncos was not even close. Seattle won 48–3 in one of the most uncompetitive finales in history. At 62, Pete became the third oldest coach to win a Super Bowl.

The locals thought he was some sort of god. And why not? He made the earth move. In one home game they were rocking and rolling in the bleachers to seismic proportions. Five minor earthquakes were recorded during a game against the New Orleans Saints, according to the Pacific Northwest Seismic Network. Carroll has had Seahawks fans wound up to such an extent that they have broken the world record for the loudest crowd noise.

There was a clamour from sports writers to unpick this Seahawk way. They wanted to know about Pete's methods. How he motivated his players. How he disciplined them. What he fed them. What he didn't feed them. How they trained. The media were curious and cynical. A nation obsessed with winning had a new winner to pedestal. How do you do it, Pete? How do you win? The problem was, the Seahawks weren't about winning. Pete's philosophy was about being competitive, about having fun and being relaxed. The sports writers didn't get that. For them, their job was about winners and losers, heroes and fall guys – about trying so hard your lungs burst. There was nothing in between.

The next season, Pete was a loser. Hero to zero. The sort of storyline a salivating media was comfortable with. He took his Seahawks team to the Super Bowl again – this time to face the New England Patriots, the team that sacked him. And with the clock ticking down they were on the very brink of back-to-back titles. For a franchise that had not even had a scent of glory for decades, here they were within a fingertip again. Literally. At USC Pete was called 'Big Balls Pete' because of the attacking, positive plays he would call. Setting the tone. Telling his players to chill. He had this. But he didn't see this coming. The Seahawks were yards from the New England Patriots end zone. A score seemed inevitable. But as the ball arrowed to its intended target, rogue Patriot digits diverted it. New England had stolen it, snaffled it and stuck it up their jersey for the win.

While the Patriots went crazy, Pete chewed gum furiously. He looked up at the big screen and swallowed hard. You could almost see the energy draining from him. His quarterback, Russell Wilson, the man who threw the pass, rubbed his head, befuddled, next to him. 'What happened?' he pleaded with big, brown puppy-dog eyes. That question – that moment – says a lot about the Seahawk way. In times of crushing disappointment, the player approaches the coach for reassurance. Like a kid who goes to his dad hoping to be told 'everything's going to be OK'. On the Secret Tapes, Pete talked about 'brainwashing' and how players were told what to think and feel by a coach's words and behaviour. And, most importantly, he spoke about showing them love. Wilson's wounded state epitomised both. He wanted to be told what had happened and why, he wanted to see the energy, the gung-ho nature. He wanted comfort.

Pete's call was labelled one of the worst plays of all time. No, he said. It was a play with the worst result. So that gap between who Pete was and who the media thought he should be widened like shuddering fault lines. They didn't *get* him or his methods. They didn't get how he turned consistent also-rans into champions in only his fourth season. To understand him and his methods a bit more, you need to read an email. One sent from Pete Carroll to Glen Albaugh on 20 October 2000 at 6.20 a.m.

'I'm kinda fired up about this!' Pete wrote. In his downtime after getting axed from the Patriots, Pete became more convinced than ever of the need for athletes to be trained to achieve extraordinary athletic feats. Just like the Esalen Sports Center had been. Pete wanted to start a 'performance enhancement centre'. But this was ESC for the 21st century. So he got in touch with an old Sports and Cosmic Forces classmate. Ted Leland was the director of athletics, physical education and recreation at Stanford University. Stanford had no official sports psychologist at the time and it seemed the perfect place for Pete's idea to take seed. Unsurprisingly, Ted was 'wide open' to the possibility and talked of 'unlimited funding'. For Pete, it was an opportunity to put together a dream team of the men who had inspired him: Glen, Mike Murphy and Tim Gallwey. Not much room on that magic carpet again.

'Now, Glen,' wrote Pete, 'if there was ever an endeavour you, me and the boys could champion, this may be the one! With the support of Michael, Tim… we may really have something here. It is all the heavyweights one project could ever hold.' He would call it The Stanford Performance Enhancement Institute. 'Are we cooking in the same pot, dude!?'

Did I mention he was excited? 'I kinda see this like the venue for us to realise our dreams in the whole realm of the sport experience and a way to share it with a community. Wow! This may just be another one of my dream/vision ideals but, then again, it may be a living, thriving example of "manifesting your own reality". Can you feel me, brother? Can I get an Amen, brother? That is all for now, send your tidings of love only when you get the feeling.'

The proposal Glen and Pete put together neatly surmised all that has come before in these pages. How the human potential movement, with their 'esoteric Eastern philosophy', had teamed up with psychologists to produce a science of 'applied sports psychology'. The goals of this applied sports psychology included accessing the siddhi states, a final frontier of sports performance.

In that regard, the pitch was like an abridged version of the First Earth Battalion's handbook. A sort of Zen playbook. This institute would 'consist of training in methods of cognitive control … by achieving mastery over one's thinking, emotional and physical states can be positively influenced and, in turn, performances can be maximized.'

The proposal included a checklist for achieving siddhis. Do all of them and you give yourself the best possible chance of lift-off. It listed them.

There were 'Cognitive Foundations', which were described as controlling self-talk, restructuring ineffective beliefs and cultivating a powerful self-worth. This was a more acceptable way of describing golfers who couldn't hit a seven iron until they imagined they were Darth Vader.

'Attention Control' was about 'learning to selectively attend to important cues and to shift the field of attention as needed'. This was akin to what Glen said with Miguel Delgado at the Peacock Gap golf course about sport being a novel. The athlete needs to see the twist in the plotline coming.

The Soviet Union's 'Psychic Self-Regulation' cropped up under the heading: 'Stress Management: understanding how reaction to stress operates in the human system, and mastering of recovery and energy management.'

Next was 'Imagery: the process of kinaesthetic, visual, auditory and tactile imagery and the methods to obtain the desired outcomes for enhanced performance.' Take your pick: Miguel seeing the shot; Mike Spino's booster button; Percy Cerutty and St Francis of Assisi.

The importance of pre- and post-game preparations was also flagged, allowing a more likely leap into optimal performance states.

Athletes and coaches would meet with a sports psychologist to implement their own personalised 'enhancement curriculum' to get those boxes ticked. They would sit in ergonomically designed chairs for relaxation training and then watch a video of empowering footage – probably of them doing something great on the field – set to their favourite music. This 'state-of-the-art audio and video production suite' would assist athletes with guided imagery so they didn't have to rely just on the pictures in their head.

There would also be 'biofeedback machinery'. 'Biofeedback' had been another term for Russia's psychic self-regulation. The body's physiological processes were recorded in front of the athlete so he could learn what thoughts, images, feelings or muscular contractions are associated with, say, heartbeat. If an athlete wanted to reduce his heartbeat or control adrenaline or electrical activity in the brain because it made him better at his sport, then he could learn to self-regulate.

All of this was different. Never before had there been an institute or programme dedicated to football players and optimal states. It was radical. Weird, even, to the layman because of where this stuff came from. These ideas had been birthed by Russian scientists trying to win the Cold War, beavering away in secret labs with KGB goons standing guard outside. They had then been adopted by the Esalen Sports Center and Mike Murphy's New Age thinkers, who were trying to change the world by rejecting aggression and rivalry, whether on the battlefield or sports field. Instead of these ideas being used to kill people or create super-soldiers, Pete Carroll was using them to win – sorry, compete – in American football. There was a lovey-dovey symmetry to the whole thing, which the counterculture would have approved. This seemed to be tangible evidence that the work of the Esalen Sports Center had been continued and that desire for people to make the best of themselves and possibly do something superhuman had not been lost to history.

Unfortunately, the Stanford Performance Enhancement Institute never existed. A little more than eight weeks later, Pete was appointed head coach at USC. But the Stanford pitch, the research and 'the dream' would not go to waste. It would form a blueprint for the programme that Pete would install at the Seahawks ten years later.

So for the Stanford Institute that never was, read the Virginia Mason Athletic Center, or VMAC, as it is known. It is where the Seahawks do all the sort of stuff you would expect a football team to do, like train, lift weights, run drills. But they also do most of the concepts that Pete outlined in that original proposal.

The sight of 300-pound guys, whose job it is to pound the hell out of the opposition, sitting crossed-legged chanting '*ommmm*' while doing mandatory yoga sessions is unusual in football lore. Or they meditate. Or – as the original vision explained – they sit down with a sports psychologist to discuss their individually tailored programmes, their hopes, their fears, their relationship with their father. That psychologist is, of course, Michael Gervais.

Gervais leads group meditation sessions or one-on-ones. 'Quiet your minds,' he soothes. 'Focus your attention inwardly, visualise success.' Established players have longer sessions and are encouraged to record them on their smartphones so they can try it at home. Players new to the Seahawk system have shorter six-minute sessions. It's inner game stuff. But it can also be called brainwashing, mind control, thought projection or brain hacking. And it is what really defines Pete and the Seahawks as different.

Remember Pete Brusso's lemon? Think about it now. Your mouth is watering, isn't it? Now think about how he talked about golfers concentrating on seeing the shot in the mind's eye before they stepped up to the ball. He argued that this was training the brain. The brain, Peter said, doesn't know what is real and what is imagined. Glen Albaugh's Think Box and Play Box routine was no different. He wanted Miguel to visualise the shot in his head. Or Dave Meggyesy when he saw the play in his head after watching hours of video footage and doing the routines that got him 'present and centred'. What Pete and Gervais are doing is all of these things but on a much grander scale. VMAC is like the Esalen Sports Center, trying to produce athletes who have the capability to go to their optimum. But it is considerably more ambitious. *They are training the Seahawks players to have experienced or 'seen' the game in their heads before it has even been played.* They are also drilling them to repeat moments when they had experienced siddhis. And they do it over and over and over again.

The game is played out in a Seahawks player's head countless times. Well, parts of a game anyway. The crucial parts that can decide whether it is won or lost. Gervais might put the quarterback in that time and space in his head when the clock is ticking, the Seahawks are losing and he has to make the pass to win the match. What do you see? How does it feel? What will you do? And repeat. This simulation means that when the quarterback *is* in a situation like that in a game, he feels less stressed, less fear. It's about reducing the anxiety players feel to reduce mistakes. It's not just the quarterback. It's anyone on the team: running back, cornerback, linebacker, tight end. 'Fear is central to what we do,' says Gervais. '[And] that allows us to master it.' If you're not afraid in a high-pressure environment, and are, in fact, feeling pretty chilled because you've 'been here' before, what can happen? You can reach for the superpowers.

Gervais focuses on those peak experiences during one-on-one sessions. He asks the players to remember when they were at their best and what it felt like. Then they work out what is stopping each player getting there more often. It could be a fitness issue, a personal problem or technical anxiety about their game. But, he says, once he asks that question they've bought in, they're interested. Why? Because the experience is so rich and pleasurable that they want to go there more often. 'It's the moment,' he says, 'and being lost in the moment is so rewarding and so engaging [that] we don't have to challenge them [to want to get there].'

Russell Okung, an offensive tackle, said, 'Meditation is as important as lifting weights and being out here on the field of practice. It's about quieting your mind and getting into certain states where everything outside of you doesn't matter in that moment. There are so many things telling you that you can't do something, but you take those thoughts captive, take power over them, and change them.' Good work, Russ. Way to go to get your cognitive foundations and awareness control in check.

Quarterback Russell Wilson is another advocate. He was pictured in *ESPN* magazine in the lotus position in 2013. It caused quite a stir. 'We do imagery work and talk about having that innovative mindset of being special,' Wilson said at the time. 'I talk to guys on other teams, and other teams aren't like this. We do stuff different here.'

Right. VMAC is not just about yoga and meditation as a means of enhancing performance. No stone is left unturned in an effort to make players feel loved and cared for. For example, the canteen serves only organic food. Above doorframes to the training ground there are signs saying, 'I'm In!' Players have to tap it with their hand to commit.

There are three rules to which everyone has to subscribe. Protect the team. No whining. Be early. Swearing is also frowned upon, and any over-the-top aggressive behaviour in practice, or bullying – either by coaches or players – is stamped out. Players are told to say 'thank you' to media after interviews.

Overall, there is a sense of fun. As Glen told Pete when at New England, 'The ultimate seriousness is non-seriousness.' So Pete is a practical joker. He has had players 'arrested' in team meetings for unpaid hotel bills, put fake snakes in ice coolers or staged a disagreement between him and a player over the shirt number they wanted to wear.

Some of these ideas might seem irrelevant. But add them all up and they contribute to the notion of the Long Body. They are designed to make everyone feel as if they are in it together. At the core is something similar to a human resources department.

When at USC, Pete was concerned that new players would join and then feel lost or displaced. So at VMAC an entire staff is on hand to help with players' problems away from the football field. This could provide help with marriage worries, advice on investments, or a tip for a good painter and decorator. The Seahawks have a player development director *and* a director of player health and performance. It sounds like the same thing. Most NFL franchises don't have a person doing even half of those two jobs.

What goes on at VMAC could easily be dismissed as athletes being cosseted. There's nothing new in that in pro sports, it might be said. In the biggest sports in the world, in the biggest leagues the superstars are afforded most luxuries. They can go talk to a psychologist if they wish. And they can try yoga or meditation too, no doubt. The difference here, though, is twofold. For a start, Pete Carroll came up with this in the form of the Stanford Performance Enhancement Institute in 2000, and the theories behind why it could work were planted by the likes of Mike Murphy, Glen Albaugh and Tim Gallwey. These were deep-rooted. Did other sports teams have such a history and ideology or did they just offer yoga and meditation as 'extras' or because they had cash to splash on the 'modern' way? Surely it had to come from a genuine desire to help somebody out rather than an expectation that it should be part of the facilities?

When Pete was formulating his philosophy in the mid-1990s and then trying to implement it at, first, the New York Jets and then the New England Patriots, sports teams around the globe didn't really do sports psychology, let alone the notion of a Long Body. Not knowingly, anyway. As an example, the England soccer team's idea to create a bond and competitive environment before the European Championships in 1996 was to go on a notorious drinking session in a Hong Kong nightclub. Players were pictured in newspapers looking the worse for wear with their shirts torn and bar staff pouring spirits down their throats. The media and the team's fans were outraged. It united the players, though, and in that tournament they celebrated goals with players pretending to pour drinks down one another's throats. But no one would advocate that approach now.

Football teams sure as hell weren't sitting around meditating and travelling forward in time to any given Sunday in their head space, practising their plays, managing their feelings and facing their fears. No wonder Pete's methods were labelled by ESPN in 2013 as 'bizarro football world'.

American football franchises, Pete and David Meggyesy would argue, are still guilty of not putting player welfare first or rejecting the dogma that pedestalled violence and brutality.

Remember that quote from the Kansas City Chiefs' player personnel manager about the team or the owner or the fans not caring about 'your problems'? There were plenty of other examples of Meggyesy's warning that the environment had not changed significantly since his playing days. Here's another. From 2009 to 2011 it was alleged that the New Orleans Saints paid out bonuses to players who injured opposition players. It was called 'Bountygate'. That sort of attitude was the motivation for Pete. As was the warning from history from Meggyesy and that very first ESC mission statement about ridding American sport of its damaging culture.

So the ESC did work. It just took a few years to come to fruition. And so inspired and motivated were the originators by how Pete Carroll had, ahem, taken their ideas and run with them, they wanted another shot. Mike Murphy, Mike Spino and Meggyesy were back. Their goal was the same: to explore the highest range of the human spirit and potential. They invited me to their first conference. And guess what? It would get weird again.

11

MONKEY BRAIN

Piiiing! A man, greying, early sixties and sporting a ponytail, clinked finger cymbals together and took an audible breath. The whole room did the same. There must have been nearly a hundred people there, some in tie-dye, some in suits (I swear I saw someone wearing hemp), but most of them in tracksuits and sports gear. Then, from a lectern looking out, in a hushed voice he said, 'Here we are … right here … right now. That's how it is. That's how it always is.' Lots of people nodded. Others had their eyes closed and were breathing deeply. I kept one eye open, beadily looking around the room.

This was the Sports, Energy and Consciousness Group's sports festival to 'awaken human potential through sport'. Good title, I reckoned, as it had, by and large, been dozing for the past 40 years, Pete Carroll aside.

They called themselves 'the SEC Group'. They were a collection of doctors, psychologists, scientists, world-class athletes and leading-edge coaches. At least, that's what the mission statement said. In private they referred to themselves as 'the Big Six'. Included in that six was the man with the ponytail, Rick Leskowitz, a Harvard psychiatrist. He was a co-founder, along with Dave Meggyesy and Mike Spino. Mike Murphy added gravitas, the revered man of mystery who would show up and sprinkle stardust on the whole thing. And I liked to think of these three old hippies mounting a comeback, even if hairlines had receded and joints stiffened. If this were a movie, the director would cut them in a slo-mo, striding in looking mean, magnificent and ready to meditate.

In reality, Spino and I arrived together. We were late, having been early. When we'd reached the Dominican University of California, just a short cab ride over the Golden Gate Bridge from San Francisco, a good couple of hours before the start, we'd wandered around aimlessly trying to find where we should be. Spino hadn't a clue. 'Don't worry,' he said. 'This is great. I can say, "We were here! Where were you guys? I was going to help set up!" So now let's go eat.'

Spino and I had buddied up. 'I think we've really connected, don't you, Big Ed?' The 'big' was a joke. At 5 feet 10½ inches, I am built like a pipe cleaner. We'd done the tourist thing, stopping for snaps at the Golden Gate Bridge, and had lunch together in the quaint and bustling community of San Rafael.

What did he know of Pete Carroll? 'The SEC guys all rave about him. Mike Murphy, too. I don't know what he actually does, but let me tell you something I probably shouldn't: he's an advisor to us at the SEC.' He nodded and winked at me.

The festival had been organised just like in the old Esalen Sports Center days. Yogis, gurus and practitioners had been invited to give workshops while Mike Murphy was due to give the big keynote speech in the evening. Spino's workshop was to publicise his True Champion mental training company, set up with a guy called Drew Mearns. Mearns used to be the agent to the disgraced Olympic sprinter Ben Johnson, who got busted for steroids in Seoul 1988. 'He lost a million bucks overnight,' he told me. Mearns, a lawyer by trade, had written rules that had allowed athletes to make money and kept Billie Jean King, the tennis player, in the black after her sponsors ditched her for coming out. The three of us formed a nice little clique over the weekend, lunching and chewing the fat.

'Everything people will talk about this weekend,' Mearns said, 'is an antidote to drugs.' The circle was almost complete, then, considering that the Russians had, according to Jim Hickman, abandoned their Hidden Human Reserves project in the eighties in favour of the juice and pills.

I was excited. It was an opportunity to see how this stuff worked first hand. Instead of people talking about it, I hoped to be doing it. And to that end I signed up for a tennis class with Scott Ford, a former tennis pro out of Denver, who promised to put me 'in the zone', as it were, within a few minutes of hitting a ball back and forth. I would be seeing auras and slowing down time in, er, no time.

If I could find somebody to hit with. I was like the kid who got picked last in school sports. No one really wanted to play with the awkward English guy who, admittedly, had come dressed for a business brunch. So I cornered a dark-haired guy called Robert, throwing a ball at him and saying, 'Let's go!' before he could say no.

Scott was another founding member of SEC, who had, quite by chance, discovered a way to slip into the alternative state of consciousness required for amazing feats. When playing tennis, of course. It was quite simple: don't look at the ball. He reckoned this simple trick was 'inspiration from the cosmos'.

'In 1978 I was playing with a friend of mine and I was having trouble with timing – hitting the balls too late,' he said. 'So I imagined I had a big window in front of me, and that if I made contact with the ball at that window then my timing would be at least consistent. So I started trying to hit the ball at the window, but what I did was this: I was watching the ball as closely as I could and I didn't see the window. And I was hitting *everything* late. So I just started to watch the window, deciding I would try to break the window with my racket swing. Every time I was successful I'd say, "Yes!" And when I wasn't I was, "No!" And if I was "yes!" like, a hundred times in a row, I was, like, "Oh my god!" I had found I could get into the zone. And that was by fixing a look on this window instead of watching the ball.'

And to think, the first thing coaches ordinarily teach kids is to watch the ball. Well, you've been doing it wrong. Try to hit the window. Any window will do. Mum and Dad will like that.

Scott was a good egg. He was warm and polite and he swapped rackets with me so I didn't have to use one that had been designed for a pre-teen girl. I think he thought it slightly odd that I was wearing brown brogues, smart pants and a button-down shirt. But he didn't let it show. He was full of what we call over here 'Yank chutzpah': back-slapping, high-fives and yelps of encouragement. I suppose I was a bit like the toddler on his first day at nursery, looking around to check if everything was OK. Everyone else was going for it. I saw someone stretching. Should I stretch? How does one stretch? This was just the beginning of my anxiety. I was worried about where, exactly, I should look for the window. To the right? To the left? Then there was the ball. Do I look at the ball? Do I keep one eye on it, warily, as if it's someone unsavoury-looking loitering outside my front window? Not surprisingly, I sure as hell could not get into any kind of zone.

Robert, some sort of sports therapist, could, annoyingly. He was shouting 'cool!' and 'awesome!' as the ball pinged off his racket. 'Hey, Scott! I'm really feeling this!' Yeah, well, Robert, you're only feeling it because I'm desperately trying to make sure that I keep getting the ball back to you, diving and rolling and fretting and sweating while you stand there, all alpha male with legs insalubriously wide apart, sounding as if you're enjoying it way too much.

I thought it might be Robert's wraparound black shades that gave him this something extra. Or maybe it was because I was wearing the wrong shoes. Maybe it was because his cries of exultation distracted me. The ball flew off the edge of my racket. 'Hey,' Robert said, and he paced over to me. Oh god, I thought, he's going to start giving me guidance on technique. He's going to coach me, isn't he? He'll call it 'friendly advice' or something else humiliating.

'Hey, man. Bit of instruction: maybe it's because your wrist is too soft. Try gripping it harder … yeah! Like that! Awesome.' Maybe it's because my wrist is too soft.

Anyway, I saw no window or vista or anything whatsoever opening out in front of me. Scott was convinced that Roger Federer, probably the greatest tennis player of all time, 'had to be using this [the window technique], or something like it'. Really? Roger Federer *not* looking at the ball? Scott had spoken in that esoteric way, suggesting that his ploy would give me 'a sense of being home … of what I'm supposed to be doing as a human being'. It was a big call, but then Scott was pretty zealous. It wasn't just about hitting a ball for him. He said it helped him define who he really was and ensured he was not only at one with tennis but also God, whether in the zone or not.

Afterwards, he bounded over and asked how I felt. I didn't find myself, God or the zone. I only told him the latter, though, as I didn't want to sound as if I was listing a bunch of grievances. And then I lied. I did have fun, though, Scott. 'You know,' I said, 'I haven't played tennis for 20 years so it felt, er, great!' I nodded enthusiastically and added 'really great!' for good measure.

'Hey, doesn't matter you didn't get in the zone,' he said. 'You had fun. That's the main thing.' I doubt Roger Federer would have been placated the same way. 'So what's your next workshop?' My next workshop was fear itself.

*

In any walk of life, humans are afraid, right? They are afraid of making a mistake that could lead to injury, humiliation, defeat, etc. Kristen Ulmer's job is to stop fear preventing folks – mostly extreme skiers, but she could cross over into any vocation – from allowing fear to dominate their lives and, surprise, surprise, achieving their full human potential. She was one of those extreme skiers. She was on the US Olympic team in the nineties, did backflips over crevasses, jumped out of helicopters and rattled down mountainsides with an avalanche raging behind her.

Ulmer put the 'world-class athlete' in the SEC. Also, she had once been interviewed by Michael Gervais, Pete Carroll's Seahawks sports shrink, for a job as a fear specialist. They talked for hours, really hit it off … but no gig. She seemed pretty peeved she never got the call. Ulmer reckoned that Pete Carroll and the Seahawks 'put fear in a box'. You can't do that, she told me. To be successful in managing fear, she said, you have to accept that you will not beat fear. You can't hide from it. You can't suppress it. Interestingly, she referenced fear being a whining child locked in a basement. Best not do that. So you had to have a conversation with fear. Pull up a chair next to you and talk to your fear. This made me afraid.

This was not because I was unnerved about facing my fears or I had locked down a dark terror deep in my subconscious. It was because I am English. There is nothing more terrifying to an English person than to not only be denied the chance to repress feelings and emotions but to be actively cajoled into doing the opposite. On the West Coast of America, they don't understand this. It is a natural state for people to let it all out there. And people, about 15 of them, were doing that left, right and centre in a small, slightly stuffy classroom. A woman a few rows ahead was shouting, '*I am out of the cage! I am free!*' The guy next to me was having a full-blown row with his fear. I put my head down and made notes, refusing to look up, when Ulmer said, 'OK, let's hear from someone else!'

I felt like an alien. I felt frustrated. How would I understand the superpowers and what Mike Murphy had been talking about for a lifetime if a stuffy heritage prevented me from loosening up? Language had been a barrier. Now it was a culture. I wanted to have some sense or feeling – literally – of what it might be like to get close to doing something extraordinary. Drew and Spino helped me out over lunch. 'Go and see the Focus Band guy,' they said. 'He's the one wearing the black beret.'

John Ruark was the guy wearing the black beret. I found him setting out his Focus Band wares. He had a ponytail, too. And he was also in his sixties. He used to fly troops in and out of Vietnam. Good, I thought, a pilot. These chaps always have their feet on the ground. Now, he was into the practical science of getting people to experience alternative states of consciousness. John was going to tell it how it was. Or, rather, show me.

He was a sales rep for the Focus Band – a black, spongy headband that measures your brainwaves to gauge whether or not you're in the perfect mental state for sporting greatness. I didn't have to imagine a window, develop a feeling of being 'home' or have a discussion with my feelings in the third person. Best of all, I would be able to see and hear what sort of mental state I was in.

Once the headband is on, it transmits the measurements to a screen on a tablet displaying an avatar of a human head. When you are using the right side of the brain, the creative part, the screen lights up green and plays soothing meditative music. When using the left, the logical part, it lights up red. And clunky electric guitar music would emerge. You could see where this was going: green, good; red, bad. Floaty pan-pipe music, good; rock 'n' roll, bad.

'When we are in the left part, research shows that we operate at about 40 pieces of information per second,' John said, his beret shifting slightly to a more jaunty angle. 'That sounds pretty fast, right?'

'Yeah, that's pretty impressive.'

'Well, in the creative part we are doing millions of bits of information per second.'

'I'm going to take a wild guess here, John. When we are playing sports at our best we are in that creative part?'

'Right,' he said. 'That's what we call being "in the zone".'

John and his Focus Band buddies had been successful in getting golfers to use their device. The Englishman Justin Rose and American Jason Day were converts. Both had won Major tournaments. Golf was the perfect stop-start sport for the Focus Band because it enabled players to look back, shot by shot, at their round on the course and know when they were in the left or right side of the brain, how immersed they were and for how long. Players were able to use it in practice and assess their state live, and the data would be 'sent to the Cloud' to analyse later. This was on-course biofeedback.

'Jason Day went from number 39 to number one in the world in two seasons using this,' John said proudly, sounding like Jason's dad. 'He's on the left side thinking about the win, the lie, where

141

the pin is. That's good. Then he immediately switches to the right. He closes his eyes, he sees the shot, goes to the ball and lets it flow.'

The best of the best, John said, are the ones who are able to flit back and forth between left and right at will. Not only that, they are able to go deep into a meditative, creative state almost immediately. It was Glen's Think Box, Play Box.

'Once we've measured what is going on with the visual feedback or with aural feedback, the brain says, "Oh, that's what you want to do," and it learns what we want it to do,' John said.

'OK, John, strap this thing on me.'

John hooked me up. The Focus Band was a little heavier than I'd anticipated. It looked like one of those ear-warmer headbands. Or, and this might be an easier visual guide, as if I had suffered a nasty head gash and had a big, thick black bandage on. We were sitting there – on a lush, green lawn outside one of the university's impressive buildings – in some plastic chairs while other SEC attendees milled around, chatting and gossiping with other stallholders. Robert, my tennis buddy from Scott Ford's class, was there plugging whatever it was he did, shouting 'awesome!' or 'yeah!' every now and again. I thought it might be difficult to concentrate. Then there was a series of bleeps and John said I was ready to go. I stared at the tablet: it showed clearly that I was in the logical part. The red was flashing and the guitar was playing.

'What this is showing you, is that everyone starts out here,' John reassured me. 'The brain is saying, "What's going on here? Tell me all about this stuff?"'

'So my left part is going, "What the hell is going on?"' I asked.

'Yeah, you're trying to work out what this is all about. So quiet down, settle down … you're *still* working out what is going on.'

'So presumably if I was intelligent I would move pretty quickly over to the right side, the creative part?' I said.

John paused.

'Er, yes. And, generally speaking, people who do meditation and yoga are able to drop into that quite quickly.' He may as well have added 'but not repressed English people'. 'We're measuring brain frequency right now so, er … umm, there's still quite a lot of chatter going on on your left side. It's what we call "monkey brain".' John laughed nervously and adjusted his beret. Terrific, I thought. I have the intelligence of an ape. This was not the sort of motivation I needed to help me relax.

'So we're still in the left brain…' he said, quietly.

Of course we're in the left brain, John. You just called me Monkey Brain. It's only natural that I'm unlikely to find this a cue for creative inspiration. Instead, my thinking part – you know, the useful part that actually keeps me alive – is whirring away: 'Come on, chimp boy, relax!'

'So let me adjust the settings here,' John mumbled. His left brain was trying to come to terms with the dunce he was dealing with. 'I'm going to find the baseline here, wait a second…'

'What does that mean?'

'Well, it's like a computer game. We don't start playing a computer game at the highest level.'

Oh, the disgrace. I was on one of the lowest levels. The sort of level they would start, say, a monkey on – if they were to ever test this on animals. The higher the baseline, the better. It went all the way up to 100.

'So we're just searching for your baseline level. So that's at five, which is, ah, pretty low…'

'Am I not doing very well, John?'

'No, you're doing fine. Everybody's different.'

'You see, I don't do yoga or meditation … and I'm not from round here.'

'Right … right, you're just very analytical. Maybe you just never switch off.'

'That's right, John, that's probably what it is.'

'That's what this is simply telling us. Sure, sure. Now, is that right or wrong? No. It's just the way *you* are.'

What I needed was time to warm up. Granted, in the breakneck hurly burly of sport this would not have stood me in any sort of stead whatsoever. I also found the clanking guitar music somewhat off-putting. It sounded like admonishment, that I *was* doing something wrong. The tone of the Focus Band was just not enough of a Pete Carroll love-in for my money. I did manage to relax a bit. It was more of a 'zone out' experience instead of an 'in the zone'. I just decided to drift off into a dream state to save face. If I had been asked to perform a basic operation in this state, like writing my name or peeling a banana, I would have looked at you with dead eyes.

When I was in the green I didn't last long because John, rather excitedly (or perhaps out of sheer relief), shouted, '*You're doing it, you're doing it!* Oh no … you've lost it again.' Nor did it help that there were constant interruptions. Scott Ford, my morning tennis coach – the irony – jolted me out of one potentially trance-like state by telling John that 'everything needed to be packed up by, maybe half-past, quarter-to', and then there was a shrill woman called Judy who insisted on a catch-up with my beret-bonneted friend. I interrupted them.

'Hey, John, I'm going to try to get to 100 now. So don't tell me how I'm getting on or anything.'

'OK, I'll say, "Goodnight," then.'

Breathing helped. As did shutting my eyes. But if I focused on the avatar I found I could go deeper. This would make green arrows shoot out of the eyes of the head on the screen. John called this 'quiet eyes'. It was a relaxed state yet I was aware and connected to what was happening around me. I was present and centred. The ideal state for performance, in other words. Yes, I could write my name, peel a banana, shoot a basket, throw a touchdown pass. And the baseline was climbing. I was up to 40.

But then somebody caught my eye in the middle distance. I recognised him. I'd seen this figure before. 'You're losing it, you're losing it,' John said. But I didn't care. The crowd had parted and he was walking towards me. Who *was* that? The silver hair, the stocky stature, the soft-rimmed spectacles. He was chewing gum. He had an easy, jocular stroll. As if he himself was present and centred. Then I saw him greet someone with boundless enthusiasm, with shoulders rocking and rolling. And I'd seen that before, too, on countless YouTube videos. And I'd read about it before.

It was Pete Carroll.

Pete was the SEC Group's secret weapon. 'We knew he might come,' Mike Spino said, after I'd torn off my Focus Band and walked up to him excitedly, jabbing him in the ribs and pointing at Carroll. 'But until he showed up no one was sure.' That night, Pete joined Mike Murphy on stage for a 40-minute talk. Sitting in a bucket plastic seat with his plaid shirt rolled up to his elbows, Carroll talked about loving his players, un-seriousness being the ultimate seriousness, the quiet mind and his competitive philosophy. And, of course, the superhuman.

'I was 23, or 24, and you guys have not left me since,' Pete said, as he wagged a finger at a beaming Murphy. 'I was tapped on the shoulder. I've been tormented by all the openness that was created back in the early days. And I have this in me because of *you*. I've watched it happen, tried to nurture, tried to create a culture for these events to take place, and they happen *all* the time. This may be the only room in the country that would understand.'

He was right about that. And this meant he spoke freely about making the players do what he wanted. The brainwashing bit again. Repeat, it's not as macabre as it sounds. That was because it came down to trust. Thanks to the brain-hacking simulations with Michael Gervais, the one-on-ones to get players in the best shape, the cosseting facilities at VMAC, the practical jokes, Long Body experiences that bind rosters and his own hyper-enthusiasm, players knew that he was going to do right by them so their anxiety levels were reduced. Reducing worry and stress would be a recurring theme. Pete had the compliance of his players. Without it, he said, 'no one can fully focus'. When there were 'no distractions', he said, 'you're available to the world'.

But practice – on the training field and in the meditation room – was where the real work was done. It was 'mind-numbing repetition'. And if you practise well enough, athletes will not only feel confident in what they are doing but they are more likely to consistently keep producing the B+ performances that can result in success – and they can also achieve the super-states.

'More opportunities, more repetitions, more practice,' Pete said. 'And when you forget that I'm trying to have some kind of experience here, all of a sudden you just have one. And you look back and just enjoy.

'When they go to game time, when it comes to performance time, they are just playing. That's the whole idea. You've shown them why they're worthy of trusting themselves. And why they should recognise that those around them are worthy of trust, that you can trust them also. And now we have this big trust thing going on where we have no concerns.'

Indeed, Pete didn't even want his players to think about the result. What he wanted was his players going out, hearing the first whistle and the last and then wondering who the hell won the game. That is quite something.

'You have to live in the moment,' he said. 'So we have to practise [those] moments all the time. And just develop a skill, which I guess is meditation in a sense. That allows you to be, "OK, clear, let it all go: play, and everything will work out." We don't even have to think about the game, the win, the loss, the match-up, the build-up, the hype, the Final Four, whatever the hell it is. None of that stuff matters. [When] the game's over … then it's "What happened?" That is the mentality we're shooting for.'

Well, the crowd lapped it up. Phrases like 'available to the world', discussions about trust and love and forgetting the result? It was like the leader had turned up to read the sacred writings to his followers. They were in raptures. Eschewing the macho stereotypes and 'win at all costs' attitude that had stained sport after sport? Ambrosia. Pete even compared his guys to being 'like a child at play' when they took to the football field. My eyebrow reached for the sky at that point because I can't remember many six-year-olds thundering into a sandpit rival over who got the bucket. But maybe I took it too literally. Didn't matter, though, because the gang were still loving it.

That night, Pete filled the room with personality. And the best example I can give of that is how powerful and in control he looked. Pete Carroll is not tall or wide. He can't be more than 5 feet 9 inches yet he fills your vision as if he is 6 foot-plus. He has an aura, you see. The only other time I had experienced that was when I was at a press conference with three sportsmen. One was a famous Australian cricketer called Adam Gilchrist, who had revolutionised the way the sport was played. The second guy was

Jonny Wilkinson, the rugby player who single-footedly kicked England to a World Cup victory. The third was late. His name was John McEnroe. When he did turn up, the room crackled and fizzed. Gilchrist and Wilkinson were sideshows, almost non-entities, in the shadow of the legend that was McEnroe. It was something to behold and difficult to explain. Some people just have an energy about them.

So Pete held that room in his hand. If he had picked on somebody, anybody, among the audience and asked them to run through a brick wall, they would have tried it, and believed they could do it. I thought back to his notion of 'brainwashing' all those years ago in his office at USC. On our way out, a woman in reverential tones said to her friend, 'What he does with his team, he was doing with *us*.'

Afterwards, Mike Murphy introduced me to Pete. I had nervously awaited my turn as scores of enraptured listeners wanted to shake his hand (never to wash theirs again) or thank him for 'everything you're doing'. When it was my go, he was less warm than I thought he would be. He didn't smile. He was serious, maybe even stern. He eyed me with suspicion, perhaps annoyance. So I apologised for bombarding him with emails, in case that was the reason.

'No, no,' he said. 'You're just being competitive. I didn't reply because I wanted to meet you.'

'Can we get together for two hours or so to talk?'

'Not possible. That almost never happens. If Mike is happy I'll be led by him.'

'So should I email?'

'Have Mike call me and then I'll have to put you in touch with my guy who looks after these things, and we'll see what we can put together.'

And with that the conversation was done. He turned to talk to another fan. And then he was gone. *Pfft.* A cloud of smoke. I didn't see him again that weekend. And I had no real commitment from him to speak with me. Had I blown it? He wasn't exactly reliable when it came to answering emails. He could just ignore me again. I was afraid. *Now* I wanted to let my fear out of its box. *Now* I wanted to talk in the third person. He did, apparently, attend workshops. He played tennis with Scott Ford, testing whether his window approach might help, presumably, his players to catch the ball. 'He liked it,' Scott said. He ordered several Focus Bands to trial. John told me that he could move from left brain to right brain at will.

'So what level did he start playing at, John? Level five, like me?'

'No, no, no,' John laughed. 'Right at the very top.'

The next day, Rick Leskowitz stood in front of us again, finger cymbals in hand. In a breathy voice he said, 'When the chimes come together, we come together and we create something wonderful. Just like we did last night.' Everyone took a big, deep breath.

12

BEAMING OUT THE MOJO

'What he does with his team, he was doing with *us*.' The woman who said that to her friend as she left Pete Carroll's talk had obviously got her money's worth. But what was he doing? Was he brainwashing us like he did with his USC players of old? Let's remind ourselves of that quote from the meeting in his office that day. 'I knew I had a chance to make a statement, and that a lot of people would hear it – control the mindset of a whole lot of people.'

Rationally, I put it down to a skilled orator with energy and confidence preaching to the converted. He was also, more simply, the most famous and successful person present (he has over 2.1 million Twitter followers). But in the context of this story, why did I have to be rational? I thought about cosmic forces, channels and the Jedi Force. I also recalled Mike Murphy's whammy at Candlestick Park and Dr Zoukhar's mind control. Pete Carroll did not put anyone on his backside that night. But could he have done? And did he get inside the heads of his audience? Probably. Maybe he was inside my head. I had, after all, spent an inordinate amount of time trying to work out what was going on inside his.

So if Pete was a good-time whammy merchant, unlike Mike when he was trying to upset baseball pitchers, or a mind-control specialist like Zoukhar, the question was, in fact, this: *how* was he doing it? The man who had an answer, of sorts, was Rick Leskowitz (the one with the finger cymbals).

A few years ago you could find Rick sitting right at the top of one of the stands at Fenway Park, the home of the Boston Red Sox baseball team. On his own. There was no game on. The place was empty. But Rick would just be sitting there, his arms folded across his waist, giving himself a cuddle and slapping each hand alternately on either bicep. Maybe rocking a little bit. And he was repeating a four-step mantra:

'Step one: release all doubts. Alternately tapping each side of your body will balance the two hemispheres of your brain.

'Step two: state your affirmations. Even though I have second thoughts about this pitcher we're facing tonight, I *really* love the Red Sox. Even though we always have trouble against this guy I choose peace of mind.'

Step three was a bit of breathing. Standing up this time. 'Breathing in through the heart, out through the heart.' While doing this he was pulling his arms in and pushing them back again so that to those on ground level it looked as though he was in some sort of distress and needed assistance. But Rick was not in distress. He was on step four. He was connecting to positive memories: 'Connect to your favourite Red Sox moments or favourite players, feel it in your body and beam those positive emotions out to the team and favourite player.' This was called 'beaming out the mojo'.

Rick and I had bonded nicely. His wife was English. She was from Edgware, London. That was on the same tube line where I had once lived. We were practically related. I didn't think he was crazy. He went to Harvard, after all, and in that very English way of being impressed/daunted/wowed by someone's schooling, we

151

can forgive a multitude of foibles. He didn't think he was crazy, either. He was different, for sure. 'I've always been an outsider,' he told me.

He wasn't mad because, he said, he had scientific proof of whatever energy or force was operating when Murphy did his whammies at Candlestick Park, Dr Zoukhar rendered poor old Viktor Korchnoi a jabbering wreck or Pete Carroll did his thing. And it had taken him seven years to figure out: 'Energy is neutral. It can be used for good or ill. I think that's what happened with those incidents Murphy talked about. He and his buddies knocking over that pitcher with directed group energy was a lower-grade application of fan energy.'

A lower grade? You bet. Rick had been looking at the bigger picture. If a small section of a baseball stadium could do what Murphy did, what could the whole stadium achieve? Well, perhaps they could cause a minor earthquake or break the world record for crowd noise. That, of course, was the level of frenzy Pete roused the Seahawks fans to. His inspiration, however, was not Murphy or Pete. It was the Red Sox winning their first World Series for 86 years in 2004.

'The team and fans generated an incredible energy which swept through New England,' he said in awed tones. 'It was the most powerful anti-depressant I'd ever seen. What was going on at Fenway Park? Could we capture it? Could we understand it? Could we use it?'

Those were a lot of questions. So he visited the Institute of Noetic Sciences in Petaluma, California. The institute had been founded in 1973 by astronaut Edgar Mitchell. Mitchell was the sixth man to walk on the moon, in 1971. And when he was making his way back to Earth he suddenly, overwhelming, felt the existence of one connecting energy force.

'I realised that the molecules of my body and the molecules of the spacecraft had been manufactured in an ancient generation of stars,' he said. 'It was a subjective visceral experience accompanied by ecstasy.'

Mitchell, as a former military test pilot and holder of a PhD on guidance systems in low-thrust interplanetary vehicles, was supposed to be too analytical to talk like that.

This experience was a conversion to the cosmic. He visited shamans, voodoo priests, experts in Tibetan Buddhist lucid dreaming, and, of course, Esalen. He believed in aliens. Told NASA to stuff it. He even grew a beard. He went the full Monty, in other words. He had also done experiments with Uri Geller, claiming that he had witnessed him 'find' two of his lost tiepins by 'teleporting' them back. One turned up in Geller's mouth when he was eating lunch. He had originally asked him to 'teleport' a camera that Mitchell had left on the moon. But no such luck.

Anyway, the Institute of Noetic Sciences was set up to explore the universe by means other than science and religion. In other words, parapsychology. Still, the man Rick went to see at the institute was very much a scientist and was very much using science to explore the universe. His name was Dean Radin, and with a neat moustache, bald pate and porthole glasses, he looked about as far from a mad scientist as you could possibly imagine. Indeed, he used to be a concert violinist.

Radin, pretty much like everybody else in this book it seems, believes that anybody is capable of psychic experiences. To prove that, he once conducted an experiment in remote healing. Subjects made dolls of themselves out of Play-Doh, dressing them with their own hair and other personal effects. They then handed the dolls to a 'healer' in a room down the corridor, who spent a few hours massaging them. Radin said that he found that the subjects' blood flow and sweat production was affected. Unfortunately, Radin has a somewhat shaky reputation among his peers. He has been criticised for ignoring non-paranormal explanations for some of his data. Maybe the air con was turned up in some rooms and not others?

Rick wasn't interested in fooling around with Play-Doh. He interviewed Radin in 2012 while the scientist sat crossed-legged in a locked bank vault, which weighed 2,000 pounds and was isolated from the floor to reduce vibration. What was he doing in there? He was busy trying to prove that meditation can affect the path of a laser beam.

'Something comes out of me and goes to you,' Radin told Rick. 'It's signal transfer. A force-like information transfer from one to another. It's interconnected.'

But it was Radin's work with 'mass consciousness' that interested Rick. The idea that if millions of people focused on one event, this energy could be recorded. Previously, Radin had worked at the Princeton Engineering Anomalies Research lab – PEAR for short. PEAR was studying extra-sensory perception. It was widely ridiculed, fellow Princeton scientists were embarrassed by it and, like a mad family member you want to keep hidden, the lab was housed in the basement of the university's engineering building.

Radin monitored the fluctuations of pinball-like machines, which, PEAR reckoned, could detect the impact of human thought and attention. Ball bearings would ordinarily fall in random fashion. But when PEAR was monitoring key moments at the Academy Awards or the O.J. Simpson trial, they found the balls would fall in strange ways. Or, as Radin said, they 'represented a significant deviation from chance'. So if the power of thought was influencing a ball bearing, could it alter the trajectory of a baseball?

Maybe to ensure it went all the way for a home run? Shivas Irons, Mike Murphy, and perhaps Pete Carroll would say, 'Yes.'

The problem for Rick was that it was not so easy to bring a hefty pinball machine into Fenway Park to prove this. Instead, he relied on a random-number generator programme on his laptop. It produced a stream of ones and zeroes and translated them to a visual indicator – a yellow ball that rotated forward if one was dominant and backward if it was zero. These rotations were recorded on a graph. To you or I, the graph looked like the thin jagged spikes we see in the movies when an earthquake is being recorded. It was all over the place. There were peaks and troughs, mountains and valleys. A line through the middle of them represented the baseline – the line of 50–50 chance. This is where, by and large, the measurement should have been. It was like tossing a coin several thousand times. You should get roughly equal the number of heads or tails.

That didn't happen. Rick's study showed that the crowd influenced the generator. It went nuts at climactic moments of the game, like when the home crowd's favourite batter came out to hit. Or when there was huge energy in the stadium – the Mexican wave or a rendition of 'Sweet Caroline'. There were so many ups and down on the graph that Rick said the chance of it behaving in such a way was 100,000 to one. Weirdly, Rick also found that the graph got consistently more jumpy in the build-up to the game as the stadium filled with spectators. He had set up a few hours beforehand when it was empty and all had been calm.

'Music, movement and heartfelt affection – those are strong enough to affect the quantum level of reality,' Rick said.

But what about the impact of this energy on an individual? Could it affect an athlete's performance, good or bad? Rick wanted to find out about that, too. So this time he took himself off to the HeartMath Institute in Boulder Creek, California, where a group of New Age thinkers reckoned that the heart had its own intuitive intelligence and was capable of emitting an energy to make people feel good, calm, sad or angry. And pretty much any other emotion you want to chuck in.

Their lead guy was a Dr Rollin McCraty. He did very much look like a mad scientist with goldfish-bowl glasses, wild hair and a penchant for turtleneck jumpers. He was another mimic of Egon from the *Ghostbusters* movies. This was how he explained 'heart-math': 'When the heart is beating out a coherent message-rhythm [it] sends signals to the brain that increase the brain's ability to synchronise its own electrical activity.

'Information contained in those fields is different depending on the emotional state you're in. If in an appreciative state, caring or passionate, that informs the patterns of the magnetic waves. Likewise, if in a negative, frustrated state the patterns are very different. You can feel the energy, electricity in the air [at sports events] … we're able to put hardcore rigorous science to show these things really do occur.'

In short, then, if your heart is happy it tells the brain and its electrical activity pumps out good vibes. If not happy-hearted, bad vibes.

Rick was Rollin's guinea pig. He sat in a room with earphones on, blindfolded. He was hooked up to a machine that recorded his heart rate. Then he sat there for a bit, twiddling his thumbs. 'He's on his own at this point,' Rollin said. 'He's 100 per cent incoherent.' What Rollin was actually saying was that Rick was unaffected by anybody else's heart.

Next, two men and two women came into the room and sat behind Rick. Their job was to send good vibes to Rick using their hearts.

'Whatever change happens will be because my nervous system responds to the energy field that the group will be able to create,' Rick had noted before being plugged in. 'Assume that also happens at a baseball game when a crowd is in appreciation and enjoyment that it affects the players and transfers to the players, enhancing their performance.'

Rather theatrically, Rollin then gave a signal to the four (what shall we call them?) heart-breakers and heart-makers, to do their stuff. This signal looked a lot like asking a waiter for the check across a crowded restaurant.

'*The experiment actually worked!*' Rollin shouted when the data had been analysed. He seemed a bit surprised. So too did Rick. 'You know, I didn't think it would show anything.'

What did it show? Well, apparently, there was a big jump on the graph – just like the one at Fenway Park – when the signal was made to send 'positive intention' from the heart-makers and heart-breakers. 'There was a profound shift at what's going on inside his body,' Rollin said. 'He had gone into an optimal state.'

But this is where it gets good. According to Rollin, when in that 'optimal state' a person's 'reaction time' is 37 milliseconds faster. 'That's ten miles an hour slower for a pitch in baseball,' he said. 'If it's thrown at 90 and you're in [that] state then it feels like it's 80.'

I was impressed by Rick. And not just because it was a nod to what the Russians and their parapsychologist programmes were trying to achieve all those years ago. What if Rick had gone and proven it all? This was the Holy Grail. The nectar. You mad, crazy, bearded, ponytailed Harvard chap. No doubt there were professional sports teams queuing up to employ Rick to teach their fan bases how to send these energies, good and bad. Sports teams who nailed it would be almost unstoppable, at their home stadium, of course. The fans *could* influence the game.

And that was why Rick had been sitting all on his lonesome at Fenway Park. He had been perfecting a routine to ensure his beloved Red Sox had a huge advantage. 'It creates energy and helps players get into the zone of peak performance.'

'Wow. You must have been pretty in demand with the pro teams?' I asked. But Rick's heart-math was not good. It was a despondent, negative beat.

'No,' he said. 'That's the disappointing part. It didn't get the wide audience I'd hoped for. The Red Sox were very helpful, but it took so much time and energy to get just 30 seconds of their attention. Maybe it's something college teams could use.'

'What about individual athletes, Rick?'

'Yeah, the ball-slowing stuff ... that should have been an eye-opener to any athlete.'

'That's slowing down time,' I said.

'That's a good way of putting it. My guess is it's not exclusive to heart-math.'

'So there are other ways?'

'Well, I think the tapping is going to be really big. Probably the next big thing.'

Now it was my heart that sank a little bit. Tapping? Seriously? This was what Rick did when he sat high in the stands, cuddling himself and tapping each bicep. Was Rick making fun of me? You could discover siddhi states just by doing that?

13

THE DOC THAT WON THE SUPER BOWL

With your forefinger, tap just above your nose. Quickly. Maybe ten times. Now do the same on both temples, under your nose, on your chin, under your throat, the side of each hand and the inside of your wrist. Do it all while humming your favourite tune. Maybe try it on public transport. Count the number of people who move away.

If it feels weird, that's because it is. It's called power tapping. And those that practise it swear by it. It turned out that my tennis partner at Scott Ford's workshop was one of the best in the world. Robert Rudelic was so good at teaching it that he had almost the entire 2015 world champion Denver Broncos roster – and I hesitate to say this – maniacally touching themselves. He was the Doc that won the Super Bowl. No wonder everything was 'awesome'.

Robert, with thick black hair and a perma-tan, was as loud and brash off court. He told me that his father had played for the Broncos and that 'as soon as he [Robert] came out of the womb he was destined to be an athlete'. But injury ruined his chances. He ended up working in advertising before finding his calling.

I met him at his San Francisco loft apartment. He stood in the living room looking up at the vaulted ceilings, arms outstretched as if he were the second coming, and said, 'This is what a million bucks looks like in San Francisco.' I think I was supposed to be impressed.

What I wanted to be impressed by was the work he did that had paid for it. As well as the Broncos, he had worked with players at the Oakland Raiders NFL franchise. Power tapping was, essentially, Robert's version of something called the Emotional Freedom Technique. Or EFT for short. EFT is a mix of psychology and acupressure. By tapping on points on the body, 'energy blockages' that cause 'negative emotions' can be cleared. It also helps the amygdala, an almond-shaped part of your brain that controls your response to fear, take a chill pill. While tapping, it helps to talk about these negative emotions. The more traumatic the better.

Robert wasn't interested in the negative stuff, though. While others were tapping 'out' the bad stuff, Robert turned it on its head. He wanted to tap 'in' the awesome. It was a shame that he didn't actually use that phrase but he did say, 'Tap in positive mantras. That stuff comes true. Believe me.'

He was not, however, of hippy nature. He was more of a belt and braces therapist who didn't sound as if he had much time for 'weakness'. Indeed, he had a typical male view of 'issues' or 'problems'. Get it fixed. What's the matter? Got depression? Right, let's get it sorted! Just tap in the awesome.

'Let me tell you something, OK?' Robert said. 'I'm a *performance* coach and I have to work as quickly as possible. If my athletes perform better right away and they can look back and see how they were performing badly two days or two weeks ago, they say, "Oh I see it now." You do not need to spend six weeks analysing and overanalysing why you were in a slump. Who cares?! Get out of the slump!'

It wasn't exactly a Pete Carroll-esque approach, was it?

'I use acupuncture points. Going in through the body to affect the mind. It's a much more effective way than to go through the mind to get to the body. The mind will notice the change if you go through the body. Psychology is not mind–body medicine, never has been. They can dress it up all they want.'

Robert didn't have time for tender loving care, then. Get out of the slump! Best of all, tapping only takes three minutes out of your day. 'Breathing and meditation,' he said, 'both takes five minutes.' Time is money, and that's what you might call a three-minute win. I'm joking. Robert didn't say that last bit. But it was working for him, even if it did look mighty odd.

'When I was with the Raiders I was pretty new to tapping but I was *so* confident. I worked with the veterans on the team. All these guys thought I was weird. When people do tapping, they think it's silly: "Oh, what am I doing?" "Nothing, 'cos you're not focused!" Then they focus. And then they're like, "Wow! What *just* happened?!"' Robert made a sort of 'told you so' face. It would transpire that 'Wow! What *just* happened?!' was his catchphrase.

'So I'd say to these guys, "How much do you think you can go do it now on a scale of one to ten? An eight? *Greeeat!* See ya later! Bye-bye!"' Robert stiffened his fingers and waved sarcastically. 'But they always said to me, "Don't tell anyone we're doing it."

'At one point I was in the locker room with Jerry Rice, one of the great wide receivers of all time, and he said, "Hey, Doc, my hamstring's bothering me." I started to feel his hamstring – nothing wrong with it. I took his hand and started tapping and he pulled it away, "Oh, no, no, no! You're not gonna do any of that *stuff!*" I go, "Jerry, almost everyone on defense and three-quarters of the offense are doing this." He said, "I know, it's crazy, they look like idiots." "Really? They're playing a lot better though, right?" And Jerry's nodding his head and then I say, "And, by the way, the two wide receivers who want your job are doing it too." I told him not to worry, no one would see us. I just rubbed some points. And he was like, "Wow! What *just* happened? The hamstring feels better." I didn't work on it, by the way, it was *all* anxiety.

'He comes in at half-time and he's like, "Doc, I feel great. I want to do some more." I said, "Jerry, you're done." He came back to me that evening and told me he did everything to extend his career, and how come he'd never come across it? It's because we're only just discovering it. He told me he'd seen a sports psychologist his whole career, and it was worthless [whereas]: "You did something immediately." "That's right," I said. "I changed you. I changed your life. That's what I do."'

Robert lounged back on his expensive-looking sofa, raised his eyebrows quickly, as if to say, "Yeah! You got that, buddy?" and just let those words sink in. He took a sip of coffee and held my gaze, nodding his head slightly. 'By the way,' he said. 'I'm not a doctor … they just called me that.'

It would be fair to say that Robert was a confident sort. But it was interesting to hear him tell me that he had, in the past, been forced to 'tap in' confidence. He was sitting on a plane once, fretting about a lecture he was going to give. He thought he would 'suck'. So he sat there, hitting the pressure points, telling himself he would be, no doubt, awesome. I didn't ask what his fellow passengers felt. I began to wonder if Robert's super-slick showboating style was just a tapped-in veneer.

He had a similar experience in 2015. The Denver Broncos had made it to the Super Bowl in one of the more unlikely underdog sports stories. They were, the media had consistently said, hopeless, one of the worst teams ever. Some of their players had started to believe the trash talk, which is when they turned to Robert. So with the Broncos on the brink and the bulk of their offence working with Robert, he felt the pressure. 'I had to tap in some positive stuff – this was the biggest game in the world.'

In the build-up to the Super Bowl, Robert spoke to his Broncos players – 12 of them – on the phone three times a week. He 'tapped in' positive mantras about how each player was going to do his job and, if something went wrong, how they would get it right the next time. One of the 12 was Michael Schofield, who had been struggling so badly that he had been benched in games and torn apart by the media. Robert banned him from using his phone in case he came across anything negative that would upset him. Another was Von Miller, who would win the Most Valuable Player award in the Super Bowl. He received one of the ultimate sporting accolades – a place on the TV show *Dancing with the Stars*.

'The Broncos were "gonna be killed". That's what they said,' Robert recalled. 'I wanted to amplify that but keep them calm, and that's what we tapped in. Proving them wrong. I don't want to take aggression away – controlled aggression, that's what I wanted. They were physically pumped and they were like, "My opposite number is a dead man." And that sounds out of control but, look, it's a saying.

'Very calmly Von would say, "I'm going straight for my man, right on the inside. I'm gonna go straight for his ass. I'm gonna drive him straight into the ground and, when I do, he's gonna know he's in trouble." That's what happened. I tapped that in. And this was "in the zone" stuff, OK. They *knew* that was going to happen.'

There was more. 'There was one guy who felt really something unbelievable during that game,' he said. 'You should talk to him.' His name was Ryan Harris.

*

7 August 2008. The eve of Ryan Harris's first start as a professional in the NFL. His Denver Broncos team are taking on the Oakland Raiders. This was what he had wanted since he was 14 years old, through high school in Minnesota and then at Notre Dame, where he had a starring college career. So why did he feel like he wanted to get the hell out of there? He paced up and down his hotel room. He couldn't sleep. He couldn't eat. He felt the same in the morning.

'I just thought, "Run. Just run. Give back the money. Go home. You're going to completely embarrass yourself. Just leave. Retire right now." But then by pure happenstance I met Robert.'

Robert had been helping out the Denver Broncos' chiropractor as a favour. The pair exchanged pleasantries, Harris asking him what he did. 'He said he "worked with a lot of athletes on the mental side of things".' Harris took him to one side and, desperate and sweating, whispered, 'You've got to help me. I. Am. Freaking. The. Fuck. Out.'

In a ten-year, five-team career, Harris would suffer similar meltdowns twice more. One of them would be before the Super Bowl. Another was his first game after a return from two dislocated toes and an ankle sprain. 'It was against Baltimore and I was just mortified that, physically, I wouldn't be able to be close to what I was.'

It was fear that gripped Harris each time. Fear that he was going to mess up so badly that he would be humiliated. That feeling of dread, he said, can do strange, damaging things to a man. 'Some guys look for other avenues to release that mental pressure, you know, substances…'

In July 2014, just a year and a half after Kansas City Chiefs' Jovan Belcher murdered his girlfriend and then took his own life, Harris signed for the franchise. Harris did not say that those 'mental pressures' played a part in that tragic incident, but I could tell he was thinking it. As eloquently as Dave Meggyesy had years before, Harris spoke of doctors patching him up and saying, 'You're ready to go' when he 'just didn't feel right'; of an uncaring attitude, of being misunderstood and a tremendous feeling of isolation. The silence in that hotel room in 2008 was deafening. He was saved by chance.

If Meggyesy was the warning from the past about how American football liked to chew players up and spit them out, Harris is a modern-day critic of the sport's brutal nature. But he didn't set himself up to be. It was pre-season and he sounded excited when we spoke. 'Just getting through the dog days of camp and then get this party going for real.' After one year with Kansas, he returned to the Broncos in 2015 and then signed for the Pittsburgh Steelers a year later for a $3.25 million contract.

He was just talking and, surprisingly, the angst came out. 'No one wants to hear about your problems when you're an athlete,' he said. I asked him to describe, in detail, the thoughts that would rampage through his head. What he told me was mental torture.

'So much of it is public, er … think about … think about it if somebody fails…' then he sighed and gathered his thoughts. 'Wait, let me put it this way, 'cos I get asked *all* the time, "What's the NFL like?" I say, "What's the most embarrassed you've ever been at work?" And they say, "Oh, I messed up this big project and my boss yelled at me." "How many people was that in front of?" "About five." In the NFL, in any given stadium, there's 70,000 there, and at any given time millions are watching on TV.

'And then you visualise those moments. Yeah. Missing a block. If I miss a block, the quarterback gets injured. These visions of your best friends texting you, "Gosh, man, that was terrible. You let the quarterback get his arm broken." Or, you know, "His knee snapped." Or something. These are things you're remembered for. Last year, for example, I was playing with Peyton Manning. People say to you, "What an honour." Awesome, yeah. But I better not get him hurt, remembered for ever as the guy that is the reason that so and so broke a leg or made a mistake costing the championship. That's where the disconnect ends, when you make a mistake and people can recognise you for it, right?'

Harris was making an unexpected point about athletes that the watching viewer probably has little understanding of. When we watch sport, we might think that the athletes in front of us are all trying to be the greatest, to pull off the match-winning moment, to save the day. Nope. Some of them are just trying to ensure they are not remembered as the guy that made an error. To do their job, unnoticed, and get out of there. In the context of this story, that was a reality check. Harris was a reality check. He didn't power tap with Robert in his hotel room before the Super Bowl because he wanted to be superman. He did it because he didn't want to mess up. Just like he didn't want to mess up on day one against Oakland.

That's a disconnect between athlete and fan. It's also a disconnect between athlete and the media, because the latter will be influencing what the fan thinks. And when you're the odd one out it gets pretty lonely. Harris talked again about how no one 'understands' what it's like to make that mistake, to lose that game, to be the guy with problems that no one will listen to. 'You think a fan wants to hear about my worries?' he said. 'They see you and they say, "He makes a lot of money, he is living *my* dream."'

If the truth came out, millions of dreams would be shattered. That's why Meggyesy became a pariah.

Not that it had always been this way for Harris. In high school, football was a breeze. No one could put him in his place: he was always faster, stronger and one step up ahead of his opponent. At Notre Dame it was tougher, but he coped. It was there he realised the need for mental focus, to get rid of all distractions. Harris was an unlikely candidate for neurosis considering the reading matter he was devouring. He became Zen, a little cosmic. 'I was into the idea of "no mind", you know.' He read the famed *Book of Five Rings* by Miyamoto Musashi, one of Japan's great samurai sword masters.

It will come as no surprise, perhaps, that before Notre Dame a certain Pete Carroll had seen and heard something he liked about Harris. Maybe on a cosmic level he knew that Harris was one of his own. Pete had tried to recruit him for his project at USC.

'There's another book you could write about the lies that are told during college recruiting, and Pete was not a liar,' Harris said. 'At the time I was interested in political science and there wasn't a professor for me to meet with so he got in the car and drove down to see me. He really took it on himself when he could have delegated to others, and he showed he wanted to connect with me, and tell me about it from his perspective. He was interested in me. That's what I took from my brief time when engaging with Coach Carroll.'

It is probable that if USC had held a political science course and Harris had joined Pete, he may never have suffered from his terrible fear of being the fall guy. He wrestled with it in college and as soon as he found himself in the NFL 'everything was exacerbated'. There was a feeling of helplessness. That a 6 foot 5 inch, 300-pound guy should not be afraid.

'That's another misconception, another disconnect. People won't talk about fear, let alone say it, but the most successful people I know understand fear and use it. But at the start I was just sitting there with these thoughts of looming, complete, embarrassment. And *certain*. Looming. Complete. Embarrassment.'

Let's massage Robert's ego a bit, then. Thank god for power tapping. 'I was ready to try anything,' Harris said. Robert and Harris tapped in positive mantras. 'I believe in my abilities. I am, I can, I will. This guy better look out for me because I'm coming.' They separated 'physical anxiety from mental', which seemed to mean that the bizarre ritual just meant that Harris was distracted. It took his mind off his troubles. It made it quiet. Even when it got noisy again on Super Bowl eve.

'So we tapped in specific situations. "I know on this play, he's turned like this. I know I can stop this move, be there for my teammates. I can see the play, I can have great vision, strike my target, have quick footwork…" Because it's not about being fast, it's about being quick, you know. Coaches will say, "Are you focused? Are you ready?" And players will go, "YEAH!" But you have no direction with those statements, right? But then if you say, "I'm going to have quick footwork. I'm going to strike my target, keep my head back and make sure my shoulders are down. And if something does go wrong I'm going to focus on the process of the next play…" That's what you're tapping.'

It worked. Harris wasn't the guy that everybody would remember for missing the block that snapped a quarterback's knee. Perversely, that torture and misery helped him.

'We weren't supposed to win any of the games we played in. And, you know what? It's un-fucking believable that that's the case. Somebody stumbles upon a Super Bowl for the first time in history? I don't think so. We were such a good team. We won it all. It was the greatest story of our lives, and we believed we'd be champions because of what we'd been through – the struggles, and how we'd learned to overcome them and the guys we had. Robert and I talked about it. "I am effective. I can help my team. I will hold that Lombardi Trophy." And we did.'

This was only half the story, though. By this time I had almost forgotten to ask Harris about his superhuman experiences. That was a good thing, considering it was the difficult question that had played on my mind for months since Meggyesy posed it. But with Harris it was easy. He had talked about far more personal things. And besides, when you reach the super-state in a Super Bowl, it would be a shame not to talk about it, right?

'For me, the thing I remember is, in a stadium of thousands of screaming people, the only thing I can hear are the footsteps and the breathing of my teammates and opponents. I *hear* the running back, where they went rather than the crowd. I *hear* the ball in this screaming moment, flying through the air, you know. It's zipping past my head and I'll know it's gone.

'And another critical thing is, when you make a mistake you're able to continue to move on in time. You don't stay in that bad moment. You don't get stuck in the past. You can make an adjustment regarding that mistake without it taking you out of those moments, without completely breaking down and getting distracted from everything you're accomplishing, because you made a mistake. So those are the kind of things that happen.

'And you lose track of time. All of a sudden the whistle will blow. And you'll be like, "What the hell's going on?" And the quarter's over. "Oh, OK." Sometimes you're in such a groove you lose track of first down and second down.'

For Harris, this was not rare. The Super Bowl did not bring out the super. 'For me, this is so frequent. They happen all the time.' It was just as Pete Carroll said.

I ran through a checklist of siddhis.

'Did you have heightened senses?'

'Yeah! It's incredible.'

'Did time slow down?'

'Absolutely, absolutely.'

'Could you predict what was going to happen?'

'Absolutely. Sometimes you can just tell from the shape of a body. Think of it like this: if you're pitching to somebody, you can tell in their body language if they're accepting what you're saying. A lawyer can read a jury. It's the same thing. A doctor can read a patient. These are the things that make people professionals. It's just that in sports you've got a million people watching.'

14

TROPHIES DON'T GO WITH YOU

Pete Carroll may be a channel for the paranormal. He may be up there now, somewhere in the cosmos, riding his magic carpet. But he was not *that* hot on space and time. Chiefly, he was over there and I was over here. Or, to be more precise, I was in London and he was in Seattle, almost 5,000 miles and a time difference of eight hours. *Pfft*. A puff of smoke. The ping of the email had woken me. 'Try calling,' it said. It was from Pete himself. It was almost 1 a.m. It was completely unexpected. I had not heard from him since the SEC Group conference. In the meantime, I had lobbied Mike Murphy and Glen Albaugh to keep reminding him that I wanted to talk. Still, I said no. Politely, but no. What was the point of conducting an interview, trying to bottom out this stuff, when I was half asleep? My mind not only needed to be quiet but free from the fug of heavy comatose. This was my sleepy self talking. In the morning, I was gripped by terror that I had blown my chance. But he rearranged it. I had gambled on his compassion.

As it turned out, Pete scrambled my brain within seconds anyway. He wasn't interested in small talk. 'You got 20 minutes,' he said from his office at VMAC. 'Let's go!'

Now, you and I know you can't possibly begin to understand Pete Carroll in 20 minutes. But I thought an easy opener, to get him on my side, was to ask him about how the media had misunderstood him. He had complained that they didn't 'get it' or 'want to get it'. So here I was, desperate to understand and see clearly. Let it all out, Pete.

'That's not a point I want to bring up because it will be misunderstood when I do,' he said. 'The stuff that we were talking about at that event [the SEC conference] has been topical for years, and so it hasn't caught on in all of this time as a mainstream topic, and I don't think it's ready to catch on now either. I don't think it should be a vocation to make it mainstream, because if it doesn't resonate it doesn't resonate – it's a long time since this conversation started. Extraordinary things are going on in sport – we understand that, but most people don't. That's unfortunate.'

A bit of a negative start. Now, I could have said, 'It doesn't need to be unfortunate … together we can make the world understand.' But I didn't. I thought Pete seemed guarded, just as he did when we first met, and that would only change if I just let him talk and talk and talk. Which, to be fair, he wanted to do. If he was ever going to speak as candidly as he did that day in his USC office on the tapes Glen had given me, it would take a while. I had to be careful with my questions. For a man who had a mind like a steel trap, getting up, down and over and round complex issues was easy. For mere mortals like me, it was more of a stretch. He enjoyed, maybe needed, to have several things going on at once. Just as Glen had warned.

'Yeah, I like that,' he drawled. 'In my office right now I have three TV screens on, music plus my computer. For some that's chaos, for others it's serene.' I didn't doubt I had his attention, though.

As a football coach, he was used to spinning plates. At practice, day in and day out, he had to be inside the heads of each and every one of his coaches and players. That could be up to 70 individuals. 'I cannot miss one single coaching opportunity,' he said. During the game, like all the other coaches, he wears a headset that gives options to listen to five different feeds, including his offense and defense coaches. Pete listened to them all. 'Some like it really quiet so they can think more clearly. I'd rather have all the input.' I checked this out with a couple of NFL experts and they both pretty much said it was really unusual to be listening to all five.

These stories reinforced Pete as an obsessive. A guy at 100 mph with no time to slow down. Had he not played 'the fat-fingered blues' (his words) on the piano as a way to switch off and relax, a psychiatrist might be interested to know why his mind had to be occupied all of the time. What thoughts would creep in when it wasn't?

'Sometimes I like to be quiet,' he insisted. 'We're talking maybe an hour and a half at the end of the week. Maybe a half hour before you go to sleep. I've tried to learn to maximise those spaces. So that does take focus. That's really just to quiet my mind in preparation for all the fun things that are going to happen.'

Just half an hour of downtime. Extraordinary. It reminded me of those hilarious 'facts' doing the rounds on the internet about famed martial artist Chuck Norris. 'Chuck Norris does not sleep. He waits.' 'Chuck Carroll does not sleep. He just closes his eyes.' 'Chuck Norris's idea of relaxing is a stroll through East Detroit at midnight.' Ah. But for Carroll this one wasn't a joke. Ever since he pitched up at USC, Pete would go out into the LA projects at all hours and try to get kids out of gangs and off violence. It helped him to switch off. He asked them to be the best they could be.

'Be competitive. The most valuable, most crucial issue to understand is, if you want to run a good organisation, be a good husband, be a good father, be a good athlete … you have to understand where you're coming from and know it so clearly so you can convey it and be consistent in all that.'

To translate, Pete meant that you had to know *what you wanted to be and how you wanted to get there.* And not deviate.

That consistency began back at Pacific, when under Glen Albaugh's wing. Pete's thesis was on Abraham Maslow's work on self-actualisation. Maslow, if you recall, had been an inspiration for the Esalen Sports Center. If Michael Murphy was the guru with the energy and the connections to get the movement up and running, Maslow was the guy who had the brains and clout to explain the theory behind it so it could take off. Maslow inspired Pete. His 1962 book *Toward a Psychology of Being* helped him form his coaching philosophy. Given American football's prevalence for the knuckleheaded, macho athlete controlled by the bullying coach, this was something of a gamble. It was also a first. He writes about Maslow's impact in his autobiography *Win Forever: Live, Work and Play Like a Champion* (2010).

> What if my job as a coach isn't so much to force or coerce performance as it is to create situations where the players develop the confidence to set their talents free and pursue their potential to their full extent? What if my job as a coach is to really prove to these kids how good they already are, how good they could possibly become, and that they are truly capable of high-level performance?

So if I got to grips with self-actualisation, then I reckoned I had a good chance of understanding what was going on inside Pete's head.

Glen had sent me the whole thesis. It had been kept pristine. It was hardbacked and its title, embossed in gold lettering, was *A Study of Self-Actualization Among Various Groups of Male Intercollegiate Athletes*. A self-actualised person was someone who fulfilled four basic needs: physiological, safety, belonging and esteem. Each had to be fulfilled before you could move on to the next one. Like a ladder. Food, water and sleep were examples of the first rung, then there was safety (having a home) followed by friendship and love. If you were struggling for food on a daily basis, it was unlikely you were going to worry about not having solid friendships. Tick all the first three boxes and you had respect. And only then could you reach your full potential. And what happens when you reach your full potential? Well, you can go *beyond*. Maslow called them 'peak experiences'. Murphy borrowed the yogic term and called them siddhis. Others might call it a flow state or 'in the zone'.

In his dissertation, Pete asked the question: If it were true that self-actualising means to operate more spontaneously, creatively and effortlessly, might it be possible that athletes self-actualise in sport? He also wondered whether good athletes self-actualised more often than average ones. After 30 neatly typed pages, including confusing mathematical charts, Pete proved precisely nothing. You could say he's been trying to prove it ever since.

That's why, at VMAC, Seahawks meditate, do yoga and eat the best food. It's why they have the 'I'm In' sign. It's why they have the two personal development officers. Each little thing is ensuring Pete's men have their basic needs fulfilled. No stone is left unturned.

'Maslow was crucial to my personal development,' Pete said.

Another 'basic need' was the practice. The Seahawks trained with more intensity than any other team, as Pete discussed at the SEC meeting. They tried to replicate the game-day experience as much as they could, so would train with a DJ pitchside to try to recreate crowd noise. The Russians did that, too. Some days, they would train without protective gear to increase feel. This got them into trouble with the NFL as it was illegal. And they would do the drill again. And again. And again. So the repetition became another form of meditation. The idea was to make it more likely that an athlete would self-actualise.

'You put so much time in, you become so adept that it is easy for you,' Pete said. He put it another way. If you play 'Mary Had a Little Lamb' on the piano every day, by the end of the year you'd get a pretty funky, souped-up version.

The Long Body, or single consciousness, was part of it, too. I quoted something he had said in a past interview.

'You said, "It takes big things to happen to draw you together so you can operate in a more connected fashion." Give me an example of a big thing?'

'Shared events, shared experiences. That's why people talk about storytelling, share stories; they eat together, they build or reconstruct together. The Long Body thing was really valuable in understanding teams and tribes and communities – really powerful stuff and fundamental. It's what coaches endeavour to do, and there's a real concept of that.'

'Can you give me just one?'

'Millions of them. Everyday stuff. It's like at the start of our meetings every day, we talk about what's happening in sports. The big stories. Sometimes when guys go out of there they're arguing about this or that. You've created a conversation that wouldn't have happened otherwise. There can be a richness to that. An ongoing process of staying connected by looking and talking about the same thing. That's what storytelling was all about, what hunting was about.'

'So,' I said, 'are peak experiences happening all the time?'

'That can be taken totally wrong,' he said. 'In any sport there are moments when clarity, you know, comes and goes for athletes. They almost go unnoticed because they're so normal. There's a tendency to want to really celebrate the peak moments, like you're asking me to do, and I don't think that way. There are extraordinary things that happen but usually they're in moments, in instances, and they come and go all the time.

'They happen in a moment when there's an explosion of energy from Lebron James when he blocks that shot. He senses something, he saw something that was going to happen and he took that opportunity and in the next second – a flash – he's running down the court doing something else.

'But I'm *not* a big advocate of seeking the peak experience. This nirvana moment. I'm just trying to help people function at their best, and those are those moments to me. I don't want to call those peak experiences. I don't want to nail it down to sensing things happening or out-of-body experiences or these peak-experience descriptions. I don't talk to players about self-actualisation. I don't talk about mindfulness.'

For a moment, it felt like I was just about to put the final piece of a jigsaw together only for Pete to have come along and swiped the whole thing off the table. But I got it. He couldn't say he was seeking peak experiences or siddhis. He was being cautious. 'Coach Carroll shoots for superpowers.' That would have made him sound like a nut. He couldn't say he was seeking them for a more important reason. It would have put pressure on players. Their minds would never be quiet. They wouldn't relax. What Pete understood was that he could build the best springboard there had ever been, and he could teach his happy, perfectly honed guys to run up and hit it perfectly. And then if they went into orbit, great! If they didn't, no biggy.

Another theory: what if he had let out just enough of the weird or esoteric to create a sense of aura or intimidation around his own team and programme? That they were doing stuff that other teams weren't? They had secret weapons or superpowers. It would have been a form of brainwashing, thought projection. I took his answer as a maybe.

'Long-term success does allow you to create an aura about a team and players – other teams can sense and feel that. I wish we could do that. There is certainly something to that, but I wouldn't use the intimidation word, but I think it's *sense*. When another team figures out they can't do anything about it and that's who you are and they can't stop it from happening.'

And that, pretty much, was that. 'OK, man, I gotta go,' Pete said. 'Talk again soon.'

We did talk again, a few weeks later. It was the day after his 65th birthday and two days before the Seahawks travelled to Los Angeles to play their second regular season game. I thought myself mighty important that Pete would break off from preparations to chat to me. But then this was Pete we were talking about. He was probably listening to music, watching three TVs, sending an email and honing a tactic or play for the upcoming game.

The Seahawks had opened their campaign with a win over Miami. I was pleased about that. A sports coach is far more likely to be in a good mood if his team had won the last time out. But, then again, for Pete winning was not the be all and end all.

I felt like testing him on that, buoyed by the easy access I suddenly seemed to have to such a high-profile figure to discuss cerebral mind and body philosophies about America's number one sport. Pete's philosophy was all about the individual maximising his potential. The more athletes that did that, the more chance they had of being successful. But what was success?

I wondered. Was it a whole roster? Pete had always said that the 'personal development of the group' was the most important. So, crudely, I took that to the extreme. And I went straight in with it. No need for small talk.

'What's more important: the development of the group or the winning of a Super Bowl?'

'The winning comes with the development, not the other way round. It's a by-product of that focus. It certainly goes to the [he let out a sigh here, as if he was frustrated] … I'm not only saying the development of the people as individuals off the field, not talking about that, I'm talking about the development of the competitor, maturity, a young man expressing his ability – we know that is what's crucial and we really focus on that. The winning, we can't control. The development we can control. And we're disciplined on that. That's always been the emphasis.'

'Hmm. So if you could choose? Development? Super Bowl?' I cupped my hands in front of me, as if weighing two imaginary footballs.

'That doesn't even make sense to me. *Why would you ask that question?* There's never that exchange, it doesn't exist – we are going to win and forget the people?'

Oh. He *was* frustrated. I had got ahead of myself. But screw it, I thought. Plough on regardless. Just keep asking questions.

'You can't win without the people?'

'The winning is not the issue, it's really not. Someone who gets beat all the time and gets fired will say different. But when building a championship-winning mentality…'

Pete had trailed off, exasperated. Shit. Got to rescue this. Quick. Ask him something that brings us back to self-actualisation, or 'being all you can be'. Both theories, I felt, I had understood. Again, I tried to sound, you know, thoughtful, unruffled, *on it.*

'Are there conflicting energies within a team when players have different ideas of what "being all you can be" means? For example, it might be taking the game to another level by playing for the pure love or playing for more selfish reasons, like a bigger contract?' Or more plainly, you can be into as much yoga, meditation and obscure philosophy as you like, but if you've got a bad apple in there the whole cart starts to stink.

'That is worth asking,' he said.

'We talk about helping the individual who can be all he can be to help his team be all it can be,' Pete continued. 'How he can best add to his team. We think by developing the individual that's the best thing they can do, but not in exchange for anything, where you'll do what's best for you but not the team. Always the team in mind, the team context.'

That brought us on to recruitment. Don't pick a bad apple. Was Pete using Abraham Maslow's theories when deciding who should join his project? It was, he said, 'a concept that supports our thinking'. But it seemed it was very much on the minds of himself and Michael Gervais, who would meet potential recruits. Pete said they used 'their intuition' to see who would fit best.

'We think the higher developed people can find their potential and get closer to their abilities. It's easier to describe the make-up in terms of the definition of *grit* – what we are looking for is passion, perseverance and resilience.'

One way of finding out if the grit was present was to ask the potential recruits to take part in a staring contest. It appealed to Carroll's sense of fun and competition. If the player saw the funny side but then showed a determination to win, that was a big tick.

I felt we were back on track. So I asked again about winning. A word that almost seemed dirty in the context of the search for the superpowers. If you were obsessed with winning, your mind wouldn't allow your body to relax. You became tight. But if you played with freedom and enjoyment, reducing the game to a pursuit rather than a goal, you would be more likely to perform better. Basically, trying was for losers. That, however, surely did not fit with the American psyche. It was what the ESC and Dave Meggyesy had fought against. Had Pete ever encountered that conflict with the US culture and his methods? Was this the big roadblock to making it mainstream? A battle between the old-fashioned winner and loser?

'It's just depth of understanding. Not a roadblock. Our stuff will sound different to those brought up in the old framework. But I don't see it as opposition. Unless someone says, "You're full of crap – I don't believe it." The conflict would come more from people who would write about it – the media – because they're not here with us. They won't buy in. "Ah, you just want to win." Of course we do, we want to win as much as anyone, but we get there in a manner which helps us sustain long-term consistency and performance. We are not tied to the end result, we are tied to the way we go about our work. I don't want to win just one championship, I want to see how many we can win and for how long, so it's a different approach … so there's a different emphasis, if you only emphasise the end result you can miss out on an awful lot along the way, and then if you get there, how do you go back? To define your best?'

It could be argued this was a major flaw with modern-day sport in the setting of this story. It wasn't about having fun. It had become a business where athletes were commodities to be bought and sold at extraordinary prices, stock market prices fluctuated on success and failure, screaming fans demanded blood for bragging rights. A good example was when Pete had finished up at USC. To define how successful he was, it is often quoted that USC athletic department revenue had almost doubled to $76 million from his first year to his last. Pick any popular sport and its top leagues in the world and you have the same. They are all soap operas. Not very Zen Buddhist, is it? So Pete seemed to be reaching for something unreachable.

'Isn't that the problem with modern sport, Pete?'

'You keep saying it's "a problem". I don't think it's like that.'

'What I meant was, how outsiders view it. That you *have* to be winning. And that's a modern problem.'

'I agree with you. That is a modern issue. I just think there's a higher level of understanding, greater depth to it, and it's more beneficial when you connect to it. Ah, I can't remember whether I mentioned this to you, but … what you've acquired during your time, how you've gained recognition, the money made and the trophies won – that's one level of character. Trophies don't go with you. Another level to aspire to is: who have you affected? Who have you impacted? Who are you serving? Who is benefiting from the way you're operating? We think that's more meaningful and will be more significant. And you have to grow to that understanding. But in the early young man's mind that's not the way you think, so it's more of a mature way of thinking about things.'

Now, I'm not sure if you have ever read Chögyam Trungpa's *Cutting Through Spiritual Materialism* (Pete definitely has – it was the book he propped on the steering wheel when driving on the freeway when he was at Pacific, studying for Glen Albaugh's Sports and Cosmic Forces class). But now you don't have to. This was, basically, it. You can't be spiritual just for the sake of your ego. To feed it by winning games and championships. To get a bigger contract, more sponsorship deals. The trophies don't go with you. And nor should you put a label on the experiences that you had when striving because, as Trungpa wrote – and as Pete pretty much said over the course of our two conversations – as soon as you put a label on something, it loses its power.

This story has been slightly bonkers at times. But, honestly, I thought this was one of the stranger moments. Pinch yourself that this is a *football coach* talking. A football coach eschewing the aggressive stereotype to analyse Buddhist masters and apply their theories. And not only that, but to prove that it can work. Pete, certainly, had enjoyed some weird experiences, and he probably was weird himself. The stories about levitation and being a cosmic channel told by Glen were fascinating, but they were mere frippery to the hardcore, almost daily grind of making it work.

Alas, it didn't work out so well for Trungpa. He was more of a 'do as I say, not as I do' merchant. He had a penchant for cocaine, women and alcohol, which was fine so long as you don't present yourself as a pure monk. Which he did. He was once so drunk he crashed his car into a joke shop in Dumfries, Scotland. I bet he had some fascinating conversations between Self One and Self Two after hitting the gin early in the morning, which he was very much prone to do.

There's a thought. Did Pete ever silently admonish himself after a bad call during the game? Or when he missed a coaching opportunity? Did he still have conversations between Self One and Self Two? He let out a hearty laugh at this question.

'Well, I do value the, er, you know, the thoughts that we have so I direct them that they're supportive. They're in line with what I need to do. I don't spend a lot of time thinking ... avoid the negativity, the dread of what might happen, basically focus on the good things that can happen and how can I influence that.

'I believe strongly in intent, what your intent is and the practice of that is beneficial. I tend to be: be well, be happy, have fun, do great things and enjoy and all. I think I have the control of that. I don't give that away to other people. That mentality you can kind of direct the reality you live in. And you can go the other way. "I'm the victim, things are going to go wrong, out of control, go bad, why me?", all that other stuff. That's the spectrum. I don't dwell on that.'

'What about negativity during a game, though, because it must be hard to control?'

'No. I've really developed a mentality to trust myself and to trust the decisions I have to make, if I … I have a quiet moment at times in the midst of it all to know what I feel and in the most part it'll work out if I don't do things for the wrong reason. One of the biggest mistakes we make is we do things to please outside influences, or what we think should happen, and that's a major pitfall. Got to do what's right and trust myself and figure it out from there. That gives me confidence and a quietness about it. So I don't struggle making decisions. I don't struggle over them, I don't dwell on them one way or the other. If I do it the way I think is the right way and the way I've trained then it'll work out.'

Then the alarm clock went off in his head. 'OK I really gotta go … let's wrap it up.'

I was scrambled again. I searched for a question. Any question. 'Who's going to win the Super Bowl?' I blurted.

'I have absolutely no idea,' he said.

Interesting that he stopped when we got talking about dwelling on the bad stuff, no? Not only that but he got a bit woolly, didn't he? There wasn't a whole bunch of sense made. Ordinarily, some of Pete's words there would have been edited to make them, well, read as if they hadn't been thrown up in the air and landed on the page. Succinctly, what he was saying was that he banished negative thoughts to feel happy and free. But I deliberately haven't touched them. That psychiatrist I was talking about? He would maybe have had his answer. Pete was filling his time, his thoughts, to keep himself safe – and therefore his project, his team, his players – from the negative. 'The dread of what might happen.' I was chuffed with myself at this little spot of amateur analysis. It wasn't entirely of my own conjuring, however. This was what was known as the Dark Side of the Force. And pretty much everybody we had met so far was afraid of it. Very afraid.

15

YODA TAUGHT MICHAEL JORDAN HOW TO JUMP

Mike Murphy raised a glass of pinot noir and said, 'To Pete …
he's one of us.' We were a few minutes' drive outside of San Rafael,
lounging around in an Italian restaurant. The SEC Group – or
the Big Six, as Dave Meggyesy had toasted – were all there. Mike's
wife, Dulce, too. I had been perched on the corner of the long
table. I hadn't really been invited, but Mike Spino had been
mischievous. He had told me it would be fine and bundled me
into the back of Rick Leskowitz's hire car before he could say
anything. Rick didn't seem that happy about it, particularly when
Spino said, 'Dulce said he could come … come on, you know
she's the one who calls the shots.'

I disagreed. Not about Dulce being the quiet powerhouse.
About Pete Carroll being 'one of us'. Literally, of course, he was.
He was an SEC Group advisor. Metaphorically, he was as well. He
was the love child of an unlikely association.

The Russians, with the shamans, gurus and mad scientists
and their alliance with Murphy's Esalen Institute, were the
beginning. Sparks flew. The seed had been planted. And from it
grew the philosophies and ideas of men who, on a sultry California

evening, sat around together eating, drinking wine and basking in the reflected light of a golden child they had helped create and advise. The likes of Glen Albaugh, Spino and Meggyesy were the wise old uncles.

But, like all young upstarts, Pete Carroll would do it his way. He had gone beyond. He really had taken their ideas and run with them. And, crucially, improved them. Pete was, instead, 'by them' rather than 'one of them'. But he was the embodiment of what all of them had so desperately wanted to create back in the 1970s. The Esalen Sports Center had spawned his coaching philosophy. Their ideology was based on creating a culture in sport that allowed room for the beautiful experiences, rather than the ugly ones. They favoured a loving environment over a bullying one, of athletes revelling in giving their all instead of obsessing about the result. At USC and the Seattle Seahawks, Pete Carroll achieved this. So, did that mean he was the superhuman? He was *everything* that they had been shooting for. While conversation continued around me, I pieced the jigsaw together in my head.

Way back in high school, Pete had shown an ability to reach the super-states. Time had slowed down in the baseball game, leaving him with a feeling that he wanted to talk about for hours and days and weeks afterwards. There was his ability to read Trungpa on the freeway. Or hold a conversation while simultaneously listening to music and watching television. This was evidence, surely, that he was a 'switchable'. Remember when Peter Brusso told me that was the learning style that I should be looking for?

Then there was his recognition that he could control people's behaviour by his own behaviour. By being gung-ho, energetic and 'Big Balls Pete'. He could determine how people thought by what he said and how he said it. He called it brainwashing in his office at USC. Years later he would repeat the trick at Dominican University. That room was in thrall to him, I swear it. An easy crowd? You bet. He was preaching to the converted. In between he had the Seahawks' home fans creating tumultuous displays of love and support for his team. I remembered something Mike Murphy had said about him: 'He could run for mayor in Seattle and win.' A profile in the *LA Times* said the same when he was at USC. Small rooms, fan bases, cities and states – he had them all in his hand.

Precognition? Yup, he had foreseen the Seahawks' rise from obscurity. He had also displayed psychic self-regulation, moving from left brain to right brain at will with John Ruark. Then there was the time he had them rocking and rolling in the bleachers in Seattle to seismic proportions. Just like Mike himself at Candlestick Park. Another, perhaps less celebrated siddhi was what Murphy had called 'Energy Transmission': an ability to inspire extraordinary performances in others. Well, Pete had this in spades.

I poked Mike Spino in the ribs to whisper my revelation.

'Is it him?' I said.

'Who?' Spino replied, looking over his shoulder nervously as if a rival from his Mafiosi family's past had caught up with him.

'Pete Carroll! He's *the* superhuman?'

Spino looked at me blankly before he twigged.

'Hmm, good theory, Big Ed,' he said.

He wasn't convinced. At all. I had forgotten that during the months on the road and in the air, criss-crossing the Atlantic, this had become *my* quest. Nobody else's. Just as Murphy had found that a spark had been lit when he heard about the Soviet programmes, I too had succumbed to the possibilities. Barry Robbins, an SEC Group founder, told me – and this wasn't as menacing as it might read in black and white – 'you're part of the family now'.

This might have been true. A distant family member eyed with slight suspicion, perhaps, because he was always writing things down or recording what people were saying, but a family member nonetheless – one who, over time, had been slowly indoctrinated into the belief system. How did that happen? How did I go from a man trying to tell a story to actively searching for a siddhi superhero? It was like I had hooked myself up to a drip of Kool-Aid. Over time, with each drop, each little hit, I became more obsessed with finding the answers.

In the past, this has put me in difficult situations when working undercover in dark, grubby corners in Africa, trying to expose human trafficking in soccer. Or getting a little too close to the Indian underworld when, again, desperately seeking the truth about match-fixing in cricket. So as soon as I first read about Murphy and the siddhis, I wanted to know it all. And I wanted to experience it all.

This is actually quite a Zen trait. The teachings from the East espouse lots of things I struggle to get my head around. But not when it comes to quests. 'Our search never ends,' a true Zen Buddhist would say. 'We value the unknowable.'

Still, I was pretty sure the Big Six probably dismissed me as a naïf because, get this, I was searching for one supreme being. Perhaps they had all worked it out years before that there was no such person. Or, more likely, that to pedestal one person above all others was just not the Zen way. That's why, in reality, I wasn't really part of the family. Indeed, I suspected that had I announced 'PETE CARROLL IS A SUPERHUMAN!' over dinner, I might have got some odd looks. Even if my glass was half full of said Kool-Aid.

Maybe it was because they might not have understood my rationale. What I actually should have told Mike Spino was, 'Pete Carroll is super-humane.' Yes, that's what I meant. For the purpose of this book it would have been wonderful to lay out the case for Pete achieving 'gnostic being' status. And, crikey, there was almost certainly a time there when I was beginning to fall for it. The way he worked the room at the SEC conference really was something. But after that speech I had gone through the Secret Tapes transcript again and there was a phrase he used that really bugged me, when he was talking carelessly about mind control and brainwashing: 'I didn't say hardly anything of substance.' Maybe he didn't say much of substance that night at the SEC. Maybe he didn't say much of substance when, finally, I spoke with him. Certainly, something popped in my consciousness when he became rather waffly when asked about allowing in the negative. He was suddenly not so smooth or mysterious any more.

This shouldn't be viewed as a criticism. If it reads that way then maybe that's just my disappointment that he's not superhuman. What he actually had shown, surely, was more prized than slowing down time or seeing the future. Sure, Pete might have displayed a wealth of the siddhi states (way more than anyone else I had encountered) but, as Peter Brusso, Dave Meggyesy, Pete himself and Ryan Harris had said, 'These things happen all the time.' And, let's face it, Meggyesy and Harris had done it in the heat of the on-field action. And Pete had never played pro sports. He couldn't be a superhuman if he had never done it at the top level, right?

Mike Murphy had a whole library full of incidents from the top athletes. Slowing down time or predicting the future didn't seem to be that big a deal to them. It is to everybody outside of that world, and maybe that's why Pete was, like me, captivated from the very start. He knew he could never make it as an athlete at the top level of sport and experience the siddhi states. Those who can, do. Those who can't, coach. Those who can do neither, write about it. Pete, when back in coaching college, had been convinced by Mike Murphy and Glen Albaugh that there was a cosmic force to connect to. Harnessing that to be successful in his football career was a no-brainer. Just like the writer who is told that, maybe, just maybe, this person exists/existed. I guess I felt a bit like Pete might have done when he was researching the Philadelphia Experiment or levitation.

Pete, when we spoke, said he did 'not want to celebrate' peak experiences. They were luxuries. It was more important to focus on an environment that might give rise to them. Meditating, yoga, having fun, taking the pressure off and practising so hard that players were operating on autopilot was all part of the plan.

Yet I think he only learned that he needed every piece of the jigsaw after failures at the New York Jets and New England Patriots. Although he was special for creating an environment to give athletes the best chance to 'go beyond', what I thought made him 'super' was something altogether more tangible, yet also beyond the reach of most of his ilk. What made Pete super-humane was that in a brutal sport like NFL, where the physical and mental wellbeing of men had largely been disregarded for decades, he made it a priority and he allowed people to be human. That had not happened before. The athletes were commodities. Nobody cared about their problems. The fans didn't care. The media didn't care. And the ownership didn't care. They cared about results.

Carroll said it was OK to make mistakes, to be afraid, to be vulnerable. And then he tried to give players the tools to get past these foibles or traits. That was level one. If they managed to experience something extraordinary on the field it was a win-win. Carroll's talent was in accepting frailty. The irony being that what elevated him to super-humane status was accepting the very opposite in all of us – our weakness, our absolutely-not-superhuman-in-any-way elements. Our commonality; the ordinary rather than extraordinary.

Being English, and therefore something of a coward when it comes to speaking one's mind, I did not share these views with the group, only Mike Spino. But after I left the Big Six in the parking lot and flew home, I did email David Meggyesy my theory. He really bought into it. Of course he did. 'God, I'd have loved to have played for Pete…' And if he had he'd never have written his book.

This story is supposed to be about the supernatural, joy and light. But you couldn't tell it without considering the reverse. Ryan Harris had reminded me of that. He had been a sobering voice, echoing Meggyesy's warning from history. For every god there were thousands of mere mortals. And there was pain, misery and gloom. If there was a Force for the good, there had to be a Dark Side. And Pete seemed to be wary of what unpleasantness could come to the fore in his downtime. The dread of failure. So to understand that a bit more, I talked to a man who had plumbed the very depths and survived. He called himself 'Yoda'.

*

George Mumford's dreams of an NBA career had ended in agony – mind and body. He'd busted up his ankles and suffered chronic back pain. His roommate at the University of Massachusetts was soaring while he was suffering. He didn't envy that kid because he respected his talent. He just thought he could have been soaring, too. That kid was Julius Erving. Better known as Dr J, Erving would become an NBA Hall of Famer.

Mumford was hurting. He had always been hurting. He grew up in Boston's Dorchester ghetto. If the cops didn't beat him, his father would. His family were poor, they lived from 'pay check to pay check'. Heroin was his escape. It was called 'skag' because it was 'inferior to white boys' heroin'. He used to sniff it off a nail file, later graduating to the needle. This was when he was in high school.

Heroin helped him forget about the darkness. It transported him to a Shangri-La of the mind. He thought it was the good side. So the drugs – mostly heroin, sometimes painkillers – were there to stay. He lived two lives. By day he was a schoolkid who would be awarded an academic scholarship. By night he would float off into space to get away from 'the physical and emotional pain'.

The double life couldn't last. By the mid-1970s he might have made it through college but he was divorced with no home, no car, no money and needing at least two hits a day. He wore long sleeves so no one could see the scars. Mumford was a dead man walking. The emergency-room doctor told him that when he came in after a needle snapped in his arm. He was sent away with painkillers. He sold them to buy more drugs.

What saved Mumford was 'stress management'. This was the East Coast's term for what the hippy West Coast was calling mindfulness, self-actualisation or the quiet mind. Mumford took a course run by Jon Kabat-Zinn, the founder of the Center for Mindfulness in Medicine at the University of Massachusetts. He got off the drugs, and through the power of meditation, positive self-talk and an obsession with Zen Buddhism he would become, from the mid-1980s, sought after in the world of sport.

He argued that his techniques could elevate athletes to the beautiful world without the need for chemicals and needles. He taught them to the Chicago Bulls, LA Lakers and New York

Knicks. Every team he has worked for has called him their 'secret weapon'. And so in demand was he that Pete Carroll tried to hire him when he was struggling at the New England Patriots. Mumford liked to talk about cosmic forces, you see. He thought that the explosion of interest in the human potential of sport in the seventies may have been due to thoughts and ideas being sent 'out there'. People were 'plucking them out' from an invisible energy field that only the mindful could connect to. Then he started talking about monkeys, which, given my experience with the Focus Band, made me a little twitchy.

'A monkey on one island started washing the coconut with sea water,' he said. 'And then all the other monkeys did the same – I'm sure he didn't text message them. There must be some sort of internet they connect to. It's an energy which is out there. It's far out stuff. If we had this conversation 20 years ago we might have been looked at as eccentric or crazy.'

Mumford had, however, learned his trade in the Dark Side. He ran a mindfulness programme in eight prisons in Massachusetts. It was his job to go in front of rapists, murderers and child molesters to tell them, 'You're frustrated, just get some space between stimulus and response. Just sit and breathe, that's enough.'

Sport was a breeze by comparison, although George wanted the same outcome for an NBA player as a criminal. He just wanted to calm them down. The language he used was the same, too, because often there would be a fine line between the guys who played street basketball and those who ran with gangs. And the philosophy was the same. 'Inside each of us is a Michelangelo masterpiece.' Mumford said he was the chisel. He put it another way as well.

'*I'm Yoda!*' he shouted. 'One day I'm sitting at home and watching this programme about Gandalf, Obi-Wan Kenobi and

Yoda. And I said, "That's me! I'm Yoda, I'm Obi-Wan, I'm Gandalf. That's me! It's my role, I'm a teacher, I'm an elder, I am wisdom…" All I do is teach somebody, and to keep them on the path, I say, "Go left" or "Go right." That's all I do. But I'm not making them who I think they are. I'm helping them to be who they already are.'

Mumford, then, was not a 'be all you can be' man. Nor was he much interested in using the word 'compassion'. How typical that an East Coast guy would do it differently to a West Coast guy. Unlike Pete, he *really* wanted to talk about the 'weird'. He was edgy.

'For me, I think some people think if you're mindful you're compassionate, and I don't buy that,' he said. 'Some of us have been programmed to be compassionate and some of us have not. These are ways of being. For me, I don't get into a process – "Let's do compassion, let's do love" – because I know the response: "Love and kindness? Compassion? Get out of here with this shit!" If you're going to tell someone to be compassionate and they don't have compassion, that's a problem.

'So I say, "Don't be hatin'." It's the opposite. So with the mindfulness you become skilful of communicating something to the audience you're talking to and the language they understand. If I say "be compassionate" they don't get it.

'I'm not trying to fix you or be all you can be against your will because some people don't want that. You have to push them out of their comfort zone, but it's a challenge, because to get out of the comfort zone is painful. So, can you be comfortable being uncomfortable? That's the question.'

'What do you mean by it's painful?'

'Change is painful because you've got to let go and because you're identifying with the way things were and they are no longer that way. When I went through my recovery and addictions, there's a mourning for that because that's what I thought I was and, "If I'm not that, then who am I?" You're going to feel lost. You're going to feel depressed, angry. You're going to be, "God, if only I can get through this I'll never smoke again" or whatever. And then there's denial about how hard it is.'

At this recall, Mumford let out a laugh that shook his shoulders. 'So it's a matter of can you be present with *everything* – the good, bad, ugly – and know how to react when it arises?'

Mumford was referring to everything that can go awry in life, whether you're a basketball player, footballer, accountant or whatever; the sort of terrifying fear that strangled Ryan Harris, a drink or drug addiction, a failing relationship, financial worries. Nagging worries that make a quiet mind almost impossible, rendering a peak state the same. The best example that Mumford could think of was Michael Jordan. Not bad, eh?

'Yeah, the main dude was MJ,' he said.

Jordan, as you probably know, was the greatest basketball player ever. He won six national championships with the Bulls, three from 1991 to 1993 and three from 1996 to 1998. Between the two 'three-peats', Jordan was in pain. His father had been murdered in 1993, so he quit the sport, a decision that prompted worldwide headlines. Instead, he wanted to become a baseball player for the Chicago White Sox to pursue the dream of his father. It didn't work out well for anybody. The Bulls were a shadow of the championship-winning team and Jordan never actually played for the White Sox.

So Jordan returned to the NBA with a two-word press release: 'I'm back.' That the Bulls and Jordan were able to recapture past glories had a lot to do with their secret weapon. Mumford said that Jordan was 'almost superhuman'. He transcended into a siddhi state more often and more easily than any other player he had worked with. And he did it when the pressure was at its most intense.

With 18 seconds left on the clock in the sixth game of the 1998 finals against Utah Jazz, Jordan produced the astonishing. He stole the ball, ghosted past one opponent, put another on his backside and nailed the shot with five seconds left. Seventy-two million people were watching on television. They say that those who saw it remember it as the greatest play of all time. Mumford, sitting a few rows behind the bench, saw it coming. He knew he had gone beyond. He likened it to remembering where you were when Neil Armstrong landed on the moon.

Jordan thought it was pretty good, too. It was, he recounted at the time, 'Zen Buddhism stuff … things start to move slowly. You see the court very well, you start reading what the defense is trying to do. I saw that moment … I never doubted myself.'

So how did Mumford help?

'I talked about being in that zone when there's no sense of self and everything's flowing and you can see everything arising. It's surreal, because your consciousness has been altered to the point you don't see yourself as a being. Or even if you're doing anything, it's just happening. Now, that's kind of weird to say. A big part of it is training ourselves to get the hell out of the way and let it happen.

'MJ had a great ability to imagine, visualise or see beyond what's there, concentrate and be in the eye of the hurricane. If you understand how something works it enhances your ability to do it even more. There's another level you can go to.'

These days, Mumford works his magic with the New York Knicks. Meditation takes place in a dark room and, just as he has done with folks from 'Yale to jail' (as he calls it), he tells them to pay attention to their breathing. I asked him to pretend I was a Knicks player, and his voice went soft and slow. And for a minute or so all he talked about was breathing. The sensation, the sound, how it might make me feel like I was sinking into the chair.

'Yes, sure, but are you mentioning the game, the ball, the crowd?' I said, somewhat impatiently.

'Yes. All of that. But the real question is, if we assume you're a player, "What do you want?"'

'Well, I guess, just that everything feels good. I'm slightly biased because I'm a long way into the process and I wouldn't have said this six months ago but I, er, reckon I would want to be present.'

'*YEEEEAH!*' Mumford shouted. I'd come a long way from John Ruark's Focus Band chimp boy, no?

The results of every team Mumford has worked for have improved. It works for the collective. Sometimes, however, the temptation for an individual not to face up to 'their pain' is too great. In 2006 Mumford worked in English soccer at Bolton Wanderers, a then Premier League club who were low on glamour, money and expectation. They needed all the help they could get. With Mumford's wisdom, they consistently outperformed teams with bigger budgets. They made the last 32 of a European competition, the UEFA Cup, and finished seventh in the Premier League. Unfortunately, Mumford was something of a bad luck omen. Coaches would hire him and they would soon leave their job, resigning or getting the sack. It happened to Sam Allardyce at Bolton after Mumford's first season. Next, he worked under Avram Grant at Chelsea in 2007. Grant would last just one year. He was then hired by Mark Hughes at Fulham for barely a season before Hughes quit. The Bolton connection was how I came to hear about Mumford. I had been talking to Mark Nesti, who was the first applied sports psychologist to work in the Premier League in England. Nesti's nickname was 'Spirit'. He was a 'believer' in Mike Murphy and had written and researched extensively about spirituality in sport and how athletes could access siddhi states. 'It messed up my career,' he said. People thought it was all 'fluff'. Nesti had been in danger of being dismissed as a kook, which frustrated him. 'I wanted to write about it because I've experienced it and I know athletes have experienced it.' The man who saved him was the Bolton coach Allardyce, who had the appearance of the archetypal bully who bawled the shots. Nesti, however, claimed that Allardyce was 'a believer', too. He had seen 'mystical' stuff. Allardyce was well known for using different methods to get results. He was one of the first coaches to embrace the use of statistics and video analysts who would pore over game footage to uncover patterns of play. It made him an unlikely success story. Nesti suggested his methods of engendering spirit and togetherness in a squad were similar to Pete Carroll's Long Body approach. 'He was all about players going over and above [their duty], forgetting the consequences, forgetting complaints or injustices, forgetting pressure,' Nesti said.

But Mumford and I didn't talk much about Allardyce. We should have done. Within a few months he had been appointed the manager of the England soccer team. Alas, the window for an interesting conversation would have been short. Allardyce may or may not have been into the cosmic forces but his demons, his dark side, got the better of him when he was exposed by an undercover newspaper reporter discussing ways to 'get around' player transfer rules. His reign lasted one match and 67 days.

Chelsea were at the other end of the spectrum to Bolton and Fulham. 'They could have probably done with some more training,' laughed Mumford. 'But I had a great time with the lads – Didier Drogba, John Terry…' Ah yes, John Terry. It was my turn to laugh. English soccer fans would find the idea of Terry attempting to be mindful amusing to say the least. When I was a reporter on the football circuit, stories abounded about Terry. I had heard that he had once taken such an exception to the way someone looked at him in a nightclub that he threatened to 'eat their eyes' if they did it again. It probably wasn't true. But Terry had far worse form, having been sacked as the captain of the England team for allegations that he had an affair with a Chelsea teammate's wife. This was a locker-room no-no. A year later Terry was investigated for calling an opposition player a 'fucking black cunt'. He maintained that what he actually said was, 'Do you think I called you a black cunt?' At the trial Terry admitted using the words 'black cunt' but said it was 'sarcasm'. He was found not guilty.

Mumford met my surprise about the vision of Terry meditating in a dark room diplomatically. It was a wonderful piece of wisdom thinly veiled as criticism. Well, that's how I heard it anyway.

'A lot of people think you can be a really good bank robber and be mindful and concentrating, but it has to come from the right place – not lying, killing, taking intoxicants and *not engaging in sexual misconduct*. If you have the mindfulness training without integrity it becomes about not creating the suffering needed to reflect. Or, as my Irish boss told me a few years ago, "Don't shit where you eat." He was Irish Catholic. "Hey, Mumford! Don't shit where you eat." I said, "OK, dude, got it."'

'Funny,' I said, 'I don't remember that being one of Yoda's catchphrases.' Mumford had an answer for that: 'Yeah, but one of the things Yoda said often [was] if somebody said, "Edward, can you do this process?" and you say, "I'll try", Yoda would say, "Do or do not. There is no try." That's when Luke Skywalker was in the swamp, and the ship went into the swamp and he said, "I'll never be able to lift that thing" or some negative, self-defeating talk, and Yoda said something like, "You have to unlearn everything you have learned." It's the same thing. You have to empty your mind.'

Another question, then: 'If Mumford was Yoda, who was Darth Vader?'

'Dude, look inside. It's like when Luke had the dream, lifted up Vader's mask and saw his own face. You heard the Cherokee story about two wolves inside you? One is love, the other fear. They are having a terrible battle. And a grandchild asks his grandfather about this battle inside of him and he says, "Which one will win?" Grandfather says, "The one which you feed."' Mumford looked at me, nodded slowly, coughed and then did his best Darth Vader impression, breathing heavily and growling: 'Don't give in to the power of the Dark Side!' he laughed.

'You can't get into your anger, all those hindrances, like sensual desire, sloth and torpor, or dumbness of mind, warrior restlessness – those are the mind killers. If you give over to that power you become Darth Vader. Don't feed the Dark Side.'

16

THE DARK SIDE

Mike Murphy and the hippy comeback crew were worried about the Dark Side. That wasn't much of a surprise. They were, after all, a self-proclaimed force for good. It was their role to help people graduate to the state where extraordinary, warm and fuzzy things happened. They were the Jedi with their slowing down of time, seeing into the future and putting thoughts into people's heads. The teachers of the Jedi mind tricks.

In the eighth episode of the *Star Wars* movie franchise, *The Last Jedi*, Luke Skywalker can be heard giving a meditation lesson: 'Just breathe … *breathe* … reach out.' His words and breathy whisper could have been copied from a George Mumford Knicks session. Or the Seattle Seahawk sports shrink Michael Gervais at VMAC, the team's training centre.

It wasn't just great marketing on the part of the human potential movement to attach themselves to the most famous science fiction story ever told – Superhuman Skywalker and a race of Jedi – and argue that this was what they were aiming for. Rather, it might have been the other way round. Not a lot of people know that it was actually Murphy's movement that inspired George Lucas, the creator of *Star Wars*.

Of course, I didn't know that, either. The references to the Force, Jedi and the Dark Side were a background hum at the SEC festival. Was it just a way of helping people to connect with what they were doing? But I did wonder. So I emailed Barry Robbins.

'George Lucas admitted that George's work was influential in creating the term "the Force",' he wrote. Two Georges. Could get confusing. The other George was George Leonard. Before his death in 2010 he used to be Barry's boss at Integral Transformative Practice, a sort of spin-off Esalen set up by Murphy and Leonard. Leonard had been in with Esalen from the start, though, and was also an important figure in the early days of the Sports Center.

Leonard, just like Murphy, believed that there was a life-force energy that flowed through everything and everybody. Some people were just able to connect to it better than others. When Leonard met Lucas, the filmmaker admitted that the Force in the movies had been based on some of Leonard's writings. There is even a line spoken by Obi-Wan Kenobi in the first *Star Wars* film that, as Leonard would often remind people, could have been taken straight from one of his workshops: 'The Force is that particular force which permeates all living things and goes to the ends of the universe.' That was exactly what he used to say.

George Leonard was with Murphy that day at Candlestick Park. Murphy told his 'whammy' story again at the SEC festival. 'It was my most fiendish experience,' he said. 'We have to look at this complexity. Lucas really picked up on this when he made *Star Wars* – the Dark Side of the Force. It's a problem. We don't want little Darth Vaders running around.'

Murphy, as was his wont, was very much of the idea that the Dark Side was the occult – using the powers for ill. Knocking pitchers over and the like. But there were other theories. Dave Meggyesy spoke at the conference about how competition, the true meaning of sport, had been forgotten because of 'fandom' and the obsession with winning. 'Athletes play, people root.' He cited a basketball match between Miami Heat and Oklahoma City Thunder in the NBA finals when the two teams hugged at its conclusion, recognising the struggle had bonded them. ('I was in tears!') The fans, of course, were not. ('Yeah! We killed them!')

Barry Robbins told a story from his time as a psychology major at the University of Michigan. Part of his training was to go to Wayne State Mental Institute to oversee hockey matches for the patients. 'They had hockey sticks and a puck – which was a ball,' Barry said. 'No other equipment. And as soon as the ball was dropped all the players immediately took off and checked each other into the boards. There was no interest in the puck at all. They just took each other out.' I wasn't sure what that had to do with the Dark Side but it was a funny image.

This had been the morning after Pete Carroll's masterclass. But there had been a point when Pete appeared irked. I did not give it much thought because at that time I had not spoken to Ryan Harris, George Mumford or, of course, Pete himself. Pete had been asked how he helped athletes cope with the Dark Side of alternative states of consciousness. Following extraordinary highs there are often extraordinary lows.

Meggyesy called it 'the dreaded transition'. Legendary quarterback John Brodie talked about it, too. 'You see, after the game [players] come down making fools of themselves sometimes, coming way down in tone level,' he said. It is a chemical comedown in the brain. When athletes go into a state where they might experience siddhis, researchers at Duke University – and scores of others – have shown that they are served up a cocktail of the good stuff. This was described brilliantly in Steven Kotler's book *The*

Rise of Superman. Dopamine, serotonin, norepinephrine, anandamide and endorphins on their own make a human feel pretty darn good. Kotler said it was like 'the meaning of life'. Together they make the athlete feel like superman – increasing focus, relaxing muscles, establishing an ability to recognise patterns, a feeling of serenity and happiness. If an athlete is capable of quietening the mind and controlling heart rate and blood pressure, as the Soviets sought to do with psychic self-regulation, then the most likely chemical reaction is a hit of dopamine. As Kotler writes, dopamine makes humans want to explore and 'to push the envelope'. It is also a skill booster. Here it acts as a potential gateway drug. If dopamine is present then it is possible that the other chemicals follow, boosting the chances of achieving something that feels otherworldly.

Studies on extreme sports professionals, like wingsuit fliers or base jumpers, have shown that they are chock full of these chemicals. This is dangerous for two reasons. Firstly, it makes them believe they are invincible, leading them to take more risks. Secondly, they seek out that high. It's addictive. Now, if you're a football player who has to wait a week until his next dose, what do you do? How do you get your fix? 'From a crazy high,' Kotler said, 'there is a very deep low.' And that was what the question to Pete was driving at: 'If they're acting without self-regard there are a lot of individuals, not just in sports, who get into trouble.' What happens in the downtime when the athlete is not at training, in the gym or playing in a game?

Pete talked about the state as akin to being a 'child at play', and to him there was 'no Dark Side to that. I don't understand that part of your question.' For Pete, there was a difference between having no self-regard and just not caring about 'what was around you'.

The query came from Brent Hogarth, a high-performance coach and doctoral student in sport and clinical psychology at John F. Kennedy University. Brent was a friend of Michael Gervais and they would go skiing together in Worcester, Massachusetts. 'He didn't like my question, did he?' Brent said to me after the discussion ended. He didn't. I didn't understand why until he told me about his need to ensure that the negative thoughts, 'the dread', did not come into his head. Pete just had his defences up.

Murphy did want to talk about it, though. He recognised that a lack of self-regard or an addiction to the feeling could cause problems of dependency, violence or other behavioural issues. That was why he had set up Integral Transformative Practice with George Leonard, he said – to help people with transition because they can't be meditating every hour of the day: 'You can use a flow state to [obstruct] your values. Certain athletes have gotten into deep trouble off the playing field. We don't have to name names. They lose track. Some of them have gone over to the Dark Side.'

One of the names that I suspected Murphy was thinking about was O.J. Simpson. He admitted as much at the SEC farewell in the restaurant. In Murphy's library of the superman states, O.J. was filed under 'mystical sensations'. O.J. had said in 1974, 'Thinking … is what gets you caught from behind. I'm not thinking about anything, so hopefully I'm thinking about everything. You just react instead of consciously thinking about it.' He had also said that the key to his success was to 'make instinctive moves without any reason for them'.

O.J.'s stories were published in the 1978 compendium of Murphy's collection of sporting feats. But in a reprint in 1995 – the same year as the former football player's trial for the murder of his ex-wife and a restaurant waiter – they were taken out, with

Murphy wary that a frenzied media would be unable to resist such salacious quotes.

O.J., who was found not guilty in the criminal trial of the century, is one of the most famous examples of a football player becoming swallowed by the Dark Side. In 2008 he was sent to prison for armed robbery and kidnapping. There are, of course, other superstar athletes who have been disgraced. Scores of them. None caught the public attention like O.J. However, there was a guy who went close. His name was Aaron Hernandez.

Hernandez was a football player with the New England Patriots. He had it all. He was living every fan's dream but had all the problems they didn't want to know about. He grew up not far from where George Mumford had in Boston. His family were poor and his father, Dennis, had died unexpectedly from complications following a routine hernia operation. It hit Hernandez hard. Dennis was his hero. At the funeral he was motionless. His brother, DJ, who would work as a college coach, sobbed and wailed. Later, he would say he could never understand why Aaron couldn't let it out in the same way. But he found another way. He went from a fun-loving kid who would do anything for anyone to an introspective thug mixing with a bad crowd. But he sure could play football.

All through high school no one could get near him on the football field. At the University of Florida he was untouchable, literally. There were rumours that he failed countless drugs tests, but the coaches protected one of their most important players. He was so good that he didn't play senior year and went straight to the NFL, although his ill-discipline had caught up with him and most teams didn't want to take the risk. The Patriots did.

So Hernandez became one of the youngest players in the NFL and on one of the smallest contracts. Two seasons later he signed a seven-year $40 million extension, the second-largest in history. The form from high school and college had carried through in to the pros. Away from the field, however, Hernandez's life was spiralling out of control. He was still hanging out with the wrong crowd. And his drug habit had not been kicked. Hernandez was getting high on PCP, otherwise known as angel dust. Its effects were similar to what an athlete might experience in a siddhi state: ultimate relaxation, euphoria, the perception of super-strength and speed.

By the spring of 2013 Hernandez was missing workouts and training sessions and the Patriots warned him he was one more mistake from being fired. The next mistake he made was big. Along with two nefarious hangers-on, Hernandez drove Odin Lloyd, his fiancée's sister's boyfriend, in a rented car to an industrial park 20 minutes outside Providence, Rhode Island. Lloyd was forced on to his knees. He raised his arms in self-defence at the first gunshot. As he fell, two more rounds were fired into his back. And then two more into his chest. The cops traced the rental car, found a bullet casing, scanned Hernandez's home security footage, which showed him leaving with a gun, and rescued data from a cellphone he smashed up. Hernandez was found guilty on 15 April 2015 and sent to prison for life. The motive was not known.

The police had known about Hernandez for some time. They knew he carried a gun. They knew the people he hung with had criminal records. He was a full-time footballer but part-time gangster. He was covered in the sort of tattoos that one would expect to see on a street thug, across his shoulders, on his neck and along his arms. Before this crime, *Rolling Stone* had already named him 'the Gangster in the Huddle'. He was suspected of being involved with a double murder and three other shootings before Odin Lloyd was killed.

On the day I was reading through notes about the Q&A on self-regard at Dominica, Hernandez caught the public eye again. In the small hours of 19 April 2017, he drew in his own blood an all-seeing eye on the wall of his cell at the Souza-Baranowski Correctional Center in Lancaster, Massachusetts, writing 'Illuminati' underneath it. He scrawled 'John 3:16' on his forehead. ('For God so loved the world, that he gave his only begotten Son, that whosoever believeth in him should not perish, but have everlasting life.') Then he attached a bedsheet from a window and hanged himself. He was 27.

It is not unusual for football players to be in trouble with the law. From the end of Hernandez's last season to the start of the next, 47 NFL players were arrested as they wrestled with what Mike would call the 'dreaded transition'. It is not unusual for football players to kill themselves, either. Hernandez became the third in the US in five months and the eighth in six years. All of the suicides – like Jovan Belcher, the Kansas City player who shot his girlfriend and then himself, or Terry Long, who drank antifreeze – were found to have suffered from chronic traumatic encephalopathy (CTE). It is a degenerative brain condition discovered in people who have suffered repeated blows to the head. It can cause extreme aggression, depression and dementia. Hernandez's family wanted his brain donated for CTE research.

Murphy, Meggyesy and George Mumford all had their theories about what the Dark Side was. This was mine. Hernandez could have just been a guy who went bad. Or he 'went bad' because of CTE. But he was far from safe from a flip from light to dark because he was an American football player. He lived the rotten culture. Football players were pawns in a world obsessed with winning and indifferent to their worries. Another symptom of that was athletes who might become depressed or angry after the comedown from a feeling of invincibility.

'Hernandez was failed by the system,' Jimmy Stewart told me sadly over the phone, 'and there will be plenty more playing who have mental health problems because nothing has changed since 1980.' That was the year Stewart left the NFL after four years as a defensive back with the New Orleans Saints and Detroit Lions, which he described as 'horrendous'. He had entered the sport with hope and joy about playing the game he loved. He left it an emotional husk and an alcoholic. Why? Because the culture that Dave Meggyesy had described was steadfast. And it's still there now. 'I'm glad someone's asking these questions,' Stewart told me over the phone. 'I cried when I read about what Pete Carroll was doing at the Seahawks. He cares about people. You can't fake that.' Stewart, who now works as the mental health coordinator for Colorado State University, has campaigned for all NFL teams to have full-time psychologists or counsellors available 24–7 to staff. With no success. He says franchises like to pay lip service to the problem – there is still a belief that talking about feelings is 'weak': 'In the NFL you are treated like an object, you don't matter, your body doesn't matter. It's like going to a strip club. It's about a woman's body and how much money the men have got. It's all about the external, and the internal gets diminished.'

Stewart put almost all of the blame on the coaches. 'It's all about strength and power for them, no one is allowed to be vulnerable.' He then listed current coaches who he believed were 'violent in their attitudes' and 'clearly' mentally unwell. There will be more casualties like Hernandez unless the NFL shines a light on its participants' mental wellbeing.

I had begun to do something that George Mumford advised nobody to do. I had fed the wrong wolf. I had fed the Dark Side.

Previously I had been skipping along happily in a world of joy and possibility. That's what, I thought, this tale would be about. But things had got decidedly black. And it was closing in fast and would only get darker. Perhaps I should have noticed a lot earlier. Perhaps I didn't because, as I said, I had been indoctrinated in some way. So fanatical had I become about the search that I had been happy to eschew rational thoughts or facts. When something didn't quite fit with what, or who, I was looking for, it didn't prick the consciousness.

For example, both Mike Spino and Scott Ford (my 'break the window' tennis coach) had told me when I first interviewed them that they had worked to assist the military to achieve siddhi states. Spino taught French military officers mental focus techniques to make them more effective fighters. Ford taught his 'don't look at the ball, look at the window' to help Navy Seals in hand-to-hand combat at their base in Virginia Beach. Scott even told me proudly, 'They told me "this will really save lives".' Sure. On the Navy Seals side. The guys they were fighting were screwed.

This now jarred horribly. Hang on, I thought, the Esalen movement was supposed to have its roots in the hippy ideal of peace and love. Not war and death. I emailed Scott to ask him whether it jarred with him, too. It was, after all, some jump from getting people to hit a ball over a net to helping trained killers to, well, kill. 'What about the loser, Scott?'

He sounded a bit irritated by my query. 'I most definitely did not feel uneasy about what we taught them,' he wrote. 'Instead, I felt extremely grateful that we have these warriors on our side when they are needed. In life and death situations, I'm "old school". I want our team to win, even if the "loser" comes off worse.'

It was also 'old school' that trained killers would be more dangerous in an altered state of consciousness because their self-regard would have been reduced. The Soviets' mad scientists were, 'like little Darth Vaders', as Murphy said, doing their work, and the American military had followed suit. So, in reality, the movement's roots were pretty much infected by the Dark Side from the beginning. When the Russians began their Hidden Human Reserves programme back in 1960, they were doing so with a reckless regard for the lives of rabbits and human beings. The response of the Americans was to try to create super-soldiers of their own. Both sides, essentially, wanted men who would show little or no self-regard in altered states to win their team the game. It was also true that in those states they would make better decisions, be faster and harder to kill. Did it matter whether people could *actually* see through walls or if they were *really* capable of slowing down time? Surely they just needed to be in a zone where they thought they could?

Was the same not true in sport? Peter Brusso's golfers were not *really* Darth Vader. Herb Elliott was not *actually* St Francis of Assisi. But the visualisation created allowed each of them to play or run with a diminished sense of anxiety, fear or self-regard. The illusion worked both ways. Remember how Dr Zoukhar got inside the head of poor Viktor Korchnoi? Zoukhar wasn't really transmitting his voice into his head, was he? Korchnoi's anxiety, fear and self-regard was at the point where he allowed himself to be spooked.

Athletes like O.J. Simpson and Aaron Hernandez, who had, as Murphy said, 'gotten into deep trouble', could have been collateral damage. It was surely impossible to argue that there had been wilful disregard for the highs and lows of peak states. Few sports coaches, certainly not one as empathic as Pete Carroll, would seriously seek to consistently place athletes in peak performance states if they knew that there was also a constant threat of those same guys doing something terrible. The Seahawks, as we have discovered, are renowned for putting players' mental and physical wellbeing first. Carroll does not dose them up and force them on to the field, for example.

No. What was whirring away in my mind was something much more unsettling. And it had really manifested itself after that exchange with Scott Ford. Sure, coaches like him were not disregarding the threats, either. But what if sport was the collateral damage? What if sport was the Trojan Horse? What if the modern-day American military had recognised, like the Russians, that sport was a breeding ground or practice field for their weird experiments? It wasn't as if the two environments were totally alien. Any football fan with the most basic understanding of the rules knows that it is, essentially, a war game. Two rival factions engage in bloody, no-holds-barred violence for each other's territory before planting the flag in the home zone. Military phrases litter the game: players are called 'warriors' and other borrowed phrases include 'blitz' and 'the bomb'. Where do you think Pete Carroll got his 'be all you can be' slogan from? It was the army's recruitment call for years.

The link between the military and sport is not unique to America. No way. We English invented that. Ever heard the quote, 'The British Empire was won on the playing fields of Eton'? George Orwell wrote that sport was war 'minus the bullets'. I could go on.

The point was, I had gone over to a bad place. Suddenly I couldn't get the words of Russell Targ out of my head. He was the CIA's 'remote viewer' who could see into the future and through walls during the Cold War. He told me, 'They were using it to kill people.' What if America was using sport to kill people?

17

BACK TO THE FUTURE

The New Age culture from the sixties and beyond argues that coincidences are not accidents but signals from the universe that guide people to their true destiny. Deepak Chopra, one of the more famous of the brethren, said that. Mike Murphy would say that about wandering into the wrong classroom that day in 1950. Had he been where he was supposed to be, Esalen would never have existed and the chain of events described in these pages would not have taken place.

There were other flukes along the way, though, that kept the storyline on a wonderful and wacky course. With Murphy just beginning his research on the siddhis he was in thrall to Abraham Maslow, who called them peak experiences. One black 1962 Big Sur night, a traveller and his wife had got lost on Highway 1 and needed a motel. They pulled in to Esalen. The man on the front desk asked him to write his name in the guest book. He recognised it immediately. Abraham Maslow. The man with whom a young Esalen community was obsessed was standing in the lobby and needed a room. '*Abraham Maslow! Abraham Maslow!*' he shouted, running to find Murphy. From that day for the next decade Maslow would become almost a resident at the retreat.

In 1979 Anya Kucharev, a Russian-American teacher, was in a book store in Monterey, California, when one of Michael Murphy's novels, about a superhuman with all the siddhi skills, fell from a shelf into her lap. She stayed up all night reading it. In the morning, the phone rang. It was Murphy, asking her to assist with Esalen's Soviet adventures. They had never met before. She became a key translator as the Esalen exchange programme whirled into action.

Back in London in the summer of 2016, I experienced a strange coincidence of my own. So strange, in fact, that I began to wonder whether it was not an accident but someone had plugged me into the Force. Rick Leskowitz, the ponytailed outsider, had predicted it: 'You'll find something will happen, and it will all come together.'

Since returning from America's West Coast I had become a little melancholy about alternative states of consciousness and their secrets. The Dark Side had a firm grip. It was not about athletes doing dumb things because they had no self-regard. It was not even about the notion that football players were injuring their brains. It was about this tale coming full circle, that sport would once again be used by governments and military to produce super-soldiers to win wars and prove that their way of life was superior.

But getting close to that world was not easy. And, as a sports writer with no expertise in defence, military or secret projects, I didn't know where to look or who to speak to. I got lucky. I had been sitting in the office of a lawyer near the Royal Courts of Justice with Chris Cairns, the former international cricketer for New Zealand. He was one of the biggest sporting stars the country had produced. He had been accused of fixing matches for gambling syndicates. And he had ended up in court not once but twice. He was found not guilty the first time around. But he had been hauled in front of a judge again to be accused of perjury after testimony emerged from two of Cairns's former teammates that said he *was* a match-fixer. One of the former teammates was the ex-captain of the New Zealand national team, Brendon McCullum.

It was salacious stuff: clandestine meetings in hotel rooms; revelations about how to hide money from the tax man, bribes of several hundred thousand dollars on the metaphorical table and speed boats in Dubai. But Cairns was acquitted of perjury in October 2015 after a nine-week trial.

He claimed he had been the victim of 'black arts'. And he wanted me to help him prove it. He handed me a witness statement. It was from a man called Kerry Schwalger, who wanted to testify in support of Cairns. It began, 'I am a neuro-human performance specialist.' Schwalger had been employed by Brendon McCullum to help him with the psychological side of his game. 'I would provide him with the mental analytics on how to mentally destabilise [the] opposition.' In other words: thought projection. I considered this a fluke. What a coincidence when researching a book on the otherness of sport to come across a practitioner purely by chance.

In the meantime, I spent several months of free time trying, and failing, to bottom out exactly what the Cairns conspiracy was for a potential exposé. I spoke to Kerry Schwalger on the phone almost every week at all hours of the day and night. He said Cairns was a victim. And that he had the documents to prove it. If correct, that was a big story so, naturally, I was desperate to get hold of the paperwork.

Schwalger lived in Auckland, New Zealand. He was skittish, even claiming that he had been beaten black and blue by people who were out to protect those who had wanted to see Cairns put behind bars. He sent me pictures of his face, swollen and purple: 'I've been bashed and brutalised.' One day he would tell me he would send 'the motherload' of emails and text messages that could bring cricket to its knees. The next he would tell me he wanted no part of it and he just wanted to crawl away and hide. And he actually did that a few times, which led to Cairns filing a missing person's report. The police called him back immediately: 'He's fine, he just wants to be on his own.'

Schwalger, eventually, decided he wanted out. Either that or he didn't have the documents that he said he did. I came to the conclusion that he enjoyed the intrigue and excitement of being the man who knew too much. Cairns wanted the documents. I wanted the documents. And there was a plethora of other journalists, I suspect, who he was courting as well. He liked the attention.

What he did instead was hand over his iPhone, which he said would give me a taste of the claims surrounding the Cairns case. He couldn't just pop it in the post, however. That would have been too dangerous, he said. It could have been intercepted. Clearly believing this was a spy thriller in the making, he said there had to be a handover agent. My sister-in-law, who happened to live in Auckland at the time, had agreed to meet him at a beachside bar. This was a meeting that Schwalger had cancelled twice before.

'Did he show up?' I texted her.

'Yes! I've got it.'

'How was he?'

'Er, it was really weird. He seemed to be wearing some sort of disguise. As if he thought he was being followed.'

'Yeah, that sounds like Kerry.'

There was nothing incriminating on his phone. This was not a surprise. But there were examples of his work as a 'neuro-human performance specialist'. There were plenty of what he called 'mental scripts', which were designed to help his athletes put the heebie-jeebies on the opposition. These appeared to be a collection of buzzwords and motivational soundbites for Schwalger's clients who, he claimed, included tennis star Ana Ivanović and golfer Adam Scott. They were supposed to make them feel unbeatable and access higher performance. They were tremendously entertaining.

'Forget about form. FIND A WAY – FIND A FUCKING WAY.'

'REDUCE HIM TO ZERO ... ANGER IS THE MOST POWERFUL EMOTION WE HAVE.'

'You are a pirate not a stuffy navy.'

'Must recall pleasant images from the past ... little puppies.'

And my two particular favourites: 'This game is gripping me like a highly sexed Victoria's Secret model' and 'No morning-after pill for that.' I had no idea whether those two were connected.

The advice was not all so obscure. There was stuff in there of which Pete Carroll would have been proud. Brendon McCullum was told to quiet his mind: 'Your brain has already registered the situation and knows exactly how to play it. Never override it by thinking you have to force or press – it will force and press automatically. You have got to let go to have mental flow!' McCullum was also told he had 'crazy and never before seen analytics' (whatever they were) and that he was 'superhuman!'

Negative thoughts could be 'fertilised' with repeated recall and they would grow into a 'real monster'. McCullum was exhorted to 'feel the shot' before he played it. I could imagine Glen Albaugh nodding sagely in agreement to some of this stuff.

McCullum, in his autobiography, would call Schwalger's form of encouragement 'outrageous and a bit disquieting'. He did, however, call Schwalger 'Genius' and 'Legend' in correspondence.

When I wasn't going round in circles with Schwalger, we spoke about his job. And we got on really well. Over time we would talk more and more about sports performance. He 'loved' my enthusiasm and even suggested I work with him as his European scout for athletic talent. 'I only take those who I connect with on a biological personality. And those who can go to the stratosphere,' he said. What did he mean by a 'biological personality'?

'I have to connect with them,' he said. Translation: he had to like them. And they like him. Schwalger was a thousand miles per hour, full of energy, his mind darting in different directions, and a conversation with him was like spinning plates. 'They have to be fun, outgoing,' he said. 'Like Ana Ivanović, we work well together because she's very engaging, smiley, flirty.'

OK. This was understood. It was like Pete Carroll making his players feel good, showing them love and commitment. But Schwalger didn't like the Carroll connection. He was doing more advanced work.

'He's pretty basic,' he said. 'I know he's heavily into visualisation and all those sorts of things – positive thinking, preparation. But if you replicate that you won't get the same results. So what is it that makes him different? It's his biological personality, which gets the players to do what he wants. They'll play for him, they'll execute for him.

'But he's been sacked a few times, then he got hold of a good quarterback [Russell Wilson at Seattle]. What happens is that the greatness comes first and then they try to develop the science behind it.'

It wouldn't be a bad idea if Schwalger actually explained to me the science behind what he did, specifically his thought projection. Schwalger insisted he could hit 'a secret neurological tripwire, which means that we can destabilise the opposition'. Again, I didn't know what that meant. 'Everyone has a cognitive security system, so all we're doing is covertly disabling it.' Riddles. Schwalger had a habit of coming up with grandstand terms for basic ideas, it seemed. 'Biological personality' being one of them. But pinning him down on the exact meaning of what he was saying was almost impossible.

'With Brendon we know how to trigger his dopamine and testosterone levels within milliseconds, so when he sees the ball it looks slower, bigger,' Schwalger said.

'What do you mean, a trigger? Do you use a word? Do they press an imaginary button?' I asked, channelling Mike Spino's running trick when he asked athletes to shout 'ping' when pushing a 'button' for an energy boost.

As he often did with my 'newbie' questions, Schwalger laughed mockingly before going off on another tangent.

'The thing about triggers is … they can change within 24 hours. You have to know your athlete so well. You start the day at ten [out of ten], but then the wife phones and there's a problem … you get to the ground and the pitch is not good, so by the time Brendon goes out to bat he's two. You have to be aware of everything they do. We talk more about arousal levels. Did you watch Federer play the other day?'

'No.'

'You're supposed to say "yes", Ed. His arousal levels were so flat. What beat Fed in that game [a semi-final loss to Dominic Thiem in the 2016 Stuttgart Open] … his shots didn't sound right. We play sound a lot – just think of the great sound of the ball hitting the racket. Fed got out-sounded in that match. The boom was so loud, so guttural, so powerful that it pissed him off.'

I was tempted to say that Federer was clearly guilty of looking at the ball instead of an imaginary window, which would help him to find God. But I didn't.

'With Brendon, Ivanović or Adam Scott we'd do a pre-mortem not a post-mortem. Post-mortems are done only by those useless sports psychologists. But it's not [the athlete's] fault they didn't perform how they wanted to do. They didn't do what the coach wanted them to because it didn't appeal. It didn't light up their dopamine centres. The biological personalities didn't connect.'

Eventually I managed to pin Schwalger down to two examples of how his athletes were able to 'mentally destabilise' the opposition. They seemed pretty basic. One of his athletes was going up against a guy who didn't like confrontation so he told him to get in his face and really snarl at him, be aggressive. It turned out that was what the 'REDUCE HIM TO ZERO … ANGER IS THE MOST POWERFUL EMOTION WE HAVE' note on his phone was for. Another was the opposite. He advised the New Zealand cricket team to be all pally and chummy when they were playing the England team, as the English were known for being aggressive. This would confuse them.

I noticed that Schwalger often used the word 'we'. I thought he was a lone operator. He did it again when I was talking to him about Mike Murphy and the SEC Group and their vision for athletes to be able to better control their minds to access higher states. Schwalger snorted. 'That's exactly what *we* do,' he said. 'For me, to manipulate minds or destabilise a person's mind, that's like having a cup of coffee for us now.'

'You keep using "we", Kerry,' I said. 'Who are "we"?'

What Schwalger told me next was unexpected. The coincidence.

'We're a cartel,' he said. 'We get together every year. It's multimillion dollar stuff. We're ten years ahead. Some of the stuff, let me tell you, is super-scary. A lot of stuff we do is derived from DARPA.'

DARPA stands for 'Defense Advanced Research Projects Agency' – one of the American military's most powerful secret organisations. It has a budget of billions to explore ways to win wars – the madder, wackier and more frightening, the better. Like robot cyborg insects, flying submarines and programmable shape-shifting matter. Programmable shape-shifting matter is taking an everyday object like, say, a mug, that suddenly morphs into a knife and slices off your hand. So DARPA is the military's version of Esalen, if you will, an organisation whose role is to think outside the margins of the rule book. They are also building computers to help soldiers communicate by thought alone, according to the renowned author Annie Jacobsen, who wrote the book *The Pentagon's Brain: an uncensored history of DARPA*.

Schwalger said his group of human performance experts got together twice a year in Russia (he refused to tell me where) to develop theories and run lab tests. Did I know that the Russians were into this back in the Cold War? he asked me. Just a little bit, I said.

'We congregate twice a year to do our stuff. Now look, when we're talking about the biggest ball players in sport we can't *afford* to be wrong. It can't be, "Give this a whirl and see how it goes." We only give it to the team or individual when it's perfected. We can't be wrong. So the money paid into it is *huge*. You'll never find any of this on the net. We go for seven weeks at a time. We always go to the same place because we have high security. We don't do anything egregious. We produce certain things for certain [teams] and sportsmen who have vested interests. I don't know how to articulate it.'

'Can I come to Russia with you next time you go?' I said.

The answer was no. 'You're an investigative journalist,' Schwalger said. 'It would be hard to convince the others involved.'

Next question. 'Who else is involved?'

'Can't say.'

'But are you telling me you are creating superhuman athletes?'

'Yes.'

Schwalger then gave me the name of an NBA player. 'XXXX XXXX is great, but he's not great through default, do you know what I mean? He is great by design.'

It didn't take long for him to spill. The 'design', though, sounded painful. Schwalger called it skeletal symmetry. Athletes, he said, were willing to be operated on to have muscles thinned down or taken away. He named more, and they were some of the biggest names in American sport. It sounded insane.

'It's like the nectar,' he said. 'How can I give you an example? Say, if you go to punch a punch bag, your skeletal system will dictate how much energy you use – you might feel a bit of pain in your shoulder. That means you're only utilising a third of your energy. And the energy is stopping at the shoulder. So you're utilising two-thirds more than someone who doesn't have skeletal symmetry.' Schwalger said surgery meant that the shoulder would be manoeuvred into a position so the energy is not wasted and is transferred down to the thigh bone and little toe. He said it made the athlete feel a million bucks. 'XXXX XXXX is a perfect example of skeletal symmetry. XXX and XXX and XXXX have fewer muscles. We've taken them away. We are doing that for central nervous system feedback. We are doing it for accuracy.'

'Those athletes have had skeletal symmetry?'

'Yes.'

Suddenly, it all seemed a very long way from Pete Carroll's Long Body or George Mumford teaching NBA players how to breathe. I said as much to Kerry.

'Yeah,' Schwalger said, enjoying being the big show again. 'We've gone beyond. It's truly monstrous what they're doing in sport now. In two or three years, who knows whether this stuff will be legal?'

But Schwalger said it was the brain that would unlock true sporting immortality. Understand how the brain works – and why some athletes are calmer, more focused and more intuitive – and you could engineer an ultimate athlete. The answer, he said, was in neuroscience. 'We're looking for neuro-supremacy,' he said. 'But we're galaxies away from knowing what the human brain can do.'

The American government and its military machine was certainly trying, however. And it had gone back to the future to do so. Not long after the CIA had said in 1975 that its ESP programmes, like the remote-viewing programme that included Uri Geller, had been 'unreliable', they cancelled their research. In 1995 the Department of Defense followed suit. ESP, psycho-kinesis (PK) and all the tricks of the First Earth Battalion manual were dismissed. Words like 'vague' and 'ambiguous' were used to describe effectiveness. Or so they said. Jon Ronson's *The Men Who Stare at Goats* book argued that the research and scheming never really stopped. In 2014, it was back on the agenda – or at least the public were allowed to know it was back – after battlefield reports from Iraq that soldiers had displayed an ability to see into the future, alerting them to the imminent attack of roadside bombs.

The Office of Naval Research investigated these claims that soldiers' intuition had prevented carnage. They spent $3.85 million and four years researching what they called 'sensemaking'. Official Department of Defense documents defined this as 'a motivated continuous effort to understand connections (which can be among people, places and events) in order to anticipate trajectories and act effectively'. This was clever. Wary of what the public would think of using terms that had a stigma like ESP and PK, not to mention 'remote viewing', they used less wacky labels. The work, for example, was called 'Perceptual Training Systems and Tools'.

But they sure wanted to train sailors and marines to be superhuman. There had also been a naval programme that had aped Stanley Krippner's dream research, helping military personnel to recover from post-traumatic stress disorder. Instead of diehard Grateful Dead rock fans sending images to a man named Malcolm to dream about, as Krippner had done, the Power Dreaming experiment transmitted soothing images through 3D glasses. When a soldier with PTSD wakes up from a nightmare, he puts on the glasses and is immediately pacified, aiding recovery. And at DARPA, the quest for the superhuman had been a constant.

Still, skeletal symmetry was probably not on their agenda. I checked that with Annie Jacobsen, the world authority on all things DARPA thanks to her bestselling exposé. 'That doesn't sound like them, it's too invasive,' she said. 'But your guy's right about neuroscience. That's a big area.'

The esoteric, therefore, had undergone a rebrand. Just like the Soviets had labelled telepathy and parapsychology a science to mute prejudices, America was using 'rubric brain computer interface technology' to build telepathic battle helmets so soldiers could communicate with one another wherever they were in the world. It sounded much better to be working with neuroscientists and human performance enhancement specialists than yogis or parapsychologists. And the size of the money pie – the Department of Defense handed out almost $275 billion in contracts in 2015 – saw a rush to grab a slice. This was no cartel, it was a community. Those contracts would be my way into what I thought was a closed world. All I had to do was follow the money and join the dots. Schwalger, despite the bluster and the bragging, was right about something. At its heart was sport.

*

One of this breed is Andrew Herr – in his mid-thirties, he's lectured on human performance enhancement at the White House. His company is called Helicase and it specialises in enhancing team performance, whether that be office workers, sports teams or US Special Forces. He wouldn't tell me who those sports teams were when I called him but he did admit 'we work a lot on pro basketball, mostly with individuals'. He is recognised as a bona fide Mad Scientist – a group the US Army collaborates with to explore the future. That's because he believes in mutant powers. Herr says that, in the future, troops could be biologically enhanced. They could be faster, stronger and smarter because technology will have been developed to 'pimp' people's minds and bodies with chemicals, neurological techniques and gene therapy (considered 'safer' than pumping people full of steroids).

Before launching Helicase, Herr was a consultant at the Virginia-based Scitor Corporation. Their research (among other bits and bobs) into what the military called biomodification was paid for by 87 defence contracts worth just shy of $195 million, from 2000 to 2015. When working for the military, Herr discovered the key to performance enhancement was reducing stress, rebalancing hormones so a soldier doesn't run away, a focused diet, exercise and good old-fashioned meditation for clarity of thought. Naturally, there would be a crossover for sport. So trained killers were directly influencing sharp-shooters in pro basketball? Herr said it was actually the other way round, suggesting it was sport that was the training ground for the military.

'A lot of the work being done in the military draws from research done in sports,' he said. 'But I think a lot of human performance research has been funded by the military. Everybody is using the same research, and it's conducted on athletes.'

Herr was just one of a cast of thousands. Just like Scott Ford when he helped the Navy Seals to kill. I couldn't possibly list them all here. But just for fun, here are two more who might interest you. Dean Radin from the Institute of Noetic Sciences also took a break from trying to make a laser beam break with the power of thought to lecture DARPA and the US Navy. And Rollin McCraty and the HeartMath Institute have provided servicemen and women with the skills to 'self-regulate' in the heat of the battle. More big numbers. They won 20 defence contracts worth more than $1.5 million. And you thought they were crazy, didn't you? It sure helped, it seemed.

What others – say, scientific peers of Radin and McCraty – might say is crazy is that two men who have had their experiments and research questioned are able to have the military in such thrall. HeartMath, for example, is listed under Quackwatch's 'questionable organisations'. Quackwatch is a US non-profit body that claims to 'combat health-related frauds, myths, fads, fallacies, and misconduct'.

So, much like the Soviets paid millions to collections of scientists – mad, crazy, questionable or not – to unlock the secrets of the superhuman states, America were funding their own. Boffins with million-dollar defence contracts were trying to find a way so that more soldiers or sailors or air force men and women could be like the Jedi and defeat whichever Dark Side was threatening their freedom that year. They didn't test on rabbits, though. They used Seahawks.

18

MIND CONTROL!

While following the money from the Department of Defense to sport, I remembered something Michael Gervais had told me. He said there were 'one hundred things I'd like to trial', telling me about processes such as 'facial recognition' and 'neurotopia brain-testing'. At the time, I was still caught up with the cosmic and the occult, reckoning that the government and military had dispensed with their strange programmes. But both those ideas Gervais had mentioned had already been the subject of vast military funding. OK, they were not as esoteric as their exponents would have argued – they were based on cold, hard scientific fact. But certainly, neurotopia brain-testing sounded, to me, like the sort of thing that could have you in a siddhi state in no time.

I wanted to find proof that the Seattle Seahawks and the great cosmic channel that was Pete Carroll had been using some of the military scientists to assist their players to reach optimal states. I thought that would be a neat way to bring the story full circle. But searching the Department of Defense contracts database with no scientist or research laboratory link to the Seahawks could have been a monumental waste of time. More than half a million contracts are awarded by the Department of Defense. Per year.

So I took the lazy way out. I Skyped Gervais – who, by the way, had also been employed by US Special Forces – and asked him. He was his usual affable self and after the usual Skype introduction – 'Can you hear me? Yes, but I can't see you? Is it working now? Wait, let me call you back?' – I tossed him up an easy question to get him rolling. You know, to build the relationship. 'You told me there were a hundred things you'd like to trial,' I said. 'Where could we be in, say, five years with putting together the best platform for athletes to reach peak states?'

'OK, so I love the question, and it's a big question. Is the question about tech?'

'Yeah, I think so. You mentioned neurotopia brain-testing last time we spoke. Are you already doing that?'

'Uh huh. Yeah, but it's not at scale. That tech is available and happening but not at scale. Can you ask the question again so I can think about it again. OK?'

'Erm, OK. So, maybe in five years' time, what tech would have been developed to allow athletes a better platform to reach these peak states?'

Gervais jabbered on for quite a while. And I could reproduce it here verbatim. But there were some big words in there, mixed with scientific terms and jargon, which, frankly, make for heavy reading. Essentially, what he told me was that coaches might be able to monitor the heart rates and brainwaves of athletes to know when they were about to go into an optimal state. At least, that's what I thought he was saying.

'Are you telling me it could be a case of a coach saying, "Let's get this guy in the game, he's about to go optimal"?' When asking this question, I mimicked what I thought was a coach's voice. Gruff and stern. But Gervais, to his credit, let it go.

'It's coming,' he replied. 'It's not three years away. We still have a very – ooh, what's the right way to say this? – deep respect for the unique traditions for sport. And what comes with that are intuitive time-tested decision-making processes. And just because someone is optimal doesn't mean they're the right fit and that might not be the way the coaches are making decisions about player personnel.'

The data then *was* available to allow sports teams to test athletes to see how likely it was that they could consistently reach optimal states. That was the point of neurotopia brain-testing.

'The art of coaching is going to be facilitated by the science of measurement. There is a great opportunity for people who are progressive thinkers on how to *apply* information coming from tech. We are moving past just looking at somebody's body shape and seeing big feet and long arms and thinking, "Swimmer!"'

'Interesting, Mike. Tell me, the neurotopia brain-testing? For the layman, what is that? What are you looking for? How's it done?'

I'm going to pause here before we let Gervais answer that question. In my small-minded, Luddite way I thought 'neurotopia' was some fancy piece of verbiage to describe the study of the brain. No. Turns out it is simply the name of a company, Neurotopia Incorporated. And this same Neurotopia Incorporated had been brain-testing Seattle Seahawks players. Having wasted hours trying to find a link in the US Department of Defense database, it turned out Gervais had told me months previously, when I was still very much unhindered by the possibility of a Dark Side. Back to Gervais.

'OK. All human beings produce electrical signals from their brain. And those signals come in four or five bands: alpha, beta, theta and delta. If one brain is making a lot of beta, that might be good or not so good for performance because we know beta is high alert, but too much creates anxiousness.

'Then we have an assessment and a baseline, and we can train your brain by giving you instant feedback to produce a different type of brainwave that will make you focus in a calm way. It's much deeper than that – that's the most basic explanation – but it's gold dust because we can get instant feedback as to how a brain is responding, and we know that particular brainwaves are correlated with particular states. And isn't that what we are trying to get to? An ideal state? It gives data-driven performers a metric so they know if they are becoming more calm. You can't fake that.'

'You described that brilliantly, Mike.'

'Well, yeah, if my peers were listening to me they'd say, "O-M-G, you just fucking butchered the science. How dare you?" But it's really complicated.'

*

Dr Leslie Sherlin is the modern-day Abraham Maslow. He wanted to know why one person could be so naturally gifted and why others would have to try so much harder. That gift might be in maths, sport or languages. (Think Michael Gervais reeling off complicated descriptions of neurological science while I flustered and fumbled around the meaning of one word.) So Sherlin took electroencephalograms (EEGs) of brains, mapping electrical activity. The brains that made good decisions, very good decisions, to allow them to get to the top of their field.

Sherlin is considered one of the world's leading experts in neuroscience performance. He was also the co-founder and chief science officer at Neurotopia Incorporated. Neurotopia were paid a cool million bucks by the military so Sherlin could develop the technology to train military brains to slip into those optimal states at will. He had also criss-crossed the US, training their best of the best – US Special Forces.

When Sherlin and his team were visiting Special Ops, he was creating individual profiles of brain and personality for each trained killer. Sensors were put on their heads and they were asked to push buttons when they saw a flashing light or particular colour on a screen. This simple test allowed Sherlin to rate them in categories like stress recovery, focus and reaction time. Once that profile had been built, Sherlin got to work training the brain in areas where it was weak. Just like an athlete would train a muscle.

Then on go the sensors again. This time, subjects play a car chase video game but one without a joystick or control pad. Players move the car with their thoughts. Stare at the car and it moves. The better your concentration, the faster the car goes. It speeds over bridges and round bends – if you crash, you're trying too hard. Lose focus, and the car stops. The more sessions you do, the harder it gets to move the car. As John Ruark might have said of the Focus Band, 'We don't start playing a computer game at the highest level, Monkey Brain.'

US Special Forces were being trained to concentrate harder when they needed to and relax when they needed to. To toggle between the two states. Sherlin said this was also important not just in the military, but in sport too. A football player needs to switch between the two from game-time to a time-out; a tennis player will do the same in the break between games and sets.

It was this inner-game training that Sherlin was doing with Pete Carroll's Seahawks. He had started working with US Special Ops in 2010. In 2011 he began applying the same methods with the Seahawks. And he's still doing it now. He also boasts an impressive roster of talent in other sports, which has included the Seattle Mariners baseball team, Carlos Quentin, the Chicago White

Sox baseball player who had been renowned for struggling to control his emotions, and two-time Olympic champion volleyball player Kerri Walsh, who had suffered a chronic confidence crisis.

Pete, by the way, according to Sherlin, did not have a particularly cosmic approach to the work. 'He was very practical,' he said. 'Not interested in the philosophy. He was like, "Who are these individuals we're looking at and what are the environments where they can maximise themselves?" So he was very strategic around the players.'

Sherlin's work was an example of how the military and sport had worked in tandem. The military benefited from these ideas being rigorously tested in environments that they could not recreate. Sport was the perfect setting for the military to continue to test. What was at stake for athlete and soldier, Sherlin said, was respectively the same. Winning or losing for the athlete was life or death to the soldier. 'For the military, sport can replicate that pressure which they can't easily do in war games.' With the Seahawks, Sherlin had tested the algorithm he had developed from thousands of soldiers' EEGs to show who was more capable of consistent high performance and therefore more likely to go stratospheric. And then he would go back to US Special Forces and update and hone the system: 'We look at how an individual shifts states between resting condition and being active, [how they] manage stress and how they recover from making a mistake. The electrical signal of the resting condition can be tweaked for optimising performance, but it's how they transition through this cycle of action and execution [that's important].'

It was a bit like the Focus Band, just more advanced. The athlete or soldier was switching effortlessly between the creative part of the brain and the logical part. The best sporting example Leslie could think of was Rickie Fowler, the golfer, who would be able to switch between the two with ease. He studied Fowler's brainwaves on a putting green. Before positioning himself over the ball to strike, Fowler had been buzzing, but as soon as he decided it was time to play the shot he drifted into a 'completely open state of mind'. And we know what happens when you reach there.

The best 'he had ever seen', however, was not a golfer, footballer or baseball player. The EEG readings had been 'off the charts'. He'd been working with the US track and field Paralympian team and there was one guy who had really maxed it out. 'This is incredible. How did you do this?' Before he was a Paralympian he'd been military Special Ops and a sniper and been trained to control his physiology. 'He would stay in a certain place for days without moving,' Sherlin said. 'He had this internal control of his heart, his breathing, his mind.'

He had Hidden Human Reserves. And that was what the military generals and the Pete Carrolls were interested in. So had Sherlin proved as fact the existence of the siddhi states that Mike Murphy and the esoteric squad had been obsessed with back in the seventies?

'Well, "fact" is a strong word,' he said. 'At least I'd say there's a huge amount of research to suggest it's real. It has scientific backing. It's not a figment of our imagination. Now it's about understanding the nuances and how it plays out for certain individuals.'

'Can we call it "Jedi"?'

'Well, we can. There's an opportunity to really get into and recreate it and explain it.'

I couldn't let Sherlin go without the tough question, though. As rewarding as his work no doubt was – and there would be tangible examples of progress when following the fortunes of the teams or individuals he worked for – there was a bottom line. And it, surely, wasn't a particularly pleasant one. He was still helping one human being to kill another. Did it ever sit heavily on his conscience?

'I don't have a strong reaction to what the soldiers, sailors, or marines may have done while performing better,' he said. 'That's a political question of which I have no control in my job. However, I realise that the training hopefully [kept] them safer while called to duty.'

I felt there was another depressing element at work here. Yes, it was dark for the military to be using this stuff to kill folks. And, yes, it was dark for sport and the military to be working together. But if we think back to the Esalen days and when the Sports Center was set up, it was done to beat the disease, the American obsession with winning. And yet here we had the much-vaunted and desired siddhi states being used to cultivate and enforce that obsession. Athletes were having electrical activity in their brains recorded to see whether they could hit the heights. And therefore take their team, or themselves, to the winners' podium.

Let's extrapolate it a bit more. With science and sport working in tandem, they had the ability to discover who was the elite and who was just 'good' – a recruitment tool to separate the wheat from the chaff. 'OK, your brain is pulsing nicely, you can play. You? Not so good. Take a walk, kid.' I'm not saying that this is wrong, I'm just pointing out that this was anathema to the very ethos of the Esalen Sports Center all those years ago. The aim was to have fun, to bring back the joy. Not to plug someone into the Matrix and see if they had the right type of brain to take to the field.

On the plus side, it was being used to improve brains. Athlete or soldier was actually being taught how to be a better person or to 'be all you can be'. In or outside of competition, or battle, the abilities Sherlin was testing for could be used for good. To keep people on the straight and narrow. Undoubtedly they could help with the dreaded comedown or the negative mindset that got athletes into trouble. Murphy and the Sports Center would have been A-OK with that.

The goal, though, for Esalen was to change the world. Picking off groups of individuals through sport? Great. Box ticked. But what about mass mind control? The notion that somebody or something could control a swathe of people to think how they wanted them to? It probably won't surprise you to learn that the American government had tried that. It was called Project MK-Ultra.

If you thought the Russians zapping death-row prisoners with death rays was beyond the pale, this CIA Cold War project was just as gruesome. It had begun in 1953 with mental patients, prisoners, drug addicts and prostitutes given LSD – some wittingly, others not – to see if the drug could act as a sort of truth serum, prompting confessions. Or maybe it could wipe people's brains clean, allowing the CIA to reprogramme them. Both were potentially useful tools in a war if they were able to get their hands on agents of the opposition. For good measure, they threw in sleep deprivation, isolation, verbal and sexual abuse and other forms of psychological torture. Some of the 'patients', picked because they could not 'fight back', died or committed suicide.

MK-Ultra ran for 23 years, officially. There had been other mind-control programmes before it, notably Project Artichoke, which, apparently, took its name from the favourite vegetable of Allen Dulles, the CIA director. In a 1952 memo, its purpose was: 'Can we get control of an individual to the point where he will do our bidding against his will and even against fundamental laws of nature, such as self-preservation?'

In ideological wars from the Cold War to Vietnam and the ongoing 'War on Terror', America has always been pushed to explore the weird, the esoteric and the downright dangerous because it can't win by traditional methods: by killing more. So as well as changing the minds of the soldiers themselves, it has needed to change the minds of their adversaries.

A less well-known psychological operation was Project Wandering Soul. It was used in the Vietnam War and had been developed to capitalise on the Viet Cong superstition that if one of their fallen fighters was not buried in his homeland then his spirit would return and indulge in much wandering, wailing and gnashing of teeth. So to give the enemy the wobbles, American PsyOps made tapes of this wailing and gnashing of teeth, with lost souls crying out, 'I'm in Hell. *Hell.* It really wasn't worth it. Give up, go home, put down your guns…' Did it work? Well, not really. On its first play in 1968, the Viet Cong were panicked and started to make a run for it, thus exposing their position to US troops, who quickly started firing. And then fire was returned. They realised it was a ruse after that.

The man who revealed Project Wandering Soul to the world was Herb Friedman, via his PsyWarrior blog. Now retired, he spent 26 years in the US military, much of them as a PsyOps specialist. I got in touch with Herb because I reckoned I had unwittingly stumbled across a possible new US mind-control programme. It didn't involve torture or drugs or anything remotely nasty.

A wizened old Swedish sports psychologist had set up a mental training school in 2015 in one of the most dangerous places on Earth. In Fallujah, Iraq, where the black flag of jihadi lunatics Islamic State once flew, Lars-Eric Uneståhl was 'changing the minds' of the locals. He told them not to worry about the crazed killers on their doorstep. All they had to do was 'go to their happy place'.

One didn't need to be an expert in world affairs to know that a project backed by the Iraqi government was, most likely, also backed by Washington. Still, I thought I'd better check with Herb. I had made contact with him right at the start of this story as I thought he would know about what the Russians were up to with their sports programme. Herb came across as a little irritated on email and he refused my request to arrange a telephone call. 'Sorry, [sport] is not a field I ever paid much attention to,' he told me, going on to explain that during his PsyOps days, when he had made contact with Russians, the CIA spooks would turn up in his house 'like two little green apples' and open his mail, warning him that he was 'now in touch with an enemy of the United States'.

But it wasn't strictly true that Herb didn't know anything about sport. He claimed that, in 1972, the US had deployed a PsyOp in the world championship chess match between Bobby Fischer, the American, and Russian Boris Spassky. It was billed as a Cold War clash and was held in Reykjavik, Iceland. The US 'did a Zoukhar', according to Herb. They absolutely had to have their man win the match because their culture and their ideology had to be shown to be superior to the Russians'.

'They just knew we were using voodoo on Spassky,' Herb wrote. I replied almost immediately, excited at the prospect of a Cold War scoop that had never been reported before. But Herb was too smart to spill. Instead, he started to toy with me. He gave me snippets of the story but not the whole plot. There had been, he claimed, a 'distant analysis of Spassky' to find weak spots and target areas. Fischer, meanwhile, was a 'mama's boy that hated his mother, a self-hating Jew anti-Semite and completely paranoid. What a great project.'

When I pressed him to give me more details, he just replied, 'None of this ever happened ... these days I just gossip but keep it light and deniable.'

Fischer won the match and was considered to be the greatest chess player ever. He was also a fugitive of the US after ignoring executive orders to not play a match in war-torn Yugoslavia. Fischer was discredited and disgraced and spent much of his later life country-hopping to avoid deportation to the US, spouting anti-Semitic and anti-American views. Coincidentally (another one) he was the brother-in-law of Russell Targ, the CIA remote viewer. I had mailed Russell to ask him what he thought about Herb's claims, but he never replied. That was odd, too, because he had always been quick to write back.

Herb hadn't finished with me yet, though. Perhaps he had launched his own Project Wandering Soul on me. Or he just fancied having some fun at the expense of the English journalist. After another flurry of questions one evening, he seemed to think that I had been asking too many. He suggested *I* was being watched. 'You are getting quite well known,' he told me. 'There will be black helicopters over your place this weekend.' I laughed it off. I doubted they came this far over the pond. But he did (sort of) answer my questions about the mental training programme in Iraq, although I suspected he knew far more than he was letting on. And, of course, he had to offer a warning.

'In general, when I get verbose they go after my friends. Would think it is an Iraqi programme, though it could well be supported by the US. We are moving Heaven and Earth to get ahead of Islamic State in the propaganda war, but so far everyone agrees they have stayed ahead of us.'

It was Mike Spino who had told me about Lars-Eric Uneståhl in the first place. 'He was the first ever sports psychologist,' Spino had said. 'An inspiration.' Mike set up a conference call between the three of us. Lars-Eric was chatty and he had a wonderful way of saying 'psychologist', putting letters in and taking them away so it sounded like 'psi-col-o-gits'. He talked for hours about his life working with athletes. He regaled me with a story about how a Swedish swimmer under his tutelage had meditated every day in the build-up to an Olympics, visualising his swim, stroke by stroke, and then looking up at the clock to see his time. When using visualisation, Lars-Eric said, it was vital to mentally rehearse every small detail. 'So when the race came he had raced it many times in his head,' Lars-Eric said. 'And when he looked at the clock it was the exact time he had practised.' He won gold.

Lars-Eric was not one for EEG readouts, complex blood tests or even convincing his athletes they were Darth Vader. He reckoned it was all way more simple than that. 'You have to teach the brain how to activate the right muscles and to relax the right ones,' he said. But for some it was inherent. Like Usain Bolt. 'When he is going to run he has an image of how he flows over the track,' he said. 'His images of running will make the brain effect the right muscles to be activated and the antagonist muscles to relax. Without thinking.'

It was quite a leap from swimmers visualising a winning time or sprinters focusing on flowing over the track to helping Iraqis combat the threat of IS, though. I asked him about Fallujah. But he didn't seem to hear me.

'Then, in '76 at the Olympics I was the only sports psi-col-o-gits—'

Mike interrupted. And shouted, for some reason, perhaps channelling his 'Finishing Clerk' uncle all those years ago: 'YOUR WORK IN FA-LOOO-JA! HE'S ASKING YOU ABOUT YOUR WORK IN FA-LOOO-JA!'

'Oh yes, of course,' Lars-Eric replied.

It was called Mental Training for Peace. In 2007 Lars-Eric had decided he wanted to create a better world. And the only way for that to happen was if we could all find inner peace. This would transfer to 'external peace'. Iraq was a pretty challenging place to implement it. Fallujah had only just been liberated from IS when Lars-Eric arrived, promising his 'basic fear and anxiety programme'. I thought they might need the deluxe version. With almost humorous understatement, Lars-Eric told me how he helped Fallujah residents cope with the daily threat of death.

'I ask them, "How many of you want to have more personal problems?" No one will raise their hand. Then I say, "How many would like to do sudoku?" Everyone. So what is the problem? So I say the problem is the task that has to be solved. What happens after solving sudoku? It feels good? Yes. They have grown more, they have greater ability to grow as a person. There are different ways of taking down fear.'

Yes, I had to read it back several times, too. I began to wonder if Lars-Eric had been backed by the Americans, whether they might worry this was money well spent. It seemed a stretch to reckon that, faced with the prospect of being beheaded by a knife-wielding psychopath or blown up by roadside bombs, the Iraqis would find the mindset to resist by comparing the problem to a maths puzzle. I couldn't let him get away with that: 'But isn't that very difficult to teach, because you are dealing with the ultimate fear? Death?'

'Yes,' he said. 'A [stressful] situation in Fallujah is *all the time*. If you get control over your reactions you will never experience negative stress. We need positive stress reactions in life.'

'What positive images can you give when there is a very powerful negative image of the black flag of Islamic State nearby?'

'We teach them to focus on the strong positive emotion in it. For instance, they put down 20 different things that make you happy. Family, birds in the forest and so on. Then they train to focus on things during the day which give a good feeling to the mind and body.'

Who knew? Family and birds in the forest. Think about those things and not only can you win Olympic gold but you can have the mental fortitude to keep IS at bay. I thought Lars-Eric was one of the most bonkers of all the people I had met. But, good for him. He was trying to change the world. Just as Esalen had promised to do all those years before.

He brought a neat end to the dark times, I thought. Yes, things had got a little murky, confusing and troubling with the military intervention into the quest for the superhuman sports star, but Lars-Eric had brought a little bit of light back. Sure, it was a crazy flickering flame dancing all on its own in a tunnel where at the other end there were people who were going to kill you, but you couldn't criticise him for giving it a go. For nearly half a century his methods had paid off in sport and so he thought there was a higher calling. It might even work. And he sure wasn't the first to enter a war zone with more mysterious methods. The First Earth Battalion were armed with indigenous flowers and floaty music. Lars-Eric had a maths puzzle and a pencil.

I never found out whether Lars-Eric was an agent of American desperation to 'change the minds' of their enemies. When I emailed to ask him if he had been backed by Washington or even received assistance from the US military when in Iraq, he didn't reply. But I didn't mind. It was time to move on from the dark government forces and focus on something joyful again. Something great.

19

THE GREATEST

One night in bed, my wife asked how the search was going. So I told her about Pete. About the Philadelphia project, brainwashing, levitation, being a cosmic channel. All that stuff.

'And what did he say when you asked him about those *things*?'

I looked at her askance. Of course I didn't ask him! I was building our relationship, I told her. Michael Gervais had taught me that. If you're on a first date with someone, you don't go in with the big questions early on, do you? 'Do you want marriage? Kids?' There would be no second date. Had I been gung-ho, Pete would have ended our relationship as quickly as the click of the receiver on the telephone.

She raised a withering lone eyebrow.

'Are you obsessed with this Pete Collins?'

'It's *Carroll*, actually,' I harrumphed.

'I think you might be,' she said, sniggering.

'NO! … *NO!* … No, I'm not. He's an important person in the story, that's all. So, you know, I need to be thinking about him…' I winced at this.

'Oh my god, you *are* obsessed with him!'

'Look, I was hoping he might be the superhuman. Technically, he is. But he's probably not. It's a bit more subtle than that. OK?'

My wife looked a little disappointed. Having told her I was searching for a superhuman – and spent many weeks away from home, not to mention a few quid on travel – the cupboard was still bare. Maybe you are relieved. Perhaps you didn't want the superhuman to be a 5 foot 9 inch, 65-year-old white football coach with a penchant for beige chinos anyway. Maybe you wanted a toned, beautiful Adonis or Venus who ruled the world. Someone who didn't tell others how to do it, but did it themselves, out there in the ferocious heat of the battle, slowing down time, employing thought projection, blocking out pain, seeing into the future. For real.

I had thought the same. If Carroll really was the best result of the quest by Murphy and the Esalen Sports Center, was there somebody outside of that cosmic sphere of influence who could rival him? I still wanted someone who could down siddhis like a fat guy did beer on his porch in the West Coast sun. There were a few candidates. The way Michael Jordan could hover in the air to make the basket, Jack Nicklaus's ability to see the golf shot before he hit it, or Babe Ruth's eerie premonitions. You didn't know about that? The Bambino once allowed two strikes against the Chicago Cubs in the 1932 World Series, knowing that he would hit the next pitch for a home run. Well, so he said.

Each of these three was a great in his own right. But I couldn't find multiple examples of the siddhis for each of them. I'm not saying they couldn't do them all, it's just that I would've thought Mike Murphy would have collated them if they'd happened. They were, perhaps, restricted by their sports, lacking the dimensions to espouse the full range. Sure, they could have all been using extra-sensory perception to will the ball into the basket, hole or over the outfield – but how much use was it to place a thought in the head of an opponent, and when would they get the chance to do so? And they didn't really need to block out pain. So maybe they learned only what they needed to. Or maybe no one actually asked *that* question.

Right at the start of this journey, I thought the sport most suited for displaying the siddhis was boxing. Mike Murphy had agreed with me, which makes you wonder why he didn't write a boxing book. If one could master them all, one could conquer the world. The heavyweight boxing champion is, after all, regarded as something of a superman. Think about that. If you can beat your opponent before you get in the ring by getting inside his head, slow down time to dodge punches, speed it up to land more and feel no pain, then you are unbeatable. So I started looking at the greatest of all time himself. Muhammad Ali.

For Ali, a man who transcended sport, culture, race and religion, developing such skills would surely have been easy by comparison. In life – and death – he has often been labelled as a super. In 1978, DC Comics produced an edition that depicted Ali fighting Superman and winning. The *Vanity Fair* obituary following his death at the age of 74 in 2016 called him 'superhuman'. But these were empty sobriquets unless in the context of the actual pursuit of such perfection. When you research Ali, it is easy to reckon that he could do it all.

Take the video of his 1977 fight against Michael Dokes as just one example of him manipulating time. He dodged 21 punches in ten seconds. His earlier fights were littered with examples of Ali bending or ducking past flailing arms, as if he had pressed a slow-motion button. His hands and feet were lightning, too. He danced and everyone was watching. He threw punches like a blur.

And so they trotted out the term that would almost become a cliché when people spoke about Ali. Boxing historian Don Cogswell wrote that he 'presented such a speed disparity between contestants as to appear supernatural. Ali was operating in another time zone.'

Sports Illustrated magazine measured that hand speed in 1969. Ali's jab broke through a balsa board 16.5 inches away in 0.19 seconds. It covered the distance in four one-hundredths of a second, the same time as a blink of an eye. He was not a man you could take your eyes off.

Speed is just one piece of the pie for a fighter. He has to be able to take punishment. Ali displayed extraordinary powers here, too. Joe Frazier, the brutal heavyweight, described it best: 'Lordy, Lordy, I hit him with punches that would have brought down the walls of a city.' Ferdie Pacheco, his fight doctor for 17 years, spoke in awe about how he could not be hurt. In Mike Murphy's library of extraordinary feats, he had a quote from Pacheco: 'Take his ability to take body shots. Why do his ribs not break when he allows someone like George Foreman to pound him? I don't know why, but they don't … And take his facial tissue. He's hardly ever marked.'

Pacheco would go on to have a successful career as an artist, boxing commentator, author, screenwriter, talk-show host, movie critic, actor, speaker, pharmacist and, of course, doctor. Sadly, a stroke had slowed down someone once known as the Renaissance Man, and when we spoke from his home in Miami, his voice was gravelly before trailing off to a whisper. His mind, however, was still sharp enough not to suffer fools. 'You're lucky I spoke to you,' he growled. 'I don't normally take these calls about *him*. I haven't taken a call for a *loooong* time. But yours interested me.'

My question was a simple one. I wanted to know whether Ali had taught himself how to change time or see the future or feel nothing.

'I must tell you something,' Pacheco said. 'This'll be a short interview, 'cos I barely did anything with him. He barely got sick, hurt – anything. If he got a cold it was gone in a day or two. It was God-given.'

'Had he trained his mind to block it out, Ferdie?'

'He was trained from birth. He had the mindset [that said] he can't lose. That's what it was. He was born that way. "Nobody's gonna beat me."'

'But how did he deal with it?'

'He ignored it. He never came back and said, "That hurt." Nothing. He was just an incredible animal when he came to taking pain. That's all there was to it.'

I quoted to him a section from Mike Murphy's research into people who could destabilise opponents by projection or suggestibility, like the samurai who, set upon by wolves, merely stared straight ahead with a 'countenance so stable and potentially explosive' that the animals were frozen in their tracks. 'Episodes,' I read seriously, 'mention men lying in ambush only to confront a victim who, simply by gazing at them, terrorised them so effectively that they were immobilised.'

'I wish you would quit quoting books to me,' snarled Ferdie. 'Books about boxing are foolish 'cos they're written by people who don't know anything about boxing.'

'OK. What about out-psyching opponents?'

'He just out-thought everybody. He didn't even have to try. He just did it. That was the way it was. It was always an easy time for him. I don't think it was premeditated, it was just him. He won fights, almost every one, before the first punch.'

'Was he superhuman?'

'Oh, yeah. Every once in a while, *something* happens in life and Ali's fights, each of them were *something* ... Now, that's it, my dear, good luck.' Click.

If it wasn't premeditated, it was arguably more impressive. Regardless of what Ferdie thought, however, it was hard not to believe that Ali knew what he was doing when he brought these powers to bear in arguably his most famous fight, the Rumble in the Jungle, against the beast that was George Foreman in Kinshasa, Zaire, in 1974. Faced with a terrifying opponent – the unbeaten Foreman had won 37 of his 40 fights by knockout – there were experts who genuinely feared that an ageing Ali would be killed. Norman Mailer, the most highly regarded of them all, insisted that Ali was scared.

But Ali was the samurai in the woods with the wolves closing in. Or, in his words, and perhaps this was where Glen Albaugh, Pete Carroll's university lecturer, got it from: 'He's the bull, *I am the matador.*' He led an orchestrated campaign of psychological pressure on Foreman. It was more than the witty barbs that had earned him the nickname 'the Louisville Lip'. His penchant for predicting the future had helped in that regard. Alex Poinsett wrote in *Ebony* magazine in 1963 that his 'uncanny knack of predicting the exact knockout round for ten of the 16 professional opponents he has faced smacks of a voodoo witch doctor which sticks psychological shafts in his victims'.

In Zaire, not only did he try to get inside Foreman's head, he exhorted Zaireans to do the same by casting himself as the returning African hero while Foreman was the white man's stooge. Wherever Foreman went, he could hear the chant 'Ali *bomaye*! Ali *bomaye*! Ali *bomaye*!' It meant 'Ali kill him!' When he entered the arena, it shook the foundations. That must have been terrifying.

It was thought projection on a large scale. Admittedly, Foreman did little to help his cause. He arrived in Kinshasa with his faithful German shepherd dog, the same breed the Belgians had used to keep the locals in check during a brutal colonisation.

The build-up to the fight was bizarre and disturbing – as you would expect, in a country run by President Mobutu, a crazed dictator. Mobutu was not a shy chap. He had changed his name to Mobutu Sese Seko Nkuku Ngbendu Wa Za Banga. Or, to you and me, 'The all powerful warrior who, because of his endurance and inflexible will to win, goes from conquest to conquest leaving fire in his wake.' He demanded TV news to begin every night with a scene of him descending from the clouds because he believed he was a demigod. Naturally, Mobutu was not a man to cross.

Norman Mailer said that under the ring, the floor was stained with blood from the stadium's former use for gladiatorial battles. Below the stands, Mobutu had imprisoned a thousand known criminals, picking out a hundred, taking them away and killing them because he didn't want the descending media hordes to experience any crime that would cast the country in a negative light. Word soon got around to the rest. He could have taught Ali a thing or two about mind control. Maybe he did.

George Plimpton, the American writer who attended the fight, claimed that Ali had visited Mobutu's witch doctor for assistance to beat Foreman. They were called '*féticheurs*'. 'Everyone had a witch doctor in West Africa,' Plimpton said. 'You'd go to one like you would a dentist.' The witch doctor told Ali that a 'woman with trembling hands' would somehow get to Foreman. A 'succubus', Plimpton said.

That Ali was prepared to consider voodoo games was an interesting insight into a not often reported side to his character. He was, actually, a bit weird. He had claimed to have seen a massive UFO mothership, and that he was being watched by extraterrestrials. A UFO expert and author, Tim Green Beckley, interviewed him extensively for a book about celebrity experiences with UFOs and little green men. 'Of all the famous folks I've spent time with discussing theories about extraterrestrial civilisations and life in outer space, no one seems to know more about the subject,' Beckley wrote in his 2015 book (deep breath), *Amazing Flying Saucer Experiences of Celebrities, Rock Stars and the Rich and Famous.* Beckley added that Ali told him he'd had '16 sightings' and they had 'been watching him for some time'. One of those had occurred in the months 'getting ready to do battle with Foreman' at his training camp high in the Pocono Mountains at Deer Lake, Pennsylvania.

It didn't seem as though Ali needed any extraterrestrial help in Kinshasa. He deployed psychological tricks as soon as the first bell rang, deliberately throwing the first punch to unsettle Foreman. He then proceeded to unleash right-hand leads at Foreman, something no fighter had had the guts, or stupidity, to do in two years against him. Why? Because professional fighters can see it coming from a mile away and it leaves them hugely vulnerable to a left hook. 'It was crazy,' Mailer said. 'It was an insult. Because it suggests he's slow enough that you can hit him with it.'

The 'projection and suggestibility' continued. At the start of the second round, Ali roused the crowd. 'Ali *bomaye!*' This riled Foreman. And he rained blows down on Ali's head and body. During the lulls, Ali would peek out from behind his gloves and taunt his assailant: 'George, you disappoint me, you're not hitting as hard as I thought you would … George, you're not breaking popcorn.'

From there on, it was a pain game. Ali took a beating but kept asking for more. As Ferdie Pacheco said, he 'ignored' it. The sort of psychic self-regulation that the Russians had held in such esteem. More colloquially in a boxing context, it became infamous as Ali's rope-a-dope tactic because he lay back on the ropes, as if he were in a hammock, and waited for Foreman to punch himself to the point of exhaustion.

And then, in the eighth round, Ali's supernatural speed returned. He countered with a devastatingly fast combination, culminating in a right that, if you blinked, you would have missed. Foreman certainly did. Plimpton turned to Mailer and said, 'The succubus has got him!' Years later, Foreman said, 'He surprised me with this lightning speed that he wasn't supposed to have at his age.' It is said that Ali was teetering on the edge of defeat before he landed those blows. But that was nothing unusual. Ali often looked beat. Against Joe Frazier, the second time the pair had met, Ali turned the bout on its head with such extraordinary skill that a biographer, José Torres, wrote, 'He is using those mysterious forces. I can't explain it any other way.' Torres was a former boxer himself, so it was not hyperbole from a hack penning an emotive line.

So Ali could do it all. And he also appeared to be open to the esoteric, given his UFO links. What seemed to confirm the latter was his conversion to the Sufi version of Islam. Sufism is the mystical arm of Islam, whose preachers are often considered to have psychic powers. Its followers believe in the 'perfectibility' of man. The superhumans or cosmic beings that Aurobindo talked about. And how do they achieve that? They meditate. They chant. And they do breathing exercises with the aim of entering into altered states of consciousness. If they're really hot at it, it is said that a link can be established to the spirit world.

I know what you're thinking. How had I suddenly become an expert in obscure religious derivatives? I hadn't. I had read one of

Mike Murphy's occult novels in which a Soviet Sufi introduces his intrepid American friend (clearly Murphy) to the faith. Together they explore a 'hyperdimensional space' that can 'support the power of angels' who can move back and forth from this world to the next like UFOs. And then I just happened to read an article about Ali's move away from religion to spirituality – Sufism. Hello, I thought, this is interesting.

Now, it could be argued that the examples of the siddhis Ali displayed in his fighting career were coincidence. Or they could be filed under the less than robust, as any lawyer might tell you, heading of 'circumstantial'. It might also be pertinent to recognise that with someone as globally revered as Ali, the myth overtakes the man quicker than one of his punches. It could be coined 'the illusion of winning'. Whatever he did was considered 'otherwordly' or 'superhuman' because the like of it had never been seen before. 'To hell with that,' I said, 'I'm calling Mike,' taking a mighty slurp of the Kool-Aid as I dialled. Yes, I was back on it, revelling in the light again after surviving the Dark Side. Like a twitch upon a thread, the cosmic force had given me a tug and I was returned to the church. It would be some swank, I thought, if I could prove that Ali had been the living, breathing 'gnostic being' that had so tantalised the movement and, ultimately, me.

'Ali!' I blustered down the phone, 'he could do it all…'

'He was *fabulous*,' Mike said. I let out an audible sigh of relief. Yes, I was right. I had found the super. I waited for Mike, in his lofty position as the godfather of the human potential movement, to reel off a story or two confirming that, yes, he thought so too, of the siddhis that he knew Ali had achieved, how he did it – and how he had trained himself in the art. Maybe he had visited Esalen. Maybe Mike himself had taught the great man. Ah ha, I could see the pair of them now, sitting crossed-legged, chanting and focusing on their chakra points. I seemed to be drifting off in a reverie, my mind had, finally, gone quiet because the quest was over. That music, the calming one from the Focus Band headset, seemed to be playing. But Mike was silent. Mike hadn't said *anything*. It was a needle-scratch-across-a-record moment. 'Er ... he was the first superhuman?' I posited.

'I wouldn't say that. We love him more now and he was glorious in so many ways.'

'But ... but ... Mike, he was a Sufi!'

'*Was* he?'

'Yes! And he could do it all! Slow down time, see the future, thought project, feel no pain,' my voice squeaked.

But Mike wasn't with me. He wasn't feeling it like I was. He had left me hanging. Instead, he just said, 'It was fun for him. It came naturally.'

I wasn't bloody having that. It wasn't fun. I didn't think it came naturally at all. Surely if I had learned anything, it was that this stuff could be sought out, taught or learned. But, alas, it was just a crazy dream. Ali had not visited Esalen. Mike had not met him. And he sure as hell didn't know – or actually seem to be that bothered – whether Ali had, in fact, been the personification of his life's work. It was slightly anticlimactic. I had gone from being pumped at the prospect of unveiling 'the Greatest' as a funky spiritualist who could exert mind control over his opponents to being, well, in a funk. This lasted a good few weeks. As my wife will attest. Then someone I had been trying to speak to since the very start picked up the phone.

To briefly continue the theme of disappointment, it is a slightly underwhelming moment when you contact the most famous psychic the world has ever known and he doesn't say, 'Hello, Ed, I've been expecting you.' But I figured Uri Geller was a busy man, juggling all manner of cosmic forces and telepathic lines of communication. Besides, Jon Ronson, the author of *The Men Who Stare at Goats*, had reckoned Uri was back working for military intelligence, reprising his role as a CIA man who could see into the future or across oceans, just like he did when he worked alongside the wild-haired, racehorse-loving and remote-viewing Russell Targ.

When Uri was 12 years old, the local football coach came to stay at the hotel his mother's partner ran in Nicosia, Cyprus. It was the same *pension* where an agent of Mossad, Israel's secret service, had also stayed and was wowed – unnerved – by the kid's ability to bend spoons and read his mind. 'I know you're an Israeli spy,' Uri had told him one day. This cover-blowing moment put Geller on a career path that would see his abilities tested by the CIA as they searched for their answer to the Soviet psychics who were stopping the hearts of frogs.

The football coach, who was Hungarian, saw Geller bend a spoon one morning over breakfast. For some unfathomable reason, he thought this kid could help his team. They were bottom of the league (he was really clutching at straws by this point). The man demanded that Geller inspire his players. So every week the boy would go into the locker room and shout and bawl at the players to score more goals, win more matches. He told them to imagine winning. That team, Geller says, went from the bottom to the top. They won the championship. Geller claims to have a picture of himself running around the pitch with the captain, holding the cup.

Fast-forward to the summer of 1996. At Wembley Stadium, the English soccer team are playing their fierce rivals, Scotland, in a European Championship match. Scotland have a penalty kick. High above the stadium is a helicopter. Inside it is Uri. He's not flying the thing. He's got a more important job than that. He is trying to move the ball with the power of his mind. Uri is wearing an England football strip. This is so he can connect to the energy of the players and the crowd. He is trying to help England win.

With the ball placed on the penalty spot, Uri focuses on trying to move the ball to confuse the player taking the shot. 'One ... two ... three ... *move*!' he says as Gary McAllister runs up. And just as McAllister is about to strike it, the ball wobbles and rolls two inches to the right. The shot is saved and England go on to win.

Apparently, Uri felt guilty about that. It was a trick too far – he'd played with a nation's emotions. Soccer in Scotland is as important as haggis, whisky and any other stereotype you wish to conjure. McAllister, he said, was an unfair victim of his superpower CIA training.

Given all this, Uri was an important person to talk to for this story. I sent him ten emails in a month via his website. I never expected him to reply, telling me he'd talk. When he answered my call, he was interested to hear about my research. 'Listen,' he said, 'you're talking to a believer.' But before we could begin he said he had another call coming through. Could I call him back? I did, but Uri suddenly sounded very grave. 'I have to go to Washington.' It seemed as though he wanted me to think that the spooks needed him for another urgent secret psychic spying mission.

A few weeks later, I got hold of him again. He wouldn't tell me what he had been doing in Washington. But he would talk about how he had been in demand from athletes and sports teams ever since that day high above Wembley Stadium (although we have to take his word he was actually up there, in his chopper).

Well, sort of. He would dangle a carrot and then whip it away. As if it were some sort of game. He told me that he had been approached to assist England in winning the match against Scotland but then gave me nothing further.

'Someone in the England team, Uri?'

'I was approached and I can't reveal by whom but I was asked to help.'

'The coach?'

'I cannot confirm or deny.'

'Someone within the England Football Association?'

'No comment on that.'

I wondered if he sensed my frustration. Perhaps I should try to butter him up? Would he see that coming, too? 'What other sports stars have you worked with, Uri? You would have given guys a great edge?'

'Exactly,' he said. 'Let me tell you, I have worked with the biggest names in soccer. And if I told you it would shock you. I've met the greatest soccer players but can't divulge.'

'Give us a clue?'

'They were Brazilian. They were German. They were Spanish. They were English … they were … er, they were the main countries that came to me. Three times a Portuguese player.'

'Is he still playing?'

'Retired eight years ago.'

'An international?'

'Yeah, world class.'

This was a game that could go on for a while. A sort of psychic version of hangman. Uri seemed to be having far more fun with it than I was.

'Other times I have worked with tennis players, Formula 1 drivers, boxers. It's always about motivation, a positive mental attitude, so I definitely believe that people in such jobs no doubt used ESP in addition to conventional skills.'

This time I wasn't about to start trying to guess who he was talking about. I knew I wouldn't get anywhere. 'Were they doing this wittingly, though, Uri?'

'Explain yourself.'

'Well, *did they know what they were doing*?'

Then he told me something quite sensational. It was another record-scratch moment.

'Very good question. All the sports people that I met, including Muhammad Ali, who I *trained*—'

What did he say? Ali? He trained him? Uri was still talking. But I just heard only the voice in my head. Did he just say he trained Muhammad Ali? 'Sorry, Uri, did you just say you trained Muhammad Ali?'

'Definitely. He knew that he had a gift. He was also into magic, the paranormal, UFOs, so no doubt he used this gift knowingly. Then there are those who are very superstitious. It's like an in-built excuse to use their powers, so good luck or superstition makes them excel, but they are actually using their own mind power. Most brilliant sports people don't know they are using a natural psychic instinct.'

Yeah, yeah, Uri. Let's get back to Ali.

'When did you first meet him?' I asked, excitedly. 'He was the greatest, and when I started to look at this subject he displayed all the characteristics, you know?'

'Oh, it was 1977 at his New Jersey training camp … I have a picture of him, which I give you permission to use,' Uri said. 'He already told me that he believed he had powers. He didn't call them supernatural but he called them "the powers of his mind". He knew about consciousness. When I met him this was not new to him, the spoon-bending was new, and when I demonstrated, he was amazed. When we did telepathy and ESP, he was amazed. That gave him a fortification – he knew when he saw these demonstrations in front of his eyes that he probably had his own power. Most people in leading roles, prime ministers, boxers [not sure these two are on a level playing field, but I let it go] – the minute I bend a spoon for them they grab one and try to do it themselves.'

Uri had spoken about his admiration for Ali before. He said that he believed he was superhuman, that Ali was the living embodiment of the paranormal powers and they had, in fact, contributed to the terrible Parkinson's disease that had, eventually, played a part in ending his life. His 'psychic powers', like the ability to feel no pain, might have meant he fought more fights than he should have. But never before had Uri revealed that he actually *taught* Ali how to use the siddhis. 'What examples of ESP did you do with Ali?'

'I trained him how to look into the eyes of his opponent. How to subconsciously, with telepathy and ESP, knock him out, visualise himself winning. Visualisation is a major tool which is attached to mind power, and those are the elements I trained in him and he just learned how to do it.'

'How long for?'

'I used to go for … I can't exactly remember, so it was the seventies. I was in New York, so not a big deal for me to drive out to his training camp.'

'You know, looking into the eyes of an opponent is thought projection?'

'Yes, or instilling fear through ESP or empowering your … you are psyching yourself up to beat your opponent. Thought transference or extra-sensory energy … that's what you're transferring.'

I mentioned Mike Murphy. Uri had visited Esalen with the astronaut Edgar Mitchell in the seventies and he remembered Mike. 'My god, is he still alive?' Uri said.

'Funny,' I said. 'I used to wonder the same.'

*

'*Uri Geller!*' I shouted, triumphantly, '*trained Muhammad Ali? Did you know?*'

'Oh my god,' Mike squeaked. Then he paused. 'Is he still alive? How old is he now?'

'Dunno, maybe early seventies,' I said, annoyed that it was this he chose to focus on. 'Listen, he trained Ali, to do whammies, to do the siddhis like they were a four-course meal, or something.'

'Well, I never heard of it … and I don't believe it, actually. And now Ali's dead, Uri can claim anything. But there's no doubt Ali could get into people's minds.'

'Yes, but—'

'If Uri was in on the act … I tell you who would have known about it. George Plimpton and Norman Mailer – very famous writers. They were at the Foreman fight in Zaire and they were into the woo-woo stuff and whammies, they really were, but *they* never mentioned it.'

'But they *did* mention it, Mike…'

Mike wasn't with me. At all. He wasn't feeling it like I was. He had left me hanging. Again. And I wasn't entirely sure why. So I emailed Adam Brucker, the man who ran the Shivas Irons Society. Why had Mike suddenly been so dismissive of my 'quest' to find the superhuman athlete?

'No idea what he *really* thinks,' Brucker replied. 'Honestly, [it] could go either way, which is a big part of what makes him a fascinating guy in my mind.' And he signed off with a smiley face.

I emailed straight back. Was it possible that Murphy, then, was just having a joke at everybody's expense?

'I think he's a serious guy with a legitimate record of accomplishments,' Adam wrote, 'who's nonetheless largely defined by his early, sometimes pretty silly, work that he's moved on from and he's just tired of people asking him about it at the expense of what he perceives as the more substantial stuff at this point. I certainly did it to him the first time we met. More of a defense/survival mechanism for him that I don't necessarily think he's doing to entertain himself. But, who knows…?'

20

WHAMMY TIME

When on that call to Mike Murphy, I also told him I thought what Pete Carroll had done was produce a 'fertile ground for siddhis to be achieved as a happy by-product of relaxed and focused athletes'. He really liked that. He didn't shoot me down all the time. 'Oh, very good, Ed, that's it,' he said. 'You've got it right there.'

I had my own 'happy by-product' from this book too. My otherwise cynical wife began to speak as if she were some sort of cosmic being. 'Of course, my dad's dad was a psychic so I think it's skipped a generation.' Then came the rundowns of dreams she had and what they meant just because, once, one came true. She had dreamed her friend had left a boyfriend for someone she met in America. It didn't matter that the relationship had been stinking the place out for years and she travelled to the US weekly.

'Ah, well,' I said. 'Mike would say that all manner of different aspects of ourselves can flower or blossom into the supernormal.'

By this point, I had been researching this book for almost two years. In our house, I like to think I had become a sort of guru mystic. Our nightly conversations had often been dominated by the 'out there' people I had spoken to that afternoon or the bizarre tales I had been told. It was, as I had said before, a bit like being part of a cult. Like a form of brainwashing. Had my wife succumbed too, by a process of osmosis? For the sake of my marriage I should probably point out she was heavily pregnant: her mind perhaps more malleable than usual.

Whatever the reason, towards the end, we were almost egging each other on. So much so that we both agreed to try hypnobirthing for the arrival of our second child. When the woman turned up at our house to teach the course, I found I could finish her sentences. It was all quiet mind, breathing, visualisation. I'd learned from the best in American sport how to deliver success, my dear, so delivering a baby would not be a problem.

It turned out my wife did have some sort of power. The trance she slipped into was so engulfing that *she didn't even realise she was in full-blown labour.* Our daughter popped out in the living room two hours after my wife had said, 'I'm feeling some twinges.' This was not planned. We had not gone so far on our cosmic journey as to reckon we could put on whale music, light some jostlicks and do it in front of the television. We were very much supposed to go to the hospital. Not least because of complications the first time. So dealing with the panic, the terror, the blood and the 'whystheambulancetakingsolong?!' by ourselves was not something I recommend.

She now does yoga every Saturday morning. This prompts my elder daughter (the one who kept interrupting important Skype calls with her wailing) to ask, 'Why don't you do yo-go, Daddy?'

'Because Daddy doesn't have the time.'

And I didn't. The search continued. And as I approached the end of this story, I realised there was no such thing as an end. Would I ever watch sport again without wondering whether the tennis player was not really looking at the ball? Was the 800-metre runner thinking he was a latter-day saint? Or was the golfer, about to putt for the Open, buoyed by his superhero cape flapping in the wind?

In the 2016 football season, Murphy and Glen had been up to some funky stuff of their own with their friend Larry Meredith, a former University of the Pacific religious studies professor who married Pete and his wife, Glena.

It was Glen himself who had told me about it. One morning an email arrived from him, championing 'the power of triangulation'. It showed a triangle with Murphy's name at the top under the header 'Spirit Force' and then Glen and Larry in the bottom two corners responsible for 'Imagination' and 'Passion' respectively. Inside the triangle was the label 'Vortex', and the picture of a twister. 'Pete came up with that,' Glen said. 'The swirling power of the vortex.'

I had to immediately look up what 'triangulation' meant. Wikipedia suggested this:

> Triangulation is a manipulation tactic where one person will not communicate directly with another person, instead using a third person to relay communication to the second, thus form-ing a triangle. It is also a form of splitting in which one person manipulates a relationship between two parties by controlling communication between them.
>
> Triangulation may manifest itself as a manipulative device to engineer rivalry between two people, known as divide and conquer or playing one (person) against another.

A whammy then. And there was me thinking Mike had given it up. On game day you could find him, Glen and Larry sitting down at the exact same time and trying to put a curse on the team the Seattle Seahawks were playing. The three of them had been at it for years, trying to influence San Francisco 49ers matches for their friend Bill Walsh, who was coach for 11 years. It looked as though it had worked. Walsh won three Super Bowls. It had been working for the Seahawks, too, although not in the season that I had met Mike, Glen and Pete. The Seahawks would end up beaten in the play-offs. The following year, they didn't qualify – the first time that had happened since 2011–12. It was small-margin stuff. They lost two matches after last-play field goal attempts were off target. Had they won one of those, they would have made it, and with a first-round bye.

There had been other issues. The injury list had been, reportedly, the worst in ten seasons. This, coupled with the Super Bowl-winning roster getting older, had made for a combination that even a cosmic channel couldn't do anything about. Mind you, there were suggestions from the in-the-know ranks of sports writers I spoke to who cover their games that senior members had become weary of Pete's 'voice and style'. Richard Sherman, the cornerback who had gushed early in Pete's Seahawk days that 'we were his guys', wasn't so enamoured. He suggested things had got stale and Pete's ways were more suited to college football. Ouch. There were also examples of Seahawks players swearing in interviews – a big Seahawk-way no-no – and clashing with opposition fans. Two coaches had also been replaced. So Pete was at a crossroads. Considering he was always about the journey rather than the destination, it seemed that some guys had, presumably, reached the end of the road. Pete wanted to mould a new, unheralded group with his philosophy. Perhaps Sherman was right. That's what he needs to make his philosophy work. The wizened pros at the New York Jets and the New England Patriots didn't fully buy into his way.

But they did at USC, where impressionable kids were desperate to get on in the game. Likewise, when Pete turned up at Seattle he had total control over the players he brought in. It was also possible that, like those players, Pete's method had a shelf life. Could he do it again with a whole new breed? He sure as hell would try. He was as gung-ho and effervescent as ever about the way he did things.

In true compassionate and diverse style, the Seahawks and Pete Carroll caused a sensation when in the April 2018 draft they signed the NFL's first ever one-handed player. Shaquem Griffin had his left hand amputated when he was four, having been born with amniotic band syndrome, which prevented his fingers from forming properly. But this was no sop. At 22 Griffin was extraordinary. He beat the ten-year record for the 40-yard dash for a linebacker. He bench-pressed 225 pounds 20 times using a prosthetic hand. His displays at the University of Central Florida, specialising in causing fumbles and turnovers, were exemplary. Maybe Pete had finally found a superhuman – in the colloquial sense, of course. Maybe, in time, Griffin will join him on a magic carpet.

Pete, all glassy-eyed, said his interview with Griffin had 'moved him'. He talked about an 'extraordinary connection' and his 'love and heart'. Griffin had the Seahawk patter, too: 'I want to show the entire world, no matter [if you have] one hand, two hands, if you're a ball player, you just play ball.'

Yep. The Seahawks would 'just play ball'. But they'd get that whammy working, too.

'There's obviously some power in it,' Glen told me on a Skype call, once he could hear me. He had started to struggle with his hearing and we had to have a chorus of 'testing, testing one-two-three' before we could begin.

'I'm sure Pete believes it. I'd send him a text saying, "We're ready." And he'd reply, "Good, let's get this thing swirling." Doesn't always equate with a win, but does equate to the power.'

I was no longer surprised that Pete would believe in something this strange. So what were the three of them thinking about, sitting down at the same time – 'you don't fool around with that' – and the same place every game day? Were they visualising a Seahawks win?'

'No,' Glen said. 'It's about playing at an epic level, playing at the highest level. Playing to win at every moment at the highest level.'

'Are Mike and Larry focusing on the same thing?'

'What was that?'

'Are Mike and Larry focusing on the same thing?'

'*WHAT?!*'

'What would Mike be focusing on?'

'Murphy?'

'Yes.'

'Well, the corner of the triangle is Spirit Force. He picked that out. He understands.'

'Spirit Force is energy from the occult?'

'You'll have to check with Murphy on that.'

When I asked Mike about it, he giggled and sounded a bit embarrassed. 'You've got to be careful,' he said, laughing again. 'This is the fans being, er, kinda crazy. I wouldn't take it seriously … this is just us doing whammies. I wouldn't put any stock in that.'

'But you're under the heading "Spirit Force"?'

'Occult backlash. Everything about that Candlestick Park story is true. No scientist would accept that, but there you go…'

It is more of a reserved whammy, though. There are no evil horns or awful cries and hollering. 'It's beams of love not cries of vengeance,' Murphy said. 'I've calmed down now, more of a quiet and contemplative whammy for our small community in the supernormal world.'

*

A few days later the ping of the email alert woke me up. 'Call,' it read. 'It's 3.41 in the morning, Pete!' The old problem of time and space. Pete sounded as though he had a cold. But he was at his most jovial, maybe because the pressure was not so intense in what was the close season. He actually seemed pleased to hear from me. What would follow would be our best talk, as he opened up and did not treat each question as if it might be a grenade that could go off at any time. I had contacted him because it was time to 'go big' and ask the questions that, had I posed them on our first or second call, would have meant there might not have been subsequent ones. I wanted to hear *him* tell *me* he was a bit weird. That he believed in something that most people would raise both eyebrows at. And not just in a football coach context. I think his approach to winning football games and dealing with athletes in these pages has been proven to be 'out of the box'. It wasn't a long conversation. 'Hey, Ed, how you doing? What's going on? What have we got? I've got 20 minutes.' So there was only one place to start – the Philadelphia Experiment.

'Did you prove it?' I asked.

'No,' he stifled a laugh. 'Where'd you get that from? That's entirely different stuff that happened along the way. Eastern philosophy is important, and that was the background which had to do with mindfulness and meditation and focus – those things have been woven into the fabric of what we talk about. More mindfulness and focus than anything.'

I thought he was getting a bit woolly on me again. So I pressed him on it. Was he still the type of person who would be captivated by a story like a warship disappearing? Would he still have the curiosity to try to find, to borrow his phrase from the Secret Tapes, 'the truth of real shit?'

'I'm more curious than ever,' he said. And with that tiny sentence I felt I had got through to him. The question, perhaps, had appealed to that competitive streak of his.

'Curiosity's never gone away,' he continued. 'I have come to understand that's a characteristic that's necessary for the kind of challenges I've faced: competing at the highest level, battling to be a true competitor and searching for an edge. That curiosity, that's where it comes from, and how you get better and [show] humility. You can always improve, you're never the finished product, and there are always ways to get advantages.'

Competition was at the root of everything. He seemed to back up my theory that him embracing the esoteric was a way of leaving no stone unturned to find a way of being more competitive.

'I am calm about it. I'm a competitor. When I realised that, a lot of things fell into place. That's where the curiosity comes from. And you're either competitive, or you're not, and trying to do things better than they have ever been done before. Competition is not about beating someone, it's about striving to be your best, and that governs everything.'

This took me back, again, to the Secret Tapes. Years ago, in his USC office, Pete had said, 'I've done a lot of weird stuff. I've had a lot of weird-encounter things. I've listened to some wild stuff that has really opened me up to figure out what's really important to me.' An example? Well, he mentioned Leonid Gissen again, the Russian sports psychologist who could tell people they had cancer, see through the skin to detect broken bones or teeth cavities. While talking about Leonid, he returned to the theme of the esoteric helping him to understand why some people were able to perform at a higher level.

'I tried to understand that better,' he said. 'I'm always trying to figure out extraordinary performances in sport and understand peak performance and what that's about. Mike Murphy is awesome at explaining that, being in the zone and how it is relevant in normal life. That has led to introductions to people who have experienced amazing things, and that just normalised it. Most people would think it's weird [being open to the esoteric] but I'd say it's part of life and part of the potential.'

This line piqued my interest: 'I'm always trying to figure out extraordinary performances in sport and understand peak performance and what that's about.' Now, the first time we spoke he said he didn't want to celebrate peak experiences or be an 'advocate'. Now here he was telling me almost the opposite. I took that as a sign that my idea about him playing fast and loose with what he really thought about superpowers was part of his grand plan. He was as much of a man of mystery as Mike Murphy.

It seemed like a good time to ask about my search for the superhuman.

'When I started this project,' I said, 'I wanted to find the person who could do it all. But, of course, having researched it for so long now, I've learned these things happen all the time, so I moderated my theory and I wanted to get your view on it. I think I wanted to prove you were the superhuman. But maybe you are super-*humane* in an environment or industry which is almost the opposite…'

'I think "superhuman" is a phrase I'd steer away from a little bit,' he said. 'But I understand what you're getting at, and I think there's room in a person's lifetime to really seek out helping others find their way. And you're able to transcend maybe normal relationships and take it to a place where ... because you can find what it takes to help others you can watch it occur, and it happens from love and that exchange of caring, and you care so much that you give whatever you can to help another person to accomplish that at a high level.'

For the first time, I felt Pete and I had really connected. We were on the same wavelength. So confident was I that I just blurted out other theories. Like this one: when he was reading *Golf in the Kingdom* in university and fascinated by Shivas Irons, had he ever thought, subconsciously, he might have been trying to be him? His answer, between laughs, was no. But it was the cue for Pete to start talking like he was that channel, that he was on his magic carpet. And I was right there. Next to him. Well, perhaps clinging on to the fringe.

'Thousands of times I've wanted to find the connection with the spirit and harmony of things around me – you know, to wind up with those kinds of visions and awareness. I know it because Mike wrote it and based it on an experience he had, and he's studied it all his life. He knows it's there, it's available, you know ... *it's there*. That was a great illustration of the experience and what it could be like. Shivas was all about it and it got reborn in the *Star Wars* movies with the Force, and it's out there, and then we let it go like a fantasy. There's a lot more to it, a lot more there. Mike has been a great influence with all he's done to unveil and reveal the existence of extraordinary experiences. It's there. We see it all the time. It's all around us. Everywhere. People are doing it all the time, sometimes in the simplest ways.'

'Do you remember George Leonard?' I asked. Leonard was Mike Murphy's whammy partner at Candlestick Park and an Esalen Sports Center cog. His teachings about the Force inspired George Lucas's *Star Wars*.

'Just listen to Yoda.'

'Did you know George Lucas took his ideas from George Leonard?'

'I did not know that! That's fascinating. I happened to know George Lucas a little bit. We did some things together and I'm not surprised.'

'I didn't know you knew him.'

'Well, he was a big USC guy, a big donor and he graduated from USC.'

'You had a similar ideology?'

'Yeah, for a long time. It was a thrill to meet him. Because I snuck onto his property one time in Marin County trying to find him and then I got thrown out. The Force was not working for me that day! OK, listen, let's wrap it up.'

'You've talked more freely than I thought. I was kinda prepared for you not to.'

'That's OK. It was terrific. I'll try to find a way for you to write another chapter this season.'

That last line sounded as though he was going to try to win the Super Bowl one more time just to help me out with book sales. Compassionate to the last. It was a decent leap from his curt reply to my question about who would win the title the second time we spoke when, if I'm being honest, I thought I'd never get Pete to talk freely. I felt mighty pleased with myself that I had managed to get him to admit to having faith in the things that folks like Glen Albaugh had always said he had. The football coach who believed in the Jedi. I almost immediately emailed

Mike Murphy to tell him how Pete had 'really opened up ... and spoke about the Force and Yoda'.

Mike had been preparing for another keynote speech at the next SEC festival. I had looked through the list of speakers, emailed to me by Mike Spino – 'It's a really great line-up ... hey, send me some pictures of your girls, I bet they're growing up fast. Will think of you often.' Dave Meggyesy, Rick Leskowitz, Scott Ford and Kristen Ulmer were all back again. And John Ruark, too, reminding anyone brave enough to give the Focus Band a go that it was not so long ago that we descended from chimps.

There were some new additions. Robert Rudelic had been added to the roster. When I saw his name, I emailed him to wonder if he wanted to use the slogan I came up with. *'Tap in the awesome* ... what do you think?' He replied immediately.

'Good morning. Thank you for the suggestion – we are running it in our heads and playing with ideas already. It may fit into our new project ... Believe in your true potential, I do!'

Rollin McCraty, the heart-math guy, was due to speak as well, in a workshop about beaming out the mojo. And I allowed myself a little chuckle at the notion of Robert and Rollin playing tennis together with Scott Ford urging them not to look at the ball. Actually, I spent a good few minutes visualising it, willing it to happen and putting that energy out there, into the cosmos, in the hope that it would be picked up and come true.

Robert: 'Oh, yeah! Awesome ... Yeah! ... Maybe hold the racket firmer, like this!'

Rollin: 'You're 100 per cent incoherent right now.'

Mike's theme would be 'expanding the zone' and getting people to talk about it. So he was interested to hear that Pete had not been shy: 'We don't have a common language, Ed. Sports is full of tough guys and they don't want to be called stupid or silly … well, you've heard me say this before.'

'Yeah, I have,' I said. 'But, hey, what we haven't talked about, you know, is that I almost thought that the superhuman might be Pete?'

'Hmm, I don't like the word "superhuman". I prefer the word "supernormal", because we're all human.'

'That's not so catchy, Mike.'

'That's true,' he said. 'But Pete's definitely superior … he's extraordinary … But, anyway, tell me, where are you now?'

'Er, well, I'm at home.'

'Now, is that a small town or village or what?'

'Well, it's a small village.'

'Oh, you lucky guy,' he said, voice squeaking again. 'Is it rolling-hills countryside or a pastoral scene, or what? I'm just living vicariously now, Ed. Are there cows? Sheep?'

I could just picture Mike's mischievous smile and flashing eyes. He was toying with me again, turning on the smoke machine and buffing the mirrors just as Mike Spino said he liked to do. And so we finished in much the same way as we had started. Him as mercurial as ever. Throughout my search for the superhuman I would turn a corner, convinced I'd found the answer, only to find another long road stretched out in front of me. From the outset, Mike had tantalised me with crumbs of 'the great untold story' about the Soviets – which he never really told – and so the mystique had been maintained throughout.

As for Mike himself, arguably no one had ever quite worked him out. Perhaps he wanted to keep everybody guessing. Did Shivas Irons exist or not? Did he ever work for the CIA or the KGB? Was he manipulating West and East solely for his Esalen values? It was, as Mike Spino had said in Fisherman's Wharf, 'all part of his mystery. You never know with Mike.' And you never really knew with Pete, either. I wonder where he got that from?

The air of mystery is important. Perhaps to pin down or label 'superhuman' is to disempower in some way. The same as if you overanalyse the magic. Like Dorothy pulling back the curtain hoping to reveal an all-powerful Wizard of Oz, only to be greeted by ordinariness, frailty. Like you. Like me. Far better to keep believing, to keep striving, searching.

*

In the 2018 season a young, untested and revamped Seahawks roster surprised everyone with a surge to the play-offs, winning six of their last seven league games. The season was compared to the 2012–13 campaign, before they won the Super Bowl. Pete was building something again. And he knew it. 'I love this team,' he said. 'I love where we're going and it's going to be more competitive than ever.'

EPILOGUE

ARE YOU A SUPERHUMAN?

If there is one thing to take from this book, it is that there are people who believe we all have the ability to do something extraordinary, no? So to give you a little bit of help, or inspiration, this is the definitive list of the siddhi states. You could be the next Pete Carroll. They were sourced, with his permission, from Mike Murphy's 1978 book *The Psychic Side of Sports*, which he co-authored with Rhea A. White. The quoted examples of siddhis are taken from that work, and from the stories I heard or read about when researching this book. The quotes below are Murphy speaking. How many can you already do?

Exceptional control of bodily processes, feelings, thoughts, imagination and other mental functions
In other words, psychic self-regulation. Controlling bodily processes like pulse, heart rate, breathing and other physiological processes. Can help to slow down time and produce a quiet mind.

Mastery of pain

An ability to block out pain was, seemingly, Muhammad Ali's great skill. But there are many examples of boxers fighting on with broken bones or football players 'playing through pain'.

The inner fire

Murphy has recorded instances where mountain climbers have summoned heat from within the body to withstand cold temperatures.

Ability to change shape, size and mass

Shape-shifting. As John Brodie, the 49ers quarterback, said, 'Five or six times … a running back got bigger once, then smaller.'

Invisibility

Murphy described this as 'ego loss, blending and harmonising with the elements'. So don't take it literally. Unless we're talking about Morihei Ueshiba, a Japanese martial artist, who is believed to have been filmed disappearing during a demonstration.

Auras, halos, the order of sanctity, emanations of extraordinary energy

If you are acting as a channel for 'other levels of the universe' then you might give off a bit of a glow. 'Manifesting the divine', qualified Murphy. Muhammad Ali, according to his assistant trainer, Bundini Brown, 'glowed in the dark'. Likewise, if you see these auras, as Dave Meggyesy did. Unless it was the acid.

Levitation

The sense of being lifted up by other energies, by the *ki* or *prana* of the Eastern disciplines or by God's grace. Some athletes, and dear Mike Spino would readily agree, have reported a feeling as if their feet are not touching the ground as they run.

Being in two places at once
Murphy termed this 'Bilocation'. This is an out-of-body experience. 'Or the power to impress others at a distance.' Like the goalkeeper in soccer who told Ken Ravizza that he watched himself playing in the game from atop the crossbar.

Ability to pass through solids, porousness
'Inner emptiness and freedom,' Murphy wrote. 'Loosening of ordinary psychic structures and boundaries. Mental and emotional fluidity.' The American military reckoned they could train psychic soldiers to walk through walls. Pelé said he felt as if he could pass through opposition players. Karate experts will tell you that they are not breaking boards or bricks but moving through them.

Incombustibility, fire immunity and impassability
Fire walking/sword swallowing. Most of these siddhis should come with a 'don't try this at home' warning. Murphy labelled these activities as 'incombustibility, fire immunity and impassability'.

Freedom from the ageing process
Anti-ageing. Eat your heart out, L'Oréal. Sports stars are playing for longer than ever, although it surely has to do with better diet, training and, indeed, practices like meditation and yoga. Murphy cites Percy Cerutty, the running coach who inspired Mike Spino, as an example here, calling it 'contact with the ever-born, ever-renewed', ironic for a man whose catchphrase was 'you'd be better dead!'

Precognition, prophecy, retro-cognition, time travel

This is psychic mobility, seeing the future or 'freedom from tyranny'. From Ali predicting what round he would win in to Meggyesy and Ryan Harris seeing the plays before they happened. Visualisation may qualify, too. The brain does not know what is real and what is imagined. So if you visualise achieving something for long enough, it will happen. So they say. Lars-Eric's swimmer is a good example. His name was Pär Arvidsson and he won gold in the 1980 Moscow Games men's 100 metre butterfly.

Telepathy

During his forays to Russia, Murphy ran an experiment with a psychic he met. They set up a call from San Francisco to Moscow with the psychic 'sending' telepathic thoughts, describing what he was looking at. The receiver correctly identified an elephant figurine. In sport, it is seen that an 'incredible power of communication often develops between members of a team'.

Energy transmission

From person to person. 'Psychological contagion; group inspiration,' Murphy said. An ability to inspire others in extraordinary ways. A big tick for Pete Carroll here.

Control of others through manipulation of their psychological processes

Thought projection. My favourite. This was Pete Brusso's party trick. He tried it with me over lunch. I sat quietly for a few minutes, cleared my mind and was to say the first thing that popped into my head. '*Bunny rabbit*,' I shouted. 'Yes. I was sending you an image of a bunny.' I was wowed. I told my wife this story, excitedly. 'You do realise he probably just agreed with you to make you both feel better?'

Power of mass hypnosis
The ability to cast a spell on an audience. Pete Carroll does well with this one, too. Muhammad Ali did this to almost every opponent, and he controlled the Kinshasa crowd against George Foreman.

Immunity to harm or danger
Bobby Orr, the Canadian hockey player, was said to have 'warded off opponents by staring at them' when his Bruins teams beat the Chicago Black Hawks in the 1970 Stanley Cup. Japanese samurai trained for this ability.

Heaviness and immovability
Football players and wrestlers have told Murphy that they seemed to be able to make themselves heavier at will.

Psychokinesis; moving objects at a distance through psychic power
'Mastery of the mind and emotions; willpower in general.' Uri Geller believes he moved the football from a helicopter above Wembley Stadium, London in 1996. Or here's that good line again from John Brodie: 'It has happened to me dozens of times. An intention carries a force.'

Extraordinary strength and endurance
This is not just a guy or gal who can run a marathon. The weirdest example is the lung-gom-pa runners in Tibet. They run in a psychic trance for consecutive days and nights. So deep is their state that to interrupt them could cause death.

Internal perception

Distance runners have reported 'seeing' their own insides during racing or training, such as bodily structures, organs, cells and molecules. 'Several distance runners have told us that they have caught glimpses ... some have seen capillaries break and heal over.'

ACKNOWLEDGEMENTS

I would like to thank everyone who allowed me to interview them for this story. There are too many to mention individually – it must have been more than 50 in the end – but special thanks must go to Mike Murphy, Glen Albaugh, Mike Spino and David Meggyesy. I pestered them so consistently over two years for facts and dates and news and views that I'm sure they were thoroughly sick of me. I owe a huge debt to Glen for the papers and thesis he sent me about, and by, his protégé, Pete Carroll. And, of course, a nod to old Supernormal himself: thanks for your precious time, Pete.

Thanks to Rick Leskowitz and all the other SEC gang. Rick kindly sent me not one but two copies of his documentary *The Joy of Sox* after the first one got stuck in the DVD player. 'I can send you another DVD,' Rick said, 'but not another player.' Chapter 12 was based on his film and the majority of quotes are taken from it. I urge you to give it a watch – it's terrific.

Murphy's seminal work *Golf in the Kingdom* was a fine companion and I also leaned on his 1978 book *The Psychic Side of Sports* as a strong source for the weird and the wonderful. Jeffrey J. Kripal's *Esalen: America and the Religion of No Religion* was an invaluable source for Chapter 2. For the Soviet side of things, Stanley Krippner's *Human Possibilities: Mind Exploration in the USSR and Eastern Europe* gave important background. You can also find Dr Zoukhar's story in there. Sheila Ostrander and Lynn

Schroeder's *Psychic Discoveries*, with an introduction by Uri Geller, provided much of the information about the Russian programmes. I got to watch *When We Were Kings*, the Academy-award winning documentary about Muhammad Ali, for 'The Greatest' and quotes and sources are taken from that film. A further bibliography per chapter follows.

A nod also to Steve Bitker for his assistance in setting the scene on that strange night in Candlestick Park all those years ago.

Many thanks to Charlotte Croft, Holly Jarrald and Charlotte Atyeo for guidance and professionalism. Finally, as always, huge portions of gratitude to F for her support, patience and gratis editing.

BIBLIOGRAPHY

1. Voodoo Games

Sports Illustrated, 'The Day We Blasted Moscow', 19 June 1989

Washington Post, 'The Moves Behind Those Moves', 13 September 1978

AP Archive, 'Karpov v Korchnoi', 7 June 2016

Golf in the Kingdom, Michael Murphy, Viking Press, 1972

Guardian.com, 'How Halifax Town were Hypnotised into Shocking Manchester City in the FA Cup', Stephen Pye, 8 January 2016

2. Back from the Dead

Esalen: America and the Religion of No Religion, Jeffrey J. Kripal, University of Chicago Press, 2007

The Psychic Side of Sports, Michael Murphy and Rhea A. White, Addison-Wesley, 1978

New York Times, 'At Home with Michael Murphy: Divine Reinvention', 2 March 1995

The Times, 'Hippy Enclave is Hip Again', 28 March 2008

3. Hidden Human Reserves

AtlasObscura.com, 'How a Famed New Age Retreat Helped End the Cold War', 8 December 2015

Houston Chronicle, 'When Boris Yeltsin Went Grocery Shopping in Clear Lake', 31 January 2018

The Power of Visualisation, Lee Pulos, Omega Press, 1990

Psychic Discoveries, Sheila Ostrander and Lynn Schroeder, Marlowe and Company, 1997

The Mind Race: Understanding and Using Psychic Abilities, Russell Targ and Keith Harary, Villard, 1984

Human Possibilities: Mind Exploration in the USSR and Eastern Europe, Stanley Krippner, Anchor Press, 1980

stanleykrippner.weebly.com, 'A Pilot Study in Dream Telepathy with the Grateful Dead'

New Dawn magazine, 'The Changing Face of Russian Psi Research', 23 April 2015

Wisdomatwork.com, 'Jedi Warrior Training for US Special Forces'

Bibliotecapleyades.net, 'How it all Started in Russia'

DailyMail.com, 'How Grateful Dead's Jerry Garcia was so Stoned He Drooled on His Mic', 1 May 2015

4. Darth Vader Can't Hit a Seven Iron

The Men Who Stare at Goats, Jon Ronson, Picador, 2004

5. Big Red

Sports Illustrated, 'Still on the Outside', 5 October 1985

Time magazine, 'Jeremiah of Jock Liberation', 24 May 1971

Out of Their League, Dave Meggyesy, Ramparts Press, 1970

Sports Energy and Consciousness: Awakening Human Potential Through Sport, edited by Eric Leskowitz, CreateSpace, 2004

The Future of the Body: Explorations into the Further Evolution of Human Nature, Michael Murphy, Tarcher/Putnam, 1992

6. The Great Wild Man

Esalen Sports Center Proposal, May 1973

Irish Times, 'A Green Mile that Got the Best from Down Under', 6 August 2007

RacingPast.ca, 'Elliott v Delany'

Sports Energy and Consciousness: Awakening Human Potential Through Sport, edited by Eric Leskowitz, CreateSpace, 2004

The Psychic Side of Sports, Michael Murphy and Rhea A. White, Addison-Wesley, 1978

7. Sports and Cosmic Forces

LA Magazine, '23 Reasons Why a Profile of Pete Carroll Does Not Appear in this Space', 1 December 2007

From Darkness to Dynasty: The First 40 Years of the New England Patriots, Jerry Thornton, University Press of New England, 2016

Yahoosports.com, 'Why Can't More Coaches Be Like Carroll?', 28 January 2014

Why Not Us: A Chronology of the Seattle Seahawks' First Super Bowl Season, Mark Arnold, CreateSpace, 2014

OfftheGridNews.com: 'The Philadelphia Experiment – Separating Fact from Fiction'

ViewZone.com: 'The Philadelphia Experiment'

ESPN.com, 'Carroll's Jets Season was a Wild Ride', 23 January 2014

New York Times, 'The Two Sides of Bill Parcells', 21 December 1997

Boston Globe, 'Pete Carroll was Always up to the NFL Challenge', 1 February 2014

USA Today, 'Carroll Admired by 9-11 Truth Movement', 30 January 2015

Win Forever: Live, Work and Play Like a Champion, Pete Carroll, Portfolio, 2010

8. I Am the Matador

Sports Illustrated, 'The Little-known Book that Shaped the Minds of Steve Kerr and Pete Carroll', 26 May 2016

Golf in the Kingdom, Michael Murphy, Viking Press, 1972

9. The Secret Tapes

Wisdom 2.0 Conference 2014: 'Sports, Performance and Mindfulness', Michael Gervais and Soren Gordhamer

Wisdom 2.0 Conference 2016: 'Mastering the Mental Game', Michael Gervais, Pete Carroll and Jon Kabat-Zinn

Outside Online, 'The Sports Shrink: Michael Gervais, Sports Psychologist to the Stars', 23 January 2013

The New York Times, 'No Foul Mouths on this Football Field', 6 September 2015

LA Times, 'Sorry, Pete, We Were Wrong', 30 December 2003

Win Forever, Pete Carroll, Portfolio, 2010

10. Zen Playbook

Espn.com, 'Lotus Pose on Two', 21 August 2013

Psychology Today, 'How Meditation Won the Super Bowl', 6 February 2014

Wikipedia.com, 'New Orleans Saints Bounty Scandal'

LA Times, 'Pete Carroll is a Man with a Plan', 7 November 2012

Mind Hacking, Sir John Hargrave, Gallery Books, 2016

11. Monkey Brain

Sports Energy and Consciousness: Awakening Human Potential Through Sport, edited by Eric Leskowitz, CreateSpace, 2004

12. Beaming Out the Mojo

The New York Times, 'The Lives They Lived: Edgar Mitchell', 21 December 2016

Cabinet magazine, 'An Interview with Edgar Mitchell', Winter issue, 2001–2

The New York Times, 'They Laughed at Galileo Too', 11 August 1996

The New York Times, 'Princeton Lab on ESP to Close its Doors', 10 February 2007

Ascent Magazine, 'An Interview with Edgar Mitchell', 2015

13. The Doc that Won the Super Bowl

Nfl.com, 'Ryan Harris signs two-year deal with Steelers', 15 March 2016

14. Trophies Don't Go with You

'A Study of Self-actualisation among Various Groups of Male Intercollegiate Athletes', Pete Carroll

Emerald City Swagger, 'Pete Carroll Makes the Seahawks Special, Different', 2015

Win Forever, Pete Carroll, Portfolio, 2010

New York Daily News, 'Texas Punter Says Seahawks Asked Him to Have a Staring Contest During NFL Combine Interview' 5 March 2018

15. Yoda Taught Michael Jordan How to Jump

The Mindful Athlete: Secrets to Pure Performance, George Mumford, Parallax Press, 2015

VICE Sports, 'The Zen Master's Zen Master', 14 July 2015

Huffington Post, 'Michael Jordan's Mindfulness Coach: the Secret Weapon of Phil Jackson, Kobe Bryant and You', June 2015

Daily Telegraph, 'Terry Sacked as England Captain', 5 February 2010

Guardian, 'John Terry: Final Speeches Pit Sarcasm Against "Straight Racial Abuse"', 12 July 2012

16. The Dark Side

Rolling Stone, 'The Gangster in the Huddle', 28 August 2013

Sports Illustrated, 'Jonathan and Aaron and …', 28 July 2016

Protecting and Promoting the Health of NFL Players: Legal and Ethical Analysis and Recommendations, Chris Deubert, I. Glen Cohen and Holly Fernandez Lynch, The Football Players' Health Study at Harvard University, 17 November 2016

Huffington Post, 'What You Need to Know About CTE this NFL Season', 8 August 2016

The Psychic Side of Sports, Michael Murphy and Rhea A. White, Addison-Wesley, 1978

17. Back to the Future

Wired, 'This Scientist Wants Tomorrow's Troops to Be Mutant Powered', December 2012

Wired, 'Real-Life Inception', October 2011

GovernmentContractsWon.com, Defense Contracts 2000–2015

Occupational Health and Wellbeing, 'The War on Stress: Resilience in the Military', 25 November 2015

DeanRadin.com, 'Biography'

Phenomena: The Secret History of the U.S. Government's Investigations into Extrasensory Perception and Psychokinesis, Annie Jacobsen, Little, Brown, 2017

18. Mind Control!

I Swear By Apollo, Dr. Ewen Cameron and the CIA-Brainwashing Experiments, Don Gilmour, Eden Press, 1987

The Devil's Chess Board: Allen Dulles, the CIA, and the Rise of America's Secret Government, David Talbot, William Collins, 2015

GovernmentContractsWon.com, Defense Contracts 2000–2015

PsyWarrior, 'The Wandering Soul Tape of Vietnam', Herbert A. Friedman

Sports Illustrated, 'The Performance Enhancer for Your Brain: How Elite Athletes are Using EEG to Get a Mental Edge', 27 February 2017

Men's Journal, 'Building the New Super-Athlete', 29 July 2013

Tennis, 'Brain Game', 26 January 2012

The Atlantic, 'Bobby Fischer's Pathetic End Game', December 2002

The Men Who Stare at Goats, Jon Ronson, Picador, 2004

19. The Greatest

BBC.co.uk, 'How the World Reacted to Boxer's Death', 4 June 2016

Daily Express, 'Ali: Aliens Watched Me', 6 June 2016

Christian Research Institute, 'Sufis: the Mystical Muslims', Vol 9, No 1, 1986

BeliefNet, 'Muhammad Ali's New Spiritual Quest', February 2005

Phenomena: The Secret History of the U.S. Government's Investigations into Extrasensory Perception and Psychokinesis, Annie Jacobsen, Little, Brown, 2017

Sports Illustrated, 'Lordy, Lordy, He's Great', 13 October 1975

An End to Ordinary History, Michael Murphy, J. P. Tarcher, 1982

When We Were Kings, directed by Leon Gast, Polygram, 1996

20. Whammy Time

YahooSports.Com, 'Carroll Takes Sherman Critiques with Grain of Salt', 28 March 2018

Epilogue: Are You a Superhuman?

The Psychic Side of Sports, Michael Murphy and Rhea A. White, Addison-Wesley, 1978

INDEX